Hannah Gurman is a clinical assistant professor at NYU's Gallatin School of Individualized Study, where she teaches U.S. history and literature, with a focus on the United States in the world. Her work has appeared in *Diplomatic History* and the *Journal of Contemporary History*, as well as *Salon*, the *Huffington Post*, and *Small Wars Journal*. She is the author of *The Dissent Papers: The Voices of Diplomats in the Cold War and Beyond* (Columbia University Press, 2012) and a columnist for the Institute for Policy Studies website Foreign Policy in Focus. She lives in New York City.

D0733845

HEARTS AND MINDS

A People's History of Counterinsurgency

Edited by

Hannah Gurman

THE NEW PRESS

NEW YORK
LONDON

Requests for permission to reproduce selections from this book should be mailed to:
Permissions Department, The New Press, 38 Greene Street, New York, NY 10013.

Published in the United States by The New Press, New York, 2013
Distributed by Perseus Distribution

LIBRARY OF CONGRESS CATALOGING-IN-PUBLICATION DATA
Hearts and minds : a people's history of counterinsurgency / edited by Hannah Gurman.
    pages cm
    Includes bibliographical references and index.
    ISBN 978-1-59558-825-8 (pbk. : alk. paper)—ISBN 978-1-59558-843-2 (e-book)
  1. Counterinsurgency—History—20th century—Case studies.
  2. Counterinsurgency—History—21st century—Case studies.
  3. Counterinsurgency—Malaysia—History—20th century.
  4. Counterinsurgency—Philippines—History—20th century.
  5. Counterinsurgency—Vietnam—History—20th century.
  6. Counterinsurgency—El Salvador—History—20th century.
  7. Counterinsurgency—Iraq—History—21st century. 8. Counterinsurgency—
Afghanistan—History—21st century. I. Gurman, Hannah, editor.
    U241.H43 2013
    355.02'1809—dc23   2013010661

The New Press publishes books that promote and enrich public discussion and
understanding of the issues vital to our democracy and to a more equitable world.
These books are made possible by the enthusiasm of our readers; the support of a
committed group of donors, large and small; the collaboration of our many partners
in the independent media and the not-for-profit sector; booksellers, who often hand-
sell New Press books; librarians; and above all by our authors.

www.thenewpress.com

Composition by dix!
This book was set in Scala

Printed in the United States of America

10 9 8 7 6 5 4 3 2 1

CONTENTS

ACKNOWLEDGMENTS

Edited volumes are by nature collaborative. Collaboration played a special role in this project, which was premised on the idea that a people's history of counterinsurgency should avoid resurrecting a simplistic grand narrative and should instead bring together more nuanced perspectives from individuals with expertise in particular areas of the world. Rather than merely reflecting a compilation of individuals' prior knowledge, however, this project became the basis for a valuable exchange of ideas, including debates about the purpose and possibility of writing a people's history of counterinsurgency. This dialogue served to deepen the individual chapters of the book and strengthened the volume as a whole. I am grateful to the contributing authors for their work and for their enthusiastic participation in this joint effort.

A conference at New York University in September 2011 provided an ideal forum to share ideas and examine the history, theory, and practice of counterinsurgency with each other as well as with other scholars, military experts, and the public. I would like to thank NYU's Gallatin School of Individualized Study, and especially Dean Susanne Wofford, for supporting the conference and Jassica Bouvier, Theresa Anderson, and Rachel Plutzer for helping me to organize the event. I would also like to thank the conference participants, including John Allison, Clint Ancker, Conrad Crane, Lloyd Gardner, Gian Gentile, Roberto Gonzalez, Bill Hartung, Vince Rafael, Dahlia Wasfi, and Marilyn Young. In May 2010, Rich Kiper and Colonel Dan Roper at the U.S. Army Counterinsurgency Center and Dan Marston at the U.S. Army Command and Staff College at Fort Leavenworth spoke candidly and openly with me about counterinsurgency and were instrumental in deepening my knowledge of how COIN was being debated within U.S. military circles.

This volume is also the product of a collaborative editing effort. I am grateful to Marc Favreau for taking this project on, supporting it throughout, and joining in the intellectual exchange. Thanks as well to Nick Turse, who played a big role in getting the project off the ground and whose masterly editing skills strengthened several chapters of this volume. My research assistant extraordinaire, Jassica Bouvier, provided invaluable editing and organizational assistance in the later stages and was key in bringing the book to fruition. Thanks to Lloyd Gardner and Marilyn Young for their contributions at the author's workshop and for reading parts of this manuscript. They are the übereditors of this volume.

—Hannah Gurman

HEARTS
AND MINDS

INTRODUCTION

From the suppression of Native American rebellions in the nineteenth century to the post-9/11 attempts to crush anti-American insurgencies as part of the Global War on Terror, U.S. counterinsurgency warfare has gone through many incarnations. The most recent "age of counterinsurgency"[1] was nearing its apex in May 2010, when I attended a conference in Fort Leavenworth, Kansas, on counterinsurgency in Afghanistan sponsored by the U.S. Army and the Marine Corps Counterinsurgency Center.[2]

Counterinsurgency, or COIN, had been making a comeback over the course of the last several years. In 2007, faced with mounting chaos in Iraq, a desperate George W. Bush grasped for a new strategy in the war. General David Petraeus was prepared for such a moment. For decades, he had been angling to bring counterinsurgency back from the ashes of Vietnam. The previous year, as head of the army's Command and Staff College in Fort Leavenworth, he directed the writing of the U.S. Army/Marine Counterinsurgency Field Manual (FM 3-24). The guide, which garnered critical acclaim and held a spot on Amazon's Top 100 list in 2007, announced the arrival of an age of "internal" or "irregular" wars in which militarily weak insurgents used political persuasion as well as force to threaten government power.

In these conflicts, the manual's authors—a group of military intellectuals and bureaucrats—explained that success would not be determined by military might alone but instead by winning the hearts and minds of the people: "At its core, counterinsurgency is a struggle for the population's support." To achieve this, COIN had to focus on the needs and interests of the civilian population, including security and the provision of basic government services, such as electricity, irrigation, and roads. Above all, counterinsurgency forces would need to avoid civilian casualties.[3]

Despite ultimately failing in each of these categories, Petraeus's "surge" of COIN-minded troops in Iraq was declared a success.[4] Counterinsurgency, which is actually a set of tactics and not a strategy, thus became the guiding doctrine of the wars in Iraq and Afghanistan, and was for a time the unofficial religion of the U.S. military. The proselytizers, dubbed COINdinistas,[5] included senior military officers, civilian policy makers, and their advisers, as well as prominent academics, think-tankers, and bloggers aligned with the military. Support for counterinsurgency transcended party lines and continued into the Obama administration—which put Petraeus's protégé, Stanley McChrystal, in charge of the Afghan War. After announcing his own troop surge, McChrystal spread the gospel of COIN: "Protecting the people is the mission. The conflict will be won by persuading the people, not by destroying the enemy," he insisted in speeches that were marketed as much to the U.S. public as to the coalition of allied troops in Afghanistan. These included the International Security and Assistance Force (ISAF) and the Afghan national security forces, including the Afghan National Army (ANA) and Afghan National Police (ANP).[6]

The conference at Leavenworth reflected the zeal for counterinsurgency that had taken root in elite circles of military and defense intellectuals at that time. In line with the doctrine's focus on public awareness and the open exchange of ideas, it was framed as a broad discussion across institutional barriers. To my surprise, you could sign up for the conference online without having to present credentials or even submit to a security clearance.[7] On arriving at Leavenworth, I discovered that the attendees consisted entirely of military personnel, State and Defense Department personnel, and government contractors. Among the more than one hundred participants, I was one of only three women and, to my knowledge, the only person with no formal ties to the national security establishment.

The event was illuminating and there was, as advertised, a remarkable openness to dialogue. But the discussion was also in many ways limited, conforming to the premise of how, not whether, to implement counterinsurgency in Afghanistan. Confined to debates over the execution of policy, the conversation paid little attention to questioning the fundamental assumptions of such policies. Despite many nods to the importance of understanding Afghan culture and history, successive PowerPoint presentations tended to reproduce superficial and instrumentalist stereotypes about Pashtun tribal culture. (PowerPoint, which typically precludes critical thought, has become the dominant form of knowledge production and exchange within the U.S. military.) The one Afghan present, a social scientist who joined the military's Human Terrain program—which was supposed to help with Afghan outreach—politely pointed out the demographic imbalance in the room. Several presenters disavowed the old taglines of "winning hearts and minds" and "nation building," but simply reframed these in less sentimental language. They spoke of getting the Afghans to "trust" and "have confidence" in their own government. While various speakers questioned the trustworthiness of our "partners" in the central government, there was no discussion of how the very presence of a foreign military could undermine the mission.

This mind-set characterized the broad enthusiasm for counterinsurgency in 2010. Military leaders framed it as a year in which counterinsurgency would prove itself in Afghanistan, but instead it proved the basic limits and contradictions of COIN, which have always plagued the doctrine. By year's end, although the era of blind faith in COIN seemed to be drawing to a close, the fundamental flaws of the doctrine remained largely unexamined.

The contradictions of COIN played out on the ground in the much-publicized counterinsurgency campaigns in Marjah and Kandahar in southern Afghanistan. Advertised as models of "population-centric" or people-centered COIN, these produced only limited security gains[8] but a wide range of grievances among the civilian population. The year 2010 turned out to be the worst to date for civilian casualties in Afghanistan.[9] In addition, the COIN campaigns displaced thousands of people—including 3,461 families in the region around Marjah (a remarkably high number given the area's sparse population, which the U.S. military had misrepresented in its attempts to elevate the mission's strategic importance).[10] Farmers scrambled in vain to obtain compensation for the destruction of their property. In the case of Tarok Kaloche, the military simply razed an entire village suspected of harboring Taliban, using 49,000 pounds of explosives.[11] In other areas, freedom of movement was obstructed in the name of security. The "Security-Commerce" Wall in the Zhari district on the north bank of the Arghandab River created an especially dire problem for farmers whose homes and fields ended up on different sides of the barrier. In the spring of 2011, heavy rains turned the wall into a dam, with one side flooded and the other starved for water.[12]

And this was supposedly "population-centric" COIN. Meanwhile, "enemy-centric" operations employed more lethal tactics. In a December 2010 statement that unwittingly belied the shallowness of the hearts and minds campaign in the south, one senior military official told the *Washington Post*, "We've taken the gloves off, and it has had a huge impact."[13]

Night raids had already been steadily increasing prior to the Marjah campaign, growing from one hundred to five hundred per month during 2009. By June 2010, they had reached a thousand a month and rose at an even faster rate after Petraeus took command, tripling between August and October 2010 and prompting fear and confusion among many civilians.[14] In these raids, armed troops, typically U.S. Special Forces, would surround the house of suspected Taliban leaders under cover of darkness, kick down the door, and kill suspected individuals or force them outside for questioning and detention.[15] According to the military's own reports, for every enemy effectively targeted in these operations, there were three civilians wrongly killed or captured.[16] Considered a violation of the sanctity of the home and an affront to Afghan culture, night raids were cited as the most significant factor in turning the population against coalition forces in 2010. Numerous studies, including one conducted by New York University's Center on International Cooperation, concluded that these operations actually inflamed the insurgency, removing older, more moderate Taliban leaders who might negotiate with the government and replacing them with younger, more radical leaders likelier to forge ties with al Qaeda.[17]

In a poll conducted by the International Council on Security and

Development in April 2011, more than 90 percent of southern Afghan men of fighting age said they believed that foreign military operations were bad for their community, and more than half said they held a more negative view of the foreign military forces than they had a year earlier. Though military spokespeople repeatedly insisted that the counterinsurgency campaigns had halted and even reversed the strength of the Taliban, these claims turned out to be exaggerated and tentative at best.[18]

To curtail the rising influence of dangerous Taliban branches in the eastern and northern parts of the country, the coalition turned increasingly to air strikes, several of which resulted in civilian casualties, including one attack in Kunar Province at the end of February 2011 that killed sixty-five civilians, forty of them children, and another a week later that killed nine Afghan children gathering firewood. The sole survivor was an eleven-year-old boy who told U.S. journalists: "The helicopters hovered over us, scanned us and we saw a green flash from the helicopters. Then they flew back high up, and in a second round they hovered over us and started shooting."[19]

After another raid on May 28, 2011, killed fourteen civilians, including eleven children, President Hamid Karzai condemned his NATO-led International Security Assistance Force (ISAF) allies: "If they continue their attacks on our houses, then their presence will change from a force that is fighting against terrorism to a force that is fighting against the people of Afghanistan." Riding the wave of popular discontent, he further warned that coalition forces were in danger of becoming "occupiers" of Afghanistan.[20]

ISAF responded by increasing air strikes to twelve a day in the following weeks.[21] This was all part of an effort to make measureable "progress" before the late 2011 deadline to begin withdrawing U.S. troops and ever so slowly wind down a war that U.S. and NATO officials refused to acknowledge they were losing.[22]

What happened to COIN? Taking stock of developments since the end of 2010, several commentators couldn't help but note an increasing rift between the coalition's avowed strategy of protecting the population and what appeared to be a turn toward a more aggressive and brutal war. John Nagl, a former counterinsurgency adviser to General Petraeus, praised the kill-capture campaign, calling it "an almost industrial-scale counter-terrorism killing machine."[23] Adopting a more critical stance, Sherard Cowper-Coles, the former British envoy to Afghanistan, observed, "Regrettably, General Petraeus has curiously ignored his own principles of counterinsurgency in the field manual, which speaks of politics being the predominant factor in dealing with an insurgency."[24] Some went so far as to declare counterinsurgency dead. "The counterinsurgency campaign in Afghanistan ends in Helmand and Kandahar," Peter Mansoor, a military historian and expert on COIN who served as Petraeus's executive officer in Iraq, told *Wired* magazine in June 2011.

In October, the Center for New American Security (CNAS), a defense think tank with close ties to the Obama administration and a key player in shaping the surge strategy in Afghanistan just a few years earlier (John Nagl is its president), issued a report that reflected how radically even the strongest advocates of COIN had shifted their positions. The report, issued as a blueprint for a responsible approach to proposed cuts in defense spending, predicted that ground forces, previously advertised as the key element in carrying out COIN campaigns, "will play a less central role in the projection of U.S. military power in the next decade than in the last" and called for a reduction of as many as 139,000 army troops (out of a total 569,000). Blog posts with titles like "Fare thee well population-centric COIN" and "A Back Somersault in the US Strategy" at the influential Afghanistan Analysts Network website served as epitaphs for the latest age of counterinsurgency.[25]

In years to come, there will no doubt be a plethora of post-mortem histories of the counterinsurgency effort in Afghanistan. Many will be written by the COINdinistas themselves. We can expect these to mirror the insights as well as the limitations that marked the excitement about COIN in 2010. They will illuminate tactical successes and failures and may even interrogate the broad strategy of the war. But they are unlikely to raise questions about the fundamental contradictions of counterinsurgency or the geopolitical contexts that give rise to them.

COINdinistas have, in fact, been writing their own versions of counterinsurgency history for a long time. Petraeus's ideas evolved out of his dissertation on Vietnam, in which he argued for the reintroduction of that war's successful counterinsurgency programs.[26] The 2006 U.S. counterinsurgency field manual and the larger body of pro-counterinsurgency literature produced in its wake relied heavily on case studies from past counterinsurgency conflicts. This official and semi-official history of counterinsurgency served as the corpus for a U.S. grand narrative of COIN that was used to indoctrinate military personnel, as well as the public, into the COIN paradigm.[27]

As with the official U.S. military reports coming out of Afghanistan, the COINdinistas molded history to fit their own purposes, reducing the individual conflicts to the vocabulary and ideology of COIN and omitting the grimmer details of these campaigns. The result was self-serving mythology that justified the wars in Iraq and Afghanistan and reinforced the image of the United States as a benevolent force in the world.

The history of counterinsurgency, as told by its proponents, is inherently reductive. The very language of insurgency flattens the varied histories, motivations, and makeup of individual groups that challenged the legitimacy and policies of their respective governments. It does not take into account the different priorities and motivations of, for example, the largely rural National Liberation Front (NLF) that posed a direct military challenge to the corrupt, postcolonial government in Vietnam in the 1950s and 1960s and the urban Salvadoran unionists in the 1970s whose demands did not even include the dissolution of the current government. The language of insurgency deliberately subsumes these and other groups under a single category linked to notions of threat, criminality, and violence. The counterinsurgency label tells us more about U.S. geopolitics and its attendant ideologies than it does about any individual conflict.

In the COIN framework, insurgencies are almost exclusively either leftist or Islamist and almost never liberal. Accordingly, while George Washington is hailed as a revolutionary, the NLF in Vietnam and the Taliban in Afghanistan are both deemed insurgencies. This division of "good" and "bad" forms of resistance has implications for the characterization of tactics across groups. The history of these conflicts includes acts of violence against the state and, in several cases, against civilians, although such tactics were typically strategic in nature and disproportionate to the violence carried out by the reigning security forces and their allies. In the COIN paradigm, no matter how violent, the actions of liberal revolutionaries are justified by the greater cause of freedom. Conversely, "insurgent" groups are virtually synonymous with their most violent tactics.

This ideological characterization of tactics changes depending on the geostrategic context. In the 1980s, President Ronald Reagan used the term "freedom-fighters" to describe the Afghan mujahideen's battle with the Soviet Union, in which the United States covertly supplied the mujahideen with weapons. The Taliban, which emerged in the internal power struggle following the Soviet withdrawal, includes some of the same groups and individuals who see their current fight against the U.S./NATO intervention as part of a much longer struggle against foreign conquest. When their improvised explosive devices began to target U.S. armored vehicles and rival factions within Afghanistan, however, the Taliban were labeled "terrorists." Only in the face of an intractable conflict and the increasing necessity to negotiate has the international coalition attempted to distinguish between the different groups and political positions that call themselves Taliban.[28]

Such caricatures of the enemy are an expected staple of war rhetoric. More complicated is the tendency of the grand COIN narrative to paint an equally simplistic picture of potential allies—the local "people" whose hearts and minds are supposed to be central to winning a counterinsurgency campaign. Despite the call to focus on the people, and ill-conceived, poorly executed attempts to integrate anthropology and other social sciences to understand the local culture, the latest generation of COIN advocates did not make a serious or sustained effort to grapple with the complex social dynamics of the populations targeted by counterinsurgency campaigns. Thus, the COINdinistas' history does little to account for demographic, political, or social differences within the civilian population. There is almost nothing in the literature that would help to differentiate, for example, between a poor twenty-five-year-old woman married to a rebel in central Luzon, the heart of the Huk Rebellion in the Philippines in the 1940s, and a well-off middle-aged man working for the government in the same region. Indeed, the very notion of a complex, let alone inequitable, social system is almost nonexistent in COIN discourse. The narrow counterinsurgency paradigm leaves little room to discuss specific historical and social forces and how they have shaped the overlapping and competing interests of individuals and groups within a region.

In COIN discourse, the only social distinction that gets any serious attention is the one between the "people" and the "insurgents." The separation of these two groups is central to the practice of COIN. "Continue to secure the people and separate them from the insurgents," declares the COIN manual time and again as the basis of numerous clear-and-hold operations across southern Afghanistan.[29] But this is one distinction that cannot be made so easily. In Afghanistan, as in the Philippines and many other sites of counterinsurgency wars, the so-called people are often husbands, uncles, sons, and fathers of the "insurgents." The "people" thus includes not only those who oppose or are victimized by the insurgency but those who physically support it, providing their relatives and friends with food, clothing, and shelter. The very idea of a neat physical divide between the insurgency and the people understates the role of family and kinship ties across these categories, while the idea of a clear ideological chasm between insurgents and the population often minimizes the degree of support for "insurgent" ideas among the people. While small-scale attempts to empower individual tribes—a tactic known as "tribal engagement"—acknowledge the local politics that motivate populations to support an insurgency, the choice to align with one group over another is made without a full understanding of these local power struggles or how U.S./NATO intervention further exacerbates them.[30] Insisting on a natural alliance between a "good" population and U.S. counterinsurgency forces against a "bad" insurgency, the American COIN narrative does not acknowledge this more nuanced dynamic or how and why it differs in each of these conflicts.

This level of social and political awareness would also entail a critical reflection on the international politics of COIN. Counter-insurgency wars have historically been mounted by imperial powers seeking to maintain or expand their spheres of influence. At the end of World War II, as the British and French struggled to manage their colonial holdings in Africa and Asia, social and political tensions came to a head in many of the colonies, including British Malaya and French Algeria, to name just two prominent examples in the COIN discourse. [31]

Though the COIN literature makes a point of citing these and other instances of colonial and imperial counterinsurgency, it largely screens out the geopolitical and economic imperatives that motivated European empires to fight resistance groups in these regions. Thus, it does not come to terms with the possibility of a fundamental tension between the goals of the powers waging counterinsurgency wars and the local population's own needs and aspirations. At the geostrategic level, the people targeted by counter-insurgency campaigns in colonial and postcolonial states mattered mainly insofar as they were potential allies in the pursuit of the empire's political and economic interests, such as maintaining a British foothold in Asia, controlling the rubber and tin production in Malaya, or protecting French property and culture in North Africa and Indochina. [32]

In the face of threats posed by groups such as the Malayan Communist Party (MCP) or the Algerian Front de Libération Nationale (FLN), colonial, quasi-colonial, nationalist, and anti-insurgent security forces employed an array of tactics to maintain order—including neglect (by such policies as propping up corrupt, unpopular, and quasi-colonial governments throughout the Third World), population control (including the issuance of identification cards, the corralling of populations into government-controlled zones, and control of food), and forced silence (via bombs and artillery or detention and torture). To the degree that they were implemented at all, hearts and minds campaigns typically existed in conjunction with or as part of these other measures. In Malaya, the COINdinistas' favorite example of a successful hearts and minds campaign, security forces rewarded the population with rice if they followed government orders and controlled food from being smuggled outside secured areas.

The United States has a long tradition of distinguishing itself from the European colonial powers, articulating its expansionist policies in the context of individual freedom and national independence. The COIN paradigm's contribution to American exceptionalism reflects an ongoing level of cognitive dissonance. Integrating the Philippine Insurrection, the Vietnam War, and the fight against the FMLN in El Salvador, as well as the more recent wars in Iraq and Afghanistan, into its COIN grand narrative, the United States situates itself as a successor to the European powers. At the same time, however, it refuses to acknowledge the implications of this framework, confirming once again what the political commentator Walter Lippmann observed in 1927—that U.S. imperialism is "more or less unconscious."[33]

In its counterinsurgency conflicts, the United States has historically attempted to advance the notion of a win-win situation in which the U.S. military explains its intervention as a gift of freedom to the local population. In the Philippines, Vietnam, Iraq, and Afghanistan, U.S. forces framed their invasion as a victory for the people, who would be freed from the yoke of Spanish, Communist, Ba'athist, or Taliban oppression. But the long and bloody wars in each of these places demonstrated the emptiness of these claims for much of the civilian population, with the important exceptions of the local elite and war profiteers. The ensuing wars not only exacerbated old tensions but produced new ones, creating what the counterinsurgency theorist David Kilcullen has called "the accidental guerrilla," in which the presence of foreign forces further fuels an insurgency that coalesces around anti-foreign sentiment.[34] Subsequently, various forms of resistance against U.S.-backed local and national authorities emerged in a messy conjuncture of international and civil wars. U.S. counterinsurgency forces, like their colonial and postcolonial counterparts, responded with an inextricable

mixture of push and shove. Refusing to acknowledge the paradoxical results that a counterinsurgency footprint can have, the latest
COIN paradigm also refuses to examine the geopolitical and structural factors that contribute to it.

This book is a response to the grand narrative of U.S. counterinsurgency. With essays from anthropologists, area experts, journalists, filmmakers, and social, military, and diplomatic historians
that critically analyze the supposed successes and mythic heroes of
past counterinsurgencies, it attempts to reconceptualize the history
of counterinsurgency without the self-serving and reductive categories of standard COIN discourse and official military spin. It is
also an attempt to consider perspectives outside the Western and
elite insurgent narratives, to gain a glimpse into the history of insurgency and counterinsurgency from "below," from the vantage point
of ordinary people caught in the maelstrom of these conflicts.

   In an effort to contrast the decontextualized nature of COIN discourse, this volume focuses on specific local, national, and international contexts in which counterinsurgency wars have been waged.
Each contributor concentrates on a different chapter in the COIN-
dinistas' history of modern counterinsurgency, from the anticolonial independence movements of the twentieth century to America's
post-9/11 wars. The first four chapters analyze counterinsurgencies
during the Cold War—in Malaya, the Philippines, Vietnam, and El
Salvador. The last four chapters offer deeper insights into the recent
history of counterinsurgency operations in Iraq and Afghanistan.

   Each contributor brings a slightly different approach to this
collective project. Some of the chapters draw from archival documents and existing scholarship, while others flow more from eyewitness accounts and on-the-ground observation. In some pieces,
the writing style is more academic and in others more journalistic.
Most important, all the contributors have their own interpretation
of the concept of "people's history" in relation to "insurgency" and
"counterinsurgency," so that the categories and their relationship become open to analysis and debate. We do not agree on everything—

including, I am sure, some of the interpretations offered in this
introduction.

To the degree that there is a shared argument across chapters, it
emanates from a mutual frustration with the grand COIN narrative.
Thus, rather than advancing an overarching or unifying history of
insurgency, this volume challenges that framework, teasing out the
specific histories, motivations, and objectives of the groups and individuals that have been reduced to "insurgents" and "terrorists" in
the COIN paradigm. And rather than perpetuate an equally reductive understanding of the civilian population, this people's history
attempts to detail the different segments of the population, their
often complex and always evolving relationship to the "insurgency,"
and the impact of counterinsurgency campaigns on their communities and their lives.

Although COIN overstates similarities across "insurgencies," it
actually understates the links across counterinsurgency campaigns.
Thus, in addition to illuminating the specific contexts of individual
counterinsurgency campaigns, this volume also demonstrates important connections between them. It shows, for example, how the
use of collective punishment in Vietnam grew out of similar operations in the counterinsurgency war against communists in Malaya
in the 1950s. Likewise, from Malaya to Afghanistan, it illustrates the
destructive effects of clearing operations on the targeted communities, one comparison that the U.S. grand narrative of COIN predictably fails to draw.

COIN tactics are increasingly being applied in the United States
and other NATO countries at the domestic level, especially in the
area of surveillance. In the United States, the FBI currently maintains a "Terrorist Watch" database containing over one million
names. As a result of the wide and racialized net of suspicion, local
and federal security forces have disproportionately targeted innocent Muslim and Arab residents and citizens of the United States.
In several instances, including a string of cases in Newburgh, New
York, they used informants and large sums of money to entrap individuals into involvement in a cooked-up plot, then swept up and

charged the suspects with attempted terrorism, resulting in convictions with life sentences. Investigative reporting by the Associated Press and others in August and September 2011 revealed that, in collaboration with the CIA, the New York City Police Department had put Muslim campus organizations as well as entire neighborhoods with a strong Muslim presence under surveillance. Not since the days of COINTELPRO, the FBI's covert intelligence program, and the CIA's analogous program, Operation MH/CHAOS, that targeted leftist political groups, including Students for a Democratic Society (SDS), the Black Panthers, and other civil rights groups in the 1950s and 1960s, has a paradigm designed for foreign enemies been so readily applied to the domestic population.[35]

Similar programs have been put into place across Western Europe as part of a broad increase in the use of surveillance technology and the normalization of a surveillance society post 9/11. In Birmingham, England, under the guise of crime prevention, police mounted one hundred fifty surveillance cameras, forty of them in undisclosed locations, to monitor the Muslim community. In March 2011, Hans-Peter Friedrich, the German interior minister, proposed collaboration between German security forces and Muslim groups to monitor extremism in their community. More broadly, concern about "homegrown terrorism" has prompted national and transnational dialogue about how to better assimilate the more moderate elements of the European Muslim population and more aggressively weed out extremists and potential extremists in their midst. The aim to "win the hearts and minds" of Europe's "good" Muslims and isolate the "bad" ones is a form of domestic counterinsurgency based in a set of shared practices across U.S. and European security establishments.[36]

Similarities in the tactics and effects of counterinsurgency serve as reminders of the structural as well as historical connections between nations that wage counterinsurgency wars. These links exist both within a particular era, in which counterinsurgency experts frequently shuttled from one war to another, and across time, in which a shared collective history, such as the one in the 2006 field manual, has been forged.

By rewriting the history of counterinsurgency, this book aims to help dispel the myths that policy makers have both propagated and labored under in recent years. In doing so, I also hope it will raise awareness of the geopolitical system that fuels counterinsurgency and the narrative structures that justify it. Thus, as in Howard Zinn's paradigm-changing *A People's History of the United States*, the "people" in *Hearts and Minds: A People's History of Counterinsurgency* does not refer only to those communities caught up in the maelstrom of COIN campaigns. It also refers to anyone with a stake in the story. This includes the people whose hearts, minds, campaign contributions, and tax dollars are used to support counterinsurgency operations and the gigantic defense establishments to which they belong. The most recent age of counterinsurgency may be on the wane, but if history is any guide, it won't be long before counterinsurgency again threatens to rise from the ashes.

I

MALAYA—BETWEEN TWO TERRORS: "PEOPLE'S HISTORY" AND THE MALAYAN EMERGENCY

Karl Hack

"Without the rich life experiences of the people, national history can only be like a plant with floating roots, or water in a shallow stream. Such is an inverted and twisted history, which is devoid of its real face."

—Fong Chong Pik, *Fong Chong Pik: The Memoirs of a Malayan Communist Revolutionary*[1]

No analysis of insurgency or counterinsurgency (COIN) can be considered securely anchored unless it is informed by "people's history": an approach that gives voice to fighters and their supporters and that captures the multiple, fractured nature of "the people." That also means avoiding a one-sided account that privileges rebels in favor of one that also includes the perspectives of victims of insurgent violence and those who resisted insurgency.[2] Such history must be not only *about* these people but *from* their perspective, including their own words.[3]

This chapter will demonstrate the significance of "people's history" for our understanding of the Malayan Emergency of 1948–60. The Emergency pitted the Malayan Communist Party (MCP) and its mainly Chinese insurgents, on the one hand, against the British colonial power and a range of anticommunist Malay, Chinese, and Indians on the other. It culminated in the grant of independence to

Malaya on August 31, 1957, and the formal ending of the Emergency three years later. The chapter will offer new insight into how most people experienced this conflict, namely, as being caught "between two terrors."[4]

THE HISTORIOGRAPHY OF THE MALAYAN EMERGENCY IN RELATION TO "THE PEOPLE"

> "The coercion and enforcement approach might ensure that the British did not lose, but neither did it give them any hope of winning . . . [until] General Sir Gerald Templer, the new High Commissioner [February 1952] . . . implemented what became known as the 'hearts and minds' approach."
>
> —Richard Stubbs, *Hearts and Minds in Guerrilla Warfare: The Malayan Emergency 1948–1960* (1989)[5]

> "In spite of the sullenly hostile population, we are making very good progress by screwing down the people in the strongest and sternest manner."
>
> —Geoffrey Bourne, Director of Operations, Federation of Malaya, to General Templer (1956)[6]

In order to know how a "people's perspective" might enrich mainstream understanding of the Malayan Emergency, we need first to outline the "orthodox" understanding of this conflict. This is all the more important since Malaya was quickly adopted as a classic case study in how to defeat insurgency through "winning hearts and minds." The resulting misconceptions have influenced the debate and practice of counterinsurgency (COIN) from Vietnam to Afghanistan.[7]

The "orthodox" narrative offered a simplified account of the Emergency. At its core was the assertion that the campaign had ground to a stalemate by 1951. In 1950–51, half a million rural Chinese had been herded into "New Villages," driving the insurgents to the jungle's edge. But this period ended with insurgent activity at near-peak levels and with the assassination in October 1951 of the

High Commissioner. According to this narrative, therefore, "Population Control" achieved a score-draw situation but would have been insufficient to tip this into a "win." It maintains that what made the crucial difference in 1952–54 was the addition—under General Sir Gerald Templer as both High Commissioner and Director of Operations (DOO)—of new ingredients. Templer added vigorous, centralized leadership (hiring and firing with vim and furiously touring New Villages). But his most important contribution is held to be the intensification of attempts to win "hearts and minds." Elections were held first at the town and local level, then at the state, and, ultimately, at the federal level. New facilities were provided for villagers, and the police launched "Operation Service" in December 1952, encouraging police officers to be helpful and approachable to the general public.

The result was supposedly that the campaign turned between 1952 and 1954, with incidents decreased by more than half over this period. Templer left Malaya in 1954 having "turned the tide." This interpretation provided a heart-warming Cold War and counterinsurgency morality tale, in which good Western democrats won because, in addition to applying carefully calibrated force, they established legitimacy by winning the "hearts and minds" of the majority.[8]

The reality, however, is that the tide had begun to turn earlier, when the "people's" experience was more predominantly one of controlled coercion, and "hearts and minds" measures were embryonic.

The campaign can best be summarized as going through three distinct phases: of "counterterror" (1948–49), "population control" (1950–52), and finally, of increased emphasis on "winning hearts and minds" combined with more dynamic, centralized control (1952–60).[9] The experiences of ordinary people varied across these three distinct phases.

In the counterterror period of 1948–49, security forces (SF) conducted sweeps, burning huts from which insurgents were presumed to have received support, and displacing or deporting their inhabitants. Nervous troops sometimes shot people they saw running away, and the government portrayed rural Chinese as liable to support whoever subjected them to greater pressure. Hence, High

Commissioner Sir Henry Gurney told the Legislative Council on November 18, 1948, "There are bound to be cases in which hardship will be caused to innocent people who do not feel that they have a duty to distinguish themselves from the guilty. I say this in no way as a threat but as a plain statement of fact."[10]

The unsympathetic view of Chinese villagers, combined with vague rules of action, translated into an official acceptance that the law would sometimes be broken.[11] Military action was loosely constrained and abuses almost inevitable. The most extreme involved the massacre of twenty-four unarmed Chinese villagers at Batang Kali by Scots Guards, and the burning of their huts, on December 11–12, 1948. The soldiers had been told that villagers were supplying the communists. All the men were locked up overnight, before being gunned down the next morning. Investigations were desultory and falsely claimed the villagers had been trying to escape. Chong Fip, the sole survivor, hid in his father's coffee shop, "scared that the white men will get me," as they had his brother. The women and children, who had been trucked away, went without compensation, further impoverished by the loss of their male relatives.[12] In more typical cases of single or limited deaths, sympathetic coroners readily recorded verdicts of justifiable homicide after unarmed Chinese were shot.[13]

In theory, huts were supposed to be burned only after possessions were removed and inhabitants screened. Suspects could then be detained without trial for up to two years. Most Chinese lacked citizenship and so could be deported. By early 1953, more than twenty thousand detainees and family members had been shipped to China, compared with a maximum of about eleven thousand in detention camps at any time.[14] The British had processes for minimizing abuses, including appeal against detention, but the MCP's *Freedom News* thought these worthless. Its January 15, 1949, issue described "such atrocious measures as arson, killing, imprisonment, mopping up and compelling the people to quit their homes by force." The "man-slaughtering and bloody war" being fought by Britain, with the help of Chinese traitors, dubbed "running dogs," included the issuance of identity cards and enforcement of censorship. Other accusations included rape.[15] *Freedom News* criticized British attempts to limit harshness, for example, characterizing the Appeals Committee as "deceitful."[16] Also highlighting the fact that the plantations and mines, mostly British-owned, took high dividends out of the country in return for low wages inside, *Freedom News* concluded in 1952, "The British Imperialists are devils that suck the blood of the Malayan People."[17]

This first counterinsurgency period nevertheless prevented the communists from establishing liberated areas, and broke up larger guerrilla units. It persuaded the communists to reorganize their civilian supporters into a more tightly structured Min Yuen (Mass or People's Movement). Incidents decreased in early 1949 as this reorganization proceeded. The MCP also shifted from a plan of setting up a few liberated areas and expanding them to surround the towns, to one of widespread sabotage of British interests while building up their own strength. It was in response to the resulting increase in incidents, from mid-1949 to early 1950, that the British instituted a second counterinsurgency phase. This centered on "population control." Lieutenant General Harold Briggs was made Director of Operations (DOO) in April 1950 and by May had drawn up what became known as the "Briggs Plan."

The Briggs Plan instituted war executive committees for every level from the district upward, which combined civil, military, and police representatives, and were authorized to order immediate action. It encouraged small-scale patrolling to penetrate and dominate villages. It also began the systematic resettlement of five hundred thousand Chinese agricultural smallholders (labeled "squatters") into Resettlement Areas (later called "New Villages"). The resulting administration and control of population and space was intended to instill security and confidence, allowing the population to offer information and support without fear of retribution. Briggs believed that confidence, and the information that would flow from it, would be the key to victory.

The Briggs Plan thus saw Britain switch from a colonial policing mode of intimidating the forest frontier population into withholding support for communists toward an approach of resource-intensive

spatial control. The British put the plan into action with remarkable speed, resettling 80 percent of squatters in over four hundred
Resettlement Areas between June 1950 and the end of 1951. That
represented 10 percent of the total population and 20 percent of the
Chinese population. In addition, they moved nearly six hundred
thousand laborers' living quarters short distances into more defen-
sible clusters. A Korean War boom in commodity prices helped to
pay for this and also contributed to an increase in plantation and
mining wages, which alleviated anger at resettlement.[18]

By mid- to late 1951, this population and space-centric approach
also provoked a furious communist response, bringing the campaign to a peak. That year, the total number of insurgents averaged
7,292, supported by many more Min Yuen, and up to a million
sympathizers.[19] British hopes rose and fell throughout 1951. Population control produced more tension before relief, as many communist supporters fled resettlement. Thus, incidents remained high
even as information started to flow more freely in some areas, especially where Chinese auxiliary police, or Home Guard (villagers
doing part-time guard duty in their own area), began—tentatively
at first—to be given firearms.[20] In addition, High Commissioner
Gurney was ambushed and killed on October 6, 1951. British nerves
were by now frayed, with further turmoil in their top leadership.

This is the point at which conventional histories of the Emergency see a stalemate. This was before General Sir Gerald Templer,
as High Commissioner and DOO, added supposedly new ingredients from 1952, namely, vigorous, centralized leadership, better intelligence, and intensified "hearts and minds" measures, which are
argued to have turned the campaign around during 1952–54.[21]

The real picture was more complicated. The communists also
reached a crisis point in 1951. That year, the Security Forces (SF) increased the ratio of enemy killed for every SF casualty, and the number
of SF-initiated encounters rose. The communist guerrilla force—now
calling itself the Malayan National Liberation Army (MNLA)—
struggled to keep larger units together. Despite support from the
Min Yuen, resettlement was affecting MNLA supplies and morale.
The MCP therefore issued October 1951 Directives, which stipulated

smaller units, the creation of armed work forces to protect civilian workers in resettlements, and increases in food production and weapons stockpiling in the jungles. Recognizing that civilian support had been weakened by overemphasis on violence and sabotage, such as derailing trains and slashing rubber trees, they also ordered that such practices be minimized. Operations should concentrate on capturing arms and attacking SF, while "avoiding harming the people." Specific excesses were forbidden. "Running dogs" must still be eliminated, but members should avoid throwing acid, killing pregnant women, or spraying crowds indiscriminately in pursuit (unless absolutely necessary to keep a traitor from escaping). The party should rebuild support to allow a future spreading of the campaign, by penetrating unions and schools, and courting the "medium national bourgeoisie," rather than relying too narrowly on rural masses.[22]

These orders filtered through to most units within a few months, while statistics for insurgent attacks and sabotage fell at their fastest rate ever. By 1952–53, the MCP Central Committee had started to move from state to state in search of an area that could support its fifty-odd members. This turned into a "Little Long March," which by 1954 had reached the Malayan-Thai border area.[23]

These changes came when life in recently established "New Villages" was still grim. Those moved were provided with an allowance (and were later offered land title), but initially they had lost jobs and plots, and the new land was often farther from potential employment or on poor ground. Malaya's Chinese initially dubbed the resettlements "concentration camps," a term used for Japanese corralling of villagers in mainland China. Han Suyin, a Eurasian author of Chinese and Flemish Belgian extraction, who in the 1950s married Special Branch Officer Leon Comber, describes these settlements in her autobiography. She writes of traveling four hours by jeep, up a road that was little more than a red gash in the jungle, to find:

> at the edge of a fetid mangrove swamp . . . behind . . . the barbed wire manned by a police post, . . . [f]our hundred beings, including children, huddled there. . . . I shall never forget their pale and puffy faces: beriberi, or the ulcers on

their legs. Their skin was the hue of the swamp. They stank. There was no clean water.[24]

Notwithstanding her disgust, she concedes that within a few years, "a good few"—not all—"became liveable." They were not as bad as the worst Malay villages, which were riddled with disease and where "the Malay peasant" was "imprisoned within his feudal village," subsisting on rice cultivation or fishing.[25] New Villages varied widely in quality, but most ultimately had perimeter barbed wire and lighting, a grid pattern of houses, limited gates to control movement, and a strategically located police post to ensure control and surveillance.

The raw angst of being moved and the grinding necessity of rebuilding lives were highest as the course of the Emergency swung in favor of the government in 1950–52. Communist defeats were driven by tough spatial and population control at the micro as well as the macro level. As the DOO said in 1956 for one obdurate area, each new problem was solved by "screwing down the people." Controls on things such as food and villagers' movements were brought to a peak in each area precisely as combined military-police operations intensified. The methods used were continuously refined and at their peak could be summarized as follows.

First, a few villages and surrounding areas within a communist committee's range were selected. Then, patrols were stepped up, and hard-line Min Yuen arrested, as they were deemed irreconcilable. This was intended to make the local MCP and MNLA lean on softer supporters. Next, food controls were increased. In November 1950, in publicizing Order Number 17 on Food Control, the DOO told villagers, "I intend to help you." He explained that he knew they could not always refuse communist demands, so he would make food controls so tight that people could legitimately say they could not smuggle out supplies.[26] Each New Village therefore had limited gates, and villagers were allowed to take out only water and a minimum of food, while shops had to account for all stock and tins were punctured. By the mid-1950s the British had also started to introduce central rice cooking for some operations. This allowed villagers to eat their fill (earlier, rice rations been cut back during operations), but since cooked rice spoiled quickly, it also prevented them from smuggling it out. Meanwhile, intensified controls made it easier to spot the new, softer suppliers who could be pressured into becoming informers due to fear or in hope of reward. Finally, security patrols were brought to a peak, sometimes leaving a "honey pot" or soft spot. Insurgents coming to this spot to meet suppliers-turned-informants would find themselves in a killing field. The SF preferred captures—to generate new information—but the grim reality was that 67 percent of insurgents eliminated up to August 1957 had been killed.[27]

Nevertheless, from 1952, "hearts and minds" measures also intensified. It had always been intended to improve village "aftercare." However, spatial control and security had come first. Changes in citizenship rules in September 1952 meant the majority of locally born Chinese could now apply for citizenship. Municipal elections began in December 1951, and New Villages were soon electing councils. The critical breakthrough in politics came at Kuala Lumpur municipal elections in February 1952, with the formation of the "Alliance" of communally based parties.[28] It was also made clear to residents of New Villages in 1951–54 that, while failure to give information would result in decreased rations and increased curfews, assistance would be rewarded. This ranged from individual rewards for information on insurgents to the declaration of "white areas," where all restrictions were lifted. There was an increasingly stark government waving of both carrot and stick.

The perception of villagers was one of "terror" and coercion from each side, as well as an extreme gap between the government-offered stick (detention, deportation, curfews, even execution for possessing a weapon) and carrot (rewards, "white areas," and political representation). This gap was intended to make the head choose cooperation with the government, even when the heart still went out to the insurgents.

In addition to intensifying the system of reward and punishment, new measures also involved more emphasis on precise targeting. During 1951–52, New Villages were divided into sections, each under a Home Guard division, so punishments for failures could be targeted at particular Home Guard and village groups. There were also plans to increase the arming of Chinese Home Guards. The mere suspicion among the MNLA that a Home Guard *might* give information hurt MNLA morale and operations. Furthermore, contact with officials on patrol or at meetings provided everyday opportunities to give information without detection by the communists.[29]

Templer built on these trends, while injecting heightened melodrama into their execution. Take Tanjong Malim. Like many "bad" areas, this was a center of wartime anti-Japanese resistance. In March 1952, District Officer Michael Codner, famous for his wartime escape from a POW camp, was among those killed by the MNLA when repairing a water pipe near Tanjong Malim. Soon afterward, Templer swooped down, personally telling the people of Tanjong Malim and nearby villages that they would be subject to twenty-two-hour curfew while sealed boxes were delivered, and that he alone would read the contents. Restrictions would be lifted only if they contained new information. Villagers had every reason to be frightened, since in November 1951 the entire village of Tras had been detained following the High Commissioner's assassination nearby. Furthermore, State War Executive Committee (SWEC) papers demonstrate how this became an established modus operandi. The SWEC would label a village "bad." Templer would be called in to berate inmates, after which they would suffer draconian restrictions as inducements to supply new information. Restrictions could include reduced rations, clearing surrounding grassland, almost total curfew, limiting of store hours, and forced renovation of public facilities.[30] In fact, the resulting information seems to have been less useful than anticipated.[31] The official visits were publicity displays, while the core work went into food-intelligence operations. In the case of Broga New Village, Templer, standing in the market square in July 1952, berated the village, which was subject to an additional series of measures up to August 1953. Afterward, villagers were described as silent, resenting what they regarded as "unjust punishment."[32]

In addition to the sanctions, such measures were accompanied by increased security for "bad" villages that the government hoped ultimately to turn around. For instance, starting in July 1952, Broga received new fencing, perimeter lighting, increased police, and assurances that those who were coerced into helping the MNLA would not be prosecuted if they reported this quickly.[33]

This was a resource-intensive battle to persuade villagers they could have "confidence" in the state, both for their immediate physical security and for their long-term economic prospects. It was an attempt to turn the experience from one of being "between two terrors" into one of being offered refuge by government spatial control against one remaining terror.

Despite the complexity of this picture and its mixing of coercion and kindness, what lingered in the world's memory was the phrase "winning hearts and minds." This was Malaya's gift (and curse) to COIN.

Putting the population at the center of the account, by contrast, helps us to avoid artificial contrasts between "winning hearts and minds" and "kinetic" or coercive approaches. It shows how British COIN blended these, and how the particular balance of ingredients changed over time. It also defies a recent trend for counterinsurgency histories to stress the more militarized sides of British COIN, rather than its true essence in population and spatial control.[34]

THE BATTLEFIELD: THE LAND, LABOR, AND PEOPLE OF MALAYA

"At present the Chinese public in the Federation, especially those in the rural areas, live in constant dread both of the Communist Terrorists and Government and are placed between the upper and nether millstones between which they stand to be crushed."

—Tan Cheng Lock, Chairman of the Malayan Chinese Association (MCA), in a memorandum to Oliver Lyttelton, Britain's Colonial Secretary, December 1951[35]

"So many things were endured in those days between two terrors, that of the police, and that of the People Inside."

—Han Suyin, a doctor and novelist in Johor and Singapore (1956)[36]

The Emergency was, on its surface, a struggle between the MCP and Malaya's British rulers and their local allies. But at a deeper level it was also a civil war: a struggle that forced Malaya's growing population (close to 5 million in 1947 and 6 million by 1960) to choose between being for or against the MCP. [37]

This internal conflict raged fiercest on the fringes of what Han Suyin describes as "jungled wilderness"—a "green hell with terrifying ferocity of growth"—that blanketed four-fifths of Malaya. [38] Forests radiated from a spine of mountains, which ran from north to south, bisecting the country. [39] At its fringe, the jungle eased into *lallang*—waist-high grasses—and then plantations of rubber trees, which covered 15 percent of the land. Finally, rubber and *lallang* gave way to coastal plains dotted with towns and *kampongs* (villages), spread with rice fields or pockmarked with tin mines from which loomed giant dredging machines.

The most critical space was the forest frontier. On one side, roads and rivers sped reinforcements to most locations within an hour or two; on the other, a platoon might hack its way through at two miles an hour. On one side, food was plentiful; on the other only the *orang asli* (aboriginal forest people) could find enough to stave off malnutrition and hunger. It was to the forest frontier that Chinese fled to escape prewar unemployment and wartime oppression from the Japanese, and to profit from high prices generated by postwar food scarcity. By 1947, around half a million Chinese lived near this frontier. Some planted vegetables or tapioca, or raised pigs and chickens. Others worked for rubber plantations or on nearby tin mines. Some owned land, but more were "squatters" with no legal title, or tenuously holding one-year Temporary Occupation Licenses (TOLs). Squatters typically lived on land owned by mines, plantations, or the state, in the latter case reserved for forestry or for the Malays. The Malays—as the main occupants of the Malay States Britain had promised to protect and advise in the late nineteenth century—had special protection. Many of the Chinese "squatters"—one in ten of the total population—therefore led a precarious existence.

This group also had a turbulent past. When the Japanese occupied Malaya, in 1942–45, Japanese troops had screened the Chinese for anti-Japanese leanings, massacring thousands. A communist-led Malayan People's Anti-Japanese Army (MPAJA) sprang up to fight the hated occupiers. The MPAJA's "mountain rats" became heroes to the squatters. But the MPAJA left a bitter aftertaste for many. Malays in the police and administration suffered most from the MPAJA's postwar reprisals against collaborators, which in places descended into Sino-Malay racial clashes. Starting in 1943, the MPAJA also received British help, as antifascist allies. At the end of the war, in December 1945, the MPAJA laid down their arms in return for a small payment. The communists converted their efforts into union work and into building a "united front" with nationalist parties in order to push for workers' rights and peaceful decolonization.

The "united front" policy sought to exploit British promises to reorganize its dependencies. Before the war, each Malay state had a sultan, who agreed to accept the advice of a British Resident, with only about half in a loose federation. Now all nine were corralled into a Malayan Union (1946–48). The British also indicated they would extend citizenship (previously restricted mainly to subjects of the Malay sultans) to most Chinese, and introduce elections soon. Singapore remained separate because it was thought that Malays were not ready to accept its inclusion and the overall Chinese majority that that would produce.

The British retreat from these positions helped to precipitate revolt. Many Malays were horrified at the union's removing the sovereignty of their sultans, at the prospect of most Chinese becoming citizens, and because they felt their community's special protections were being abandoned. They formed the United Malay National Organization (UMNO), whose protests persuaded the British to limit Chinese citizenship and negotiate a new "Federation of Malaya," inaugurated on February 1, 1948. The federation gave some powers back to the sultans in their states, and as protectors of the Malays. Meanwhile, the communal tensions this aroused delayed elections. By early 1949, feelings ran so high that the British started a Communities Liaison Committee, in order to restart intercommunal discussions in private.

The British calculated that, although they still aimed for

common citizenship and multiracial politics, they could not *force* the Malays to embrace this vision. Hence, they resolved to appease the UMNO in the short term and work toward rapprochement between the communities. Meanwhile, in 1946–47, a range of parties, including the MCP and the Malayan Democratic Union (which included MCP members and non-communists), bitterly opposed British retreat. In a wider front that also included the Malay Nationalist Party (MNP), the MCP proposed a "People's Constitution," to include common citizenship and a quick move to elections for a majority of seats in the Legislative Council. They organized a nationwide *hartal*—combined work stoppage and demonstration—in October 1947, all without winning any concessions.

According to MCP Secretary-General Chin Peng, the inauguration of the new federation helped persuade his colleagues to abandon their "united front" approach. The new Legislative Council was to include 16 representatives nominated from employers, six for English-speaking unions, but none for the MCP and its affiliates.[40] On February 1, 1948, discussions between Chin Peng and his colleagues were interrupted by the sound of guns firing on Kuala Lumpur's *padang* (green space), to mark the inauguration of the federation. MCP leaders finally agreed to drop the "united front" and devise a new set of policies, which included a commitment to support the labor movement by coercing and killing *kongchak* (labor thieves), fomenting more disputes and refusing conciliation, and mobilizing ex-guerrillas. This was to culminate in all-out warfare after September 1948. But the resulting escalation of violence prompted the British to declare a nationwide state of emergency on June 18, 1948, giving the High Commissioner the power to make such orders as he saw fit for security purposes: the "Emergency Regulations."[41] The British arrested more than a thousand people, badly hitting the MCP and Malay radical organizations and ensuring that their plans went off half-baked.

In reality, the communist call to arms was massively overdetermined. Beginning in late 1947, the international communist movement was moving away from the united front. As a Chinese party facing a partly hostile Malay population, the MCP wanted reassurance that its actions fit into a world picture—that they might be part of a Third World *iskra*, or spark—to foment a Western capitalist disaster. The former MCP leader Lai Teck had absconded in early 1947, discrediting his "united front" policies. The communists and British were also at violent loggerheads over strikes in 1947 and over squatters being thrown off their plots as TOLs expired and mine and plantation owners got businesses going again.[42] Any two or more of these factors might have been enough to set the country alight: together they supercharged the rush to violence.

Before we talk more about the Emergency itself, it is important to give some background on the union struggle that preceded it.

Wages of Field Workers, Rubber Industry, Federation of Malaya

	1939	1949	1950	1951	1952	1953
Wages	100	315	348	565	485	457
Cost of Living	100	412	372	586	604	580
Real Wages	100	77	94	96	80	79

SOURCE: Victor Purcell, *Malaya: Communist or Free?* (London: Victor Gollancz, 1954), 148.

From a worker's perspective, a number of things were clear by 1947–48. First, wartime inflation had been ferocious. Second, although tin mine managers and plantation owners did raise postwar wages (and living allowances), they refused to compensate fully for inflation. Third, many workers and their organizers had been radicalized by wartime association with the MPAJA or, for Indians, with the Japanese-sponsored Indian National Army (INA). The INA had fought the Raj on its Burma border in 1944. Some ex-INA became postwar union leaders and were in no mood to buckle in the face of management's use of trespass laws (stopping unionists from going onto plantation land), dismissals, and replacing strikers with new workers. The wartime MPAJA and INA had produced large numbers of eighteen- to twenty-four-year-olds able to organize workers. Fourth, when such organization occurred, intimidation and violence readily became an option. The Annual Reports for Malaya of 1947–48 noted that wartime violence, black markets, and crime had

produced "a reduction in the value of human life," a generation of
young people used to turmoil and removed from family influence,
and easy availability of weapons. It is true that after the war, crime
then fell in successive years, with murders reaching record lows in
early 1948, but the weapons, memory, and repertoires of action were
there to be grasped when the MCP decided to increase the violence.
One might argue that the MCP chose to revivify this violent potential before it atrophied.[43]

Violent Crime in Malaya: The Trend in the Immediate Postwar Years

	Murder Rates	Gang Robbery with Firearms	Robbery with Firearms
1946	421	853	764
1947	220	290	459
1948	470*	217	186

* Up until March 1948, the monthly murder rate was falling, with record lows of seven
murders a month (including political murders) in January and March. Then, from
May 1 to June 9, there were thirty-three "terrorist" crimes in Malaya alone. (*Straits
Times*, September 6, 1948, 1)

SOURCE: *Federation of Malaya Annual Report, 1948* (Kuala Lumpur: Government Press, 1949), 8, 123–25.

Fifth, the workforce was faced with managements increasingly
determined to restore their right to manage, backed up by a legal
system and police action that often seemed one-sided and overly violent. In February 1947, planters and police in Kedah decided that a
display of force was necessary to discourage labor unrest. In May
1948, Chinese employers reduced wages by 20 percent.[44] Sixth, the
MCP overplayed a strong hand—many workers looked to it for leadership and it delivered victories—by easy recourse to intimidation
and by politicizing disputes.

The MCP funneled unions into wide agglomerations, first General Labor Unions, then Federations of Trade Unions, culminating
in the Pan-Malayan Federation of Trade Unions (PMFTU).[45] Strikes
soared in 1947–48, and by early 1948, demands included a 100

percent wage increase. The British responded by trying to weaken communist federations and get noncommunist unions to compete. A new Trade Union Ordinance was introduced on May 31, 1948, restricting officials to people of a union's particular trade and federations to unions of similar trades. This, coupled with the banning of those convicted for intimidation or other serious crimes from being officials, was the final provocation, since it would dismantle the federations and exclude many MCP members from union positions.

In addition, an October 1947 legal decision confirmed the right of an employer to fire three plantation workers for "breach of contract" in striking. Clearly, the majority of Malaya's rural workers needed union protection, and worked in arduous jobs for real wages that remained low. As Han Suyin recalls:

> I stayed for a short time with a Chinese rubber tapper, a patient of mine, on a small plantation near Johore Bahru. The family rose at three in the morning; three of the five children went with their parents into the darkness of rubber, their heads shrouded in black cloth to ward off the myriad stinging mosquitoes. They ran from tree to tree; two hundred, three hundred trees. . . . [T]he tapper was paid by the load of latex he tapped. . . . Then children went to school tired out.[46]

These workers relied on the plantations for their homes, for medical dispensaries, and for small schoolhouses for their children's education. But this reliance meant that most tappers also needed to minimize lost wages and the risk of dismissal and eviction.

The politicization of struggles left them "between two terrors" even before the "Emergency" was declared. On Dublin Estate (a rubber plantation) on April 28, 1947, police were called to remove an outside union official from a meeting in one of the plantation's buildings on grounds of trespass. Managers believed this was legally justified as a means to prevent "intimidation." The speaker, Lim Soo, objected that he was a member of a registered union holding a peaceful meeting. From the worker's viewpoint, when they lived in labor lines, where else could they meet? When police tried to remove Lim Soo, he shouted *misti lawan* ("let's fight"). Missiles were hurled and punches thrown at the thirty policemen by a crowd of two hundred fifty to three hundred. Some police then opened fire without orders, killing one and injuring several.[47]

In other cases, there is clear evidence for communist-orchestrated intimidation, as well as for employer and official obduracy. On June 1, 1948, police tried to arrest some men at a Johor rubber plantation, in connection with an earlier assault (again resulting from an attempted eviction). Workers felled a tree and wielded *parangs* (long curved knives) and *changkols* (hoes). The police charged, leaving several dead and thirty injured. But the background was murky. Some laborers had threatened to take over the plantation, and the management fled.[48]

On June 2, police also descended on two oil-palm plantations near Slim River, Perak. According to the procommunist *Min Sheng Pau* ("The People's Livelihood Newspaper"), eight hundred armed military and civil police were "used to besiege the oil-palm estate [plantation] in Kuala Slim, and ousted seventy-nine fellow workers from the estate . . . taking away . . . cutleries . . . wrist-watches and other valuables. . . . They even threw the foodstuffs of the workers on the floor, . . . urinating on them. All the above acts are not unlike the 'round up' which the Japanese did during the occupation."[49] At first this looks like just another heavy-handed employer action, calling in police to evict people linked to a strike and to demands for a 25 percent pay increase and six-hour day. The management said it would close the plantation and refuse negotiations until these men left. The police trucked them out. But in response, Chong Sam Chew, a female communist, and others ordered twelve hundred laborers off the plantation under threat of violence and destruction of their homes. On June 8, after her arrest, the laborers returned, to rejoin Malay workers who had never left.[50]

By this point, threats were in deadly earnest. Even before March–May 1948, there were elements willing to use paramilitary approaches. A.M. Samy, an elderly shopkeeper and founding member of the Kedah State Indian Union, ran the *Thondar Padai* (Tamil for "Volunteer Corps"). It picketed plantation toddy (alcohol) stores and used stick-wielding youths to set up roadblocks, enforce pickets, and resist police detention.

Following MCP orders of March and May 1948, labor violence took a deadlier turn. The *Straits Times* of June 4, 1948, reported two laborers killed at a mine eleven miles south of the capital, Kuala Lumpur. Ch'ng Chin and See Chong had broken a strike: "The two men were dragged from their beds at two o'clock in the morning." One was taken to the mine office and shot through the chest; the other suffered a similar fate behind the "*kongsi* house." Beginning in April, the MCP's Workers Protection Corps were stepping up violence. One Perak MCP Area representative, a "tough gun-man type," explained that, "Anyone not for the M.C.P. is against the M.C.P. and must be eliminated—hence the recent killings. . . . By eliminating all opposition M.C.P. would then get full support of the people, and a democratic government could be formed. Amongst the main obstacles were labour contractors, and 'running dogs', those who worked for the government or passed information to it." [51] Yet, despite government repression, "There has been quite a bit of controversy over the question of change of policy to one of violence and bloodshed" with one "clique" arguing it would not get far, another that "extremist methods and finally an armed rebellion" were the only ways to self-government.

The latter "clique" won. The entire Perak setup had been reorganized in early May, splitting the single political committees into two: one for politics (including supplies), another for military matters. Open "united front" trade unions had been replaced with "Red" secret organizations. Those thought to be potentially unreliable (for instance, some who had escaped from Japanese capture in the war) were removed. Indian organizations remained separate, with R.G. Balan's unions cooperating with the MCP's Rubber Workers Union. Finally, in Perak, a headquarters section had been established on the jungle's edge and started calling up fighters. [52]

The Emergency itself intensified pressure on workers. Some were recruited as Home Guards. The PMFTU was banned on June 13, 1948. Many Indian unionists went into the jungle, and union membership slumped. Despite the temporary increase in wages in 1950–52 as a result of stockpiling for the Korean War, less than 20 percent of the workforce was now unionized, with Chinese underrepresented. Plantation employers agreed to new pay scales in 1953, but gains in real wages remained limited.[53] During the first few years of the Emergency, the MCP neglected union penetration. Ironically, some of the main results of communist-led insurgency were, therefore, the vitiation of the Malayan labor movement and the weakening of left-wing politics.

By the time the British declared a state of emergency, some unionists were already going underground. P. Veerasenan had been shot dead on May 3, 1949. S.A. Ganapathy, the first president of the PMFTU, had been caught in possession of firearms in April 1949 and was executed on May 4. Approximately two hundred "insurgents" were hanged over the course of the conflict, over one hundred of them by 1951.[54] When unionism did become a major force again from the mid-1950s, it was in Singapore rather than Malaya.

WINDOWS ON A CONFLICT

What I want to do next is to provide windows onto a wider range of "people's" responses to the Emergency, from "fence-sitting" villagers up to the Secretary-General of the MCP. This will allow us to glimpse how insurgency and counterinsurgency worked in Malaya from the inside, from the perspective of the Min Yuen, fence-sitters, and anti-insurgents inside the New Village/Concentration Camps. It will also offer additional insight on how many of these people saw themselves as pressed "between two terrors."

The Min Yuen

Jungle fringe "squatters" had been the guerrillas' wartime suppliers.[55] Beginning in June 1948, the insurgents wandered into squatter areas to collect food. The villages with the strongest communist support thus became battlegrounds. The British swept through with hooded or hidden informants, picking out bandit supporters.[56] The communists returned to intimidate anyone identified as helping the British. As Security Forces (SF) numbers escalated, the MNLA had to build a more resilient network. In 1949, it rearranged supporters into the more secretive Min Yuen (Mass or People's Organization). By 1951, the Min Yuen was underpinning the struggle of more than seven thousand guerrillas, pitted against forty thousand British and local troops, seventy thousand police, and two hundred fifty thousand Home Guard.

There was, however, a fatal flaw in the MNLA and Min Yuen. Less than 10 percent were non-Chinese.[57] There were significant numbers of Malay and Indian supporters, but these remained small minorities of their respective communities. Hence, the United Malay National Organisation (UMNO) emerged as the largest Malay nationalist party, built around conservative leaders from the aristocracy and administration, supported by teachers and journalists. It was anticommunist, and some members remembered MPAJA intimidation at the war's end. Some of the Malays who did join radical postwar groups had partnered with the MCP in political campaigns. A significant portion found themselves in danger of arrest in 1948, or were inspired by tales of historic Malay resistance to colonialism and went into the jungle. In particular, a Malay 10th Regiment of the MNLA was formed. A significant number of these Malays had recent links to Indonesia.[58] For Indians, there were two obvious routes to the jungle. Many had been trade union leaders. Others had been inspired by the wartime, Japanese-sponsored INA and found the communists the most rigorous anticolonial allies.

By 1947, Malaya's population was around 49 percent Malays and related groups, 38 percent Chinese, 11 percent Indians, and less than 2 percent Europeans, Eurasians, and others.[59] The Chinese made up a small percentage of those with citizenship until an amendment in September 1952 automatically extended this to around 50–60 percent, with the option for more to apply.[60] Different groups tended to mix in the marketplace without mingling cultures. They kept their own languages, ceremonies, and schools, thus sustaining a plural society. Only a minority enjoyed common education, mainly in English-language schools. All this complexity was crammed into a relatively small country. At just 50,850 square miles, Malaya was similar in size and shape to England without Wales, and only slightly smaller and less populous than the state of Alabama.

Because the MNLA and Min Yuen remained overwhelmingly Chinese, Chinese smallholders were thus the main human battle-ground. In addition to being targets of government "counterterror" in 1948–49, these smallholders were also targets of terror commit-ted by the Min Yuen, whose jobs included raising supplies, collect-ing money, and reporting "running dogs" (traitors) for punishment. Enforcement could be brutal. In April 1951, four tappers lay in wait for two nights for Chin Ah Chen on a Penang rubber plantation, then "pounced on him and kicked him to death." When they were sentenced to hang in 1952, the press branded them "weekend ban-dits."[61] As government pressure on Chinese settlements increased, many of these weekend bandits and people's representatives gradu-ated to become full-fledged fighters.

The Fighters

"I joined the guerrillas because I knew that they were good people. My family life was hard; I had no chance to study. The Communists taught me a lot. I felt this was the path I should take to a have a decent future."

— Huang Xue Ying, a female guerrilla who
joined in 1948, about fourteen years old [62]

Why did people become fighters? For some, the experience or ex-ample of wartime fighting is the answer. Insurgency was not only a response to socioeconomic exploitation. For many, the "Great Asian War" that started in 1937—the struggle between China and Japan—was a more potent motivation, followed later by elation over the new, communist China.

The most dramatic example of the political journey made by many Chinese is provided by Ong Boon Hua, alias "Chin Peng." Chin Peng was born in October 1924 to Chinese immigrants who ran a bicycle and motor parts shop in Perak. He has said, "If my parents had approved my [teenage] request to go to join the Military

Academy, perhaps I would have joined the Kuomintang." [63] But he was too young. Instead, he stayed in school reading everything he could about the China conflict. Mao's *On Protracted Warfare* (1938) persuaded him that the communists knew best how to defeat Japanese aggression. So he joined communist-led anti-Japanese organizations. Thus, he started as an overseas Chinese patriot who wanted to help his homeland by whatever means possible: boycotts, fund-raising, organizing others, or volunteering to go and fight. He graduated from student and labor work for the MCP to full party membership in 1940, and in the war rose to be the main MCP liaison officer with Britain's clandestine military unit in Malaya (Force 136). Only in the war did he complete his metamorphosis to self-consciously "Malayan Chinese," ideologically committed to the country of his birth and to communism, and inspired by Soviet resistance to Germany. The conversion was made easier by the proximity of capitalist exploitation in Perak's tin mines, and by the example of Chinese classics that championed the underdog's fight for justice, such as Han Suyin's *The Water Margin*. Han Suyin echoes this osmosis between cultural roots and insurgency when she has the fictional fighter Sen sing an old Chinese saying:

> I will go to the forest for justice.
> The wind for my garment I wear.
> Together with my many companions,
> The wind for my garment AND THE RAIN MY DRINK,
> We build a new heaven and earth. [64]

Yet for Han Suyin, these passionate young were also too impatient, their "eyes merciless with truth, twin judges without passion or pity for the foolish old ones who claimed wisdom, and preached patience, and had forgotten to provide for the dreams of the young." [65] On a less intellectual level, many had become emotionally committed to the communists during the war, or because of the MCP's postwar unionism. From 1948 to 1949 the MPAJA's successor, the MNLA, won yet more people through propaganda against feudal (including gender) exploitation. They courted others by practical solidarity with poor farmers, tappers, and their children—for example, teaching people to read in night schools.

For poor villagers such as Huang Xue Ying, whose rubber tapper father died during the war, a blend of education and indoctrination made her feel, "This was the path I should take to have a decent future." She joined in 1948 despite family opposition. Huang Xue Ying's oral testimony confirms the scholarly analysis of the American sociologist Lucien Pye, who, after visiting Malaya and analyzing interviews with surrendered insurgents, concluded that joining the party was less about ideology than about personal connections to leaders they thought would help them into the modern world. It was about "their desire for personal security and personal advancement," in a world where poverty or war had prevented more than a minimal education. Han Suyin similarly noted that communism seemed to offer a pathway to modernity.[66] It also placed the insurgents' lives in an international context, linked to "progressive" forces led by the Soviet Union and inspired by the communist march to victory in China. The declaration of the People's Republic of China (PRC), in October 1949, and British diplomatic recognition of the PRC, in January 1950, boosted confidence. Until the communist march was halted in Korea in 1950–53, it seemed to many insurgents that they were backing a winner.

But there was a more bitter side to becoming a fighter, as many found out in the war. Attacks on the Japanese invited discovery of your base or retribution against surrounding villages. The British also wanted to preserve guerrillas to assist future reoccupation. As Freddie Spencer Chapman, a British officer in Force 136, reported, "[T]he only action that was encouraged was the wholesale removal of spies and informers."[67] His 1945 report provides a fly-on-the-wall view of life inside the jungle camps he stayed in, stuffed with "rural coolie types," tin miners, "rubber tappers, vegetable gardeners, squatters, timber workers," with a sprinkling of Chinese schoolmasters, "foremen, mechanics, tailors, small contractors, barbers, and shopkeepers." Even the occasional businessman's son or daughter who had "swung left" to communism inhabited the camps. There were few urban types, and—according to Chapman—the best jungle men were wild jungle rubber tappers and "dulangers" (illicit tin washers). Mandarin was the official language, but there was a cacophony of Chinese dialects.[68]

The mission of bringing justice produced impressive discipline. Violence was reserved for "Japanese sympathizers" and what little thievery there was. But there was a pervasive dread of betrayal, which might lead to capture and torture. Hence, informers, Chapman noted, "are burnt with brands, cut with knives, and beaten almost unconscious with rattan before being shot or bayoneted to death." Chapman added, "Informers are dealt with summarily, and rightly so. On one occasion, in the middle of a concert, the scene suddenly changed and I found we were trying an informer in grim earnest. Although, as always, he was allowed to defend himself and call witnesses to his defence, within half an hour he was condemned to death and, while the play went on, a party was detailed to carry out the sentence."[69]

Camp life, meanwhile, was necessarily harsh. Camps were usually located two to three hours' walk (three to six miles) from a *kampong*, screened by swamps or "across mountain torrents," up to two thousand feet up on a ridge or over a summit. Nearby *orang asli* or villagers might provide advance warning of attack. Initially they had a headquarters, hospital, parade ground, and huts with raised platforms, festooned with propaganda posters. As the Emergency wore on, they shrank, and the need for frequent moves and invisibility from the air made life increasingly spartan. At the best of times, food was limited, except when they could visit villages, or fortuitously kill a jungle animal. Often there was but a single "vegetable" (for Chinese, meaning any accompaniment with rice), low calorie intake, and continual problems with malaria, fevers, and deep, running, suppurating sores that remained stubbornly open for weeks or months.

What relieved this picture in the early part of the Emergency was the easy communication across the jungle frontier of 1948–49. In that period, fighters could slip quietly into the village or villagers could visit comrades during Chinese New Year, "to give them treats, snacks and cakes" and watch the plays the MCP delighted in staging.[70] Later, as resettlement restricted supplies, food shortages could become desperate, and many guerrillas' worst memories were of prolonged hunger.[71]

Refugees and Fence Sitters

There can be no doubting the enthusiasm of some "revolutionary families" and of individuals who went to the mountain. But others wanted to avoid trouble—understandably so, when you look at casualty figures. Until 1957, over ten thousand people had been killed, or were missing and presumed dead. The insurgents had lost 6,398 of their number. They had killed just 1,851 SF, compared to 2,461 civilians. Another 807 civilians were missing.[72]

Somewhere between the ardent revolutionary and the "fence-sitter" (as British documents dubbed the uncommitted majority) was another category, the "refugee." One of these, calling himself "Tan Chin Siong," wrote to Tan Cheng Lock in May 1950.

Tan Cheng Lock was a wealthy businessman and president of the Malayan Chinese Association (MCA), an organization set up in 1949 to provide social welfare to squatters and so lure them away from communism. The MCA subsequently became a political party and aligned itself with the UMNO, winning the vast majority of seats in town, state, and federal elections between 1952 and 1955, and persuading the British to grant full independence on August 31, 1957. This meant that the anticommunist Chinese (businessmen, English-educated Anglophones, and traditional leaders of clans and associations) had accepted influence on government as vital but remained junior Alliance partners of the UMNO.

In his letter to Tan Cheng Lock, Tan Chin Siong wrote, "Now you may call me a terrorist, or you may call me a refugee" from the mass arrests of 1948–49. He had been a union committee member who ran away to work as a Min Yuen subscription collector. Why, he asks, had insurgent numbers ballooned since 1948? In answer, he related the story of the insurgent unit he helped to supply. In 1948, it comprised around forty low-skilled members surrounded by a "fence-sitting" public. Slowly, arrests created a flow of "refugees." In 1949 the unit grew to one hundred fifty, becoming more organized, though still with poor technique. As of 1950 it had grown to around 180 and was becoming more effective.

Tan Chin Siong characterized this group as being 10 percent high-caliber leaders, 20 percent MPAJA veterans, and 70 percent refugees, adding, "It could be said that the Government helped the Malayan Communists to recruit." He conveyed the pervasiveness of police bribery, arguing that it not only alienated the population but undermined security. The letter reported that Special Constables were accepting bribes from communist organizers in exchange for identity cards. It also alleged that the police were shooting people after disputes, so that "if any one had disagreement with the police he should be careful even when walking on a public road."

But Tan Chin Siong held that there was still another factor in communist recruitment. This was the creation of "heartache" by forcing people to "evacuate" their homes and crops; displaced youths provided the most ardent recruits. A government that knew only how to use force, not political means, was stoking the fires. "The slogan that since death is everywhere they should fight against the Government to the end is common throughout the rank and file."[73]

Tan Cheng Lock put the latter case to Oliver Lyttelton, the new Secretary of State for Colonies, in a memorandum dated December 2, 1951. The Chinese were, he said, being crushed between the upper and lower millstones, between demands from the government and fear of communists. Government must improve its attitude to the Chinese and trust their leaders more. Tan's warning reflected the fact that, by this point in late 1951, the government policy of population control was subjecting the rural Chinese population to intense—and intensifying—pressure.

Conflicts in New Villages

> The Bamboo music was lively and rousing
> How miserable Tras resettlement was
> Here another meal with dried and salted fish
> A deeply bitter experience we suffer in silence
>
> —Hakka song by Tras New Villagers,
> composed at the Ipoh detention camp[74]

"There were many severe restrictions placed on us in the concentration camps. Layers and layers of barbed wires fenced
us in. . . . They could fence us in physically; they could not
fence in our hearts. As long as their heart is in the struggle,
people will always think of ways to support the revolution."

—Chen Xiu Zhu[75]

By 1952–53, New Villages were seeing improved perimeter security
(barbed wire, lighting), facilities (halls, schools, clinics or Red Cross
Nurse visits), and organization (village committee elections, raising
of Home Guard, and increases in its arming and security responsibili-
ties). Government provided compensation (though goods sold were
not always fully reimbursed), but the land chosen was sometimes bad.
Controls were most severe when local operations peaked; this was
especially true starting in 1950–52, when disruption occurred with
frequency. Villagers had dangled in front of them the prospect of intensified pressure, including the possibility of mass detention, if they
refused cooperation, and the prospect of rewards, including cash and
the removal of all Emergency controls, if they helped.

By 1954 there were approximately four hundred eighty New Villages. By 2002 some four hundred fifty were still in existence, and
their population had almost doubled. By 2007 there were 1.256 million (82 percent Chinese, 13 percent Malay, and 4 percent Indian) in
New Villages, representing around 21 percent of Malaysia's Chinese
population.

New Villages in Malaysia, 1954–2002

	1954	1970	1985	2002
New Villages	480	465	452	450
Population	572,917	1,023,000	1,650,000	1,250,000

SOURCE: Malaysian Chinese Association (MCA), *The Guardian*, Vol. 4 (2007),
"Revisiting Our Roots: New Villages": mca.org.my/Chinese/Guardian%20
pdf/GUARDIAN%20AUG.pdf

The history of New Villages has recently been the subject of
new studies, including oral history, novels, and online projects. The

authors of these projects are mostly Chinese speakers and, as such, are well placed to bring a "people's history" of "New Villages" to fruition.[76] Their work confirms that the experience of many New Villagers was one of being "between two terrors" and highlights the social ferment within the villages. Resettlement did not instantly domesticate villagers to government desires. While some Min Yuen went to the mountains, others remained. As Chen Xiu Zhu, a courier, supplier, and fighter from northwest Malaya, recalls, Min Yuen who stayed told storekeepers not to enter all stock into their books, passed food over the wire, hid food under fertilizer, or bribed police to look the other way. Chen Xiu Zhu even used her smaller siblings to observe supply convoys in order to warn of approaching security forces.[77]

Another window onto this world is provided by the *Report on the Food Searches at Semenyih in the Kajang District of the State of Selangor,* which recorded disturbances and protests at Semenyih New Village in reaction to searches at the New Village gates from late 1955 to January 1956.[78] Semenyih New Village was surrounded by a three-mile lighted and guarded perimeter fence, and in early 1956 was subject to a house curfew from 7 P.M. to 5 A.M., with no exit from the gates before 6 A.M. It was also subject to food control measures. Semenyih had been assembled around an old settlement twenty-one miles south of Kuala Lumpur, with resettlement swelling its population from 2,308 in 1947 to 5,150 in 1955. As workers were paid a proportion of rubber tapped, it had a "thriving appearance."

Why did this village experience protests? In part, it was a matter of logistics. Around 2,500 tappers (60 percent women) wanted to leave through one gate (Kachau Gate) every morning. Yet they had to be searched thoroughly, since the surrounding areas had seen much "bandit" activity, "including the murder of a Chinese rubber tapper who was found tied to a tree and who had been shot twice and stabbed in the throat." Food control had begun in 1952, but at the time of this report, supplies were increasingly seeping out. As of September 1955, controls intensified, in preparation for a major operation. In one incident, in November 1955, an impatient crowd forced their way through Kachau Gate. The key problem was how to process 2,500 people so they could tap early when latex flows best, when most wanted Kachau Gate, and could only leave their houses at 5 A.M. and the gate at 6 A.M., when they rushed to their tapping. The police manned two searching booths, one for women and one for men, outside the gate. Most tappers were just frisked on their way out, but if the booth was empty, a person was directed inside to have their undergarments searched.

Protests emerged for two reasons. First, delays made it diffi-cult for tappers to get to work on time. Second, for more personal searches, the army provided burlap tents with a lamp outside. These proved translucent in particular combinations of light and angle. By January 13, 1956, protesters were going to local representatives, and the press ran articles entitled "Strip-Tease Riles Village," and "Women Forced to Expose in the Nude." The official report did not automatically blame Min Yuen agitation, but noted tensions between the female searchers and the searched, resulting in cloth-ing (on occasions removed to leave cotton underpants and a cotton undershirt) sometimes being thrown outside the tent.[79] Semenyih was atypical in having temporarily used very unsuitable searching huts, but it otherwise offers a window onto the world of the tightly controlled New Village.

A recently published novel, *Deep in the Jungle* (2010), written by Liu Dan, suggests that such incidents were the inevitable result of an incendiary clash among at least three categories of political leaning within villages. Basing his writing on interviews with ex-fighters, he paints a picture of fermenting tensions between these groups.[80] There were the "fence-sitters" keen to keep out of trouble. But alongside them were passionate procommunists and anticom-munists. On one side were the Min Yuen and the MNLA sympa-thizers, many with relatives in the jungle, in detention, or already deported. On the other side were people who were actively helping the government, whether as Home Guard section leaders, in the police, on village committees, as MCA representatives, or through informing.

Chen Xiu Zhu described herself as being from one of ten "revo-lutionary families" in her New Village, representing around fifty to one hundred people out of at least several hundred. This toxic cocktail of hatreds and suspicions could fuel petty sexual insult and verbal jousting, which could end fatally. The aggrieved might tell the communists a person was a running dog, or the authorities that they were communist. Chen Xiu Zhu recounted confrontations with "the traitor at the gate" and "the Head of the New Village." Her family was even told at one point to leave the village because they would not tell where their brother was. He was with the MNLA.[81]

Intense control and pressures in small communities contributed to a brewing cauldron of emotions and dangers. This was brought to its most intense pitch as government operations peaked in each particular area.

Loyalists

"Everyone lived in fear of the communists during the Emergency."

—Sheah Choi Yea, a former auxiliary policeman at Simpang Tiga New Village, eighty-two years old[82]

In the battle to control the New Villages, the people willing to stand for election to village committees, search fellow villagers, pass information, or lead Home Guard patrols were vital. Some joined the MCA and were particularly vulnerable to attempted assassination. Tan Cheng Lock himself had suffered a grenade attack. In another case, in Kuala Pilah, two grenade attacks were launched on successive MCA representatives, the second killing three of one committee member's children.[83] The MCA ran a lottery, distributed funds, helped screen detainees, and then reorganized itself as a centralized political party in October 1951. This enabled it to join UMNO in the Alliance in February 1952, and afterward, as part of that Alliance, to govern postcolonial Malaya. The MCA had turned itself into a truly mass organization, for instance, having sixty thousand members in Perak alone by 1952, out of the state's 444,000 Chinese. That meant that 13 percent of Perak's Chinese were members. In the 1950s and 1960s, many New Villagers looked to the MCA to try to influence government.[84]

The MCA, an agglomeration of people with anticommunist interests, was not "loyal" to the colonial government per se. They might be supporters of the Kuomintang in Formosa/Taiwan, businessmen, store owners, or association leaders. They aligned with government insofar as it shared their anticommunist interests but quarreled with it over its insufficient sympathy to Malaya's Chinese population. Furthermore, beginning in 1952, they showed a preference for a partnership of communal parties. Britain had hoped that cross-communal politics would emerge, but they gradually gave way as the Alliance won election after election.[85]

If there is one glaring hole in our understanding of the Emergency, it is of the MCA. Thus far, we can garner little more than glimpses of its perspectives. From oral history collections, we know, for example, that one Home Guard in Bukit Tinggii joined at eighteen and became a patrol leader. In an interview, he recalled that most of his generation joined. Some were killed as "traitors," whereas he was wounded. He explained that the communists knew who they were and would try to win them over, while at the same time, his group believed they identified about a hundred people as communists: "We Home Guards knew who they were."[86]

This interview illustrates the intimate contest for loyalties within the village. It also shows how little we know of anti-insurgent actors in the villages. From the MCA leaders at the top to individual Home Guard section leaders and village committee members, we need more research on why and how individuals align against an insurgency, and how their "confidence" was gradually won over by security measures and by ratcheting up opportunities to help the government. In short, we need a new understanding of the dynamics of the different groups at work inside the villages that insurgents and counterinsurgents compete over.

CONCLUSION

By its nature, any attempt to write a "people's history" cannot fit within the bounds of a single chapter, unless those cover very specific events or narrow themes. It demands a multivocal and bottom-up view of history that devours pages.

For that reason, I have concentrated on giving a taste of the perspectives on insurgency that this approach might generate, with particular regard to how some of these are essential to understanding the Emergency specifically, and insurgency and counterinsurgency in general. In this way, I have attempted to give a glimpse of the perspectives of the rural villagers at the epicenter of these struggles in order to understand how intimately their world was tied to that of the insurgent, supporter, refugee, anti-insurgent, administrator, soldier, and policeman. In doing this, I have also sought to emphasize to what extent the majority who actively participated in insurgency probably did so not as fighters and Min Yuen, but rather as Security Forces, Home Guard, and MCA members. If we truly want to understand the world of the village-at-war, we must place as much weight on understanding these groups as we do on reconstructing counterinsurgency policy making and insurgent stratagems. In particular, the conditions under which people can acquire sufficient confidence in government to take sides must be central to our understanding of why the Emergency unfolded as it did. It is only in increasing our understanding of the hypersensitized, intimate world of the villager and the way in which people inhabiting these villages interact that we can get closer to the core of what makes insurgency and counterinsurgency tick.

2

THE PHILIPPINES— "ENGENDERING" COUNTERINSURGENCY: THE BATTLE TO WIN THE HEARTS AND MINDS OF WOMEN DURING THE HUK REBELLION IN THE PHILIPPINES

Vina A. Lanzona

INTRODUCTION

From the beginning, women have been at the forefront of the U.S. war in Afghanistan. The burka-clad woman was the symbol of Taliban hostility to women. In both official and popular U.S. representations of the war, their uncovering marked their freedom as well as their reinstatement into their rightful place in the home and society. But according to the correspondent Ann Jones, in the ensuing counterinsurgency (COIN) war against the Taliban and other hostile forces, the women of Afghanistan, "whom George W. Bush claimed to have liberated so many years ago, are still mostly oppressed, impoverished, malnourished, uneducated . . . and mad as hell."[1] Despite women's roles as "combatants, cooks, dependents, supporters of armed groups, community peace advocates, spies and informers," in Afghanistan's long history of war and conflict,[2] the current COIN strategy advanced by the U.S. and Afghan military continues to ignore and marginalize women. Women have been scarcely consulted or considered by "American military leaders" who "slip easily into the all-male comfort zone," "probably relieved to try to win the 'hearts and minds' of something less than half 'the population.'"[3]

Military and academic critics of the COIN program in Afghanistan, especially those who point to the campaign's lack of attention to women, echo similar sentiments raised earlier about the U.S. counterinsurgency wars in Vietnam and the Philippines from the 1950s to the 1970s. These two wars, waged by the United States more than seventy years ago in Southeast Asia, had radically varying results: while COIN experienced utter failure in Vietnam, it was more successful in the Philippines, which partly explains its potency and persistence as a war strategy in subsequent conflicts. In Vietnam, the U.S.-supported South Vietnamese government fell, paving the way for the reunification of the country under the socialist government of North Vietnam.[4] In the Philippines, however, the Communist-led Huk Rebellion was defeated by a comprehensive counterinsurgency program conducted by both the Philippine and U.S. governments.

The conflict in the Philippines succeeded the decades-long fight for national independence. When the Philippines finally achieved independence in 1946, after more than four hundred years of colonial rule, its new republic was immediately confronted by the massive Huk insurgency. Also known as the Huk Rebellion (1942–56), the movement began in March 1942, at the height of World War II, when leaders of peasant organizations and the Partido Komunista ng Pilipinas (Communist Party of the Philippines, or PKP) formed the Hukbo ng Bayan Laban sa Hapon (Anti-Japanese Army), or Hukbalahap, or Huk for short, to resist the Japanese Imperial forces.[5] At the end of the war, the new Philippine republic vowed to work with the Huks in rebuilding the nation. But with the onset of the Cold War, the Philippine government closely aligned itself with the United States, which immediately moved to discredit and harass the Huks to undermine their popular support. By August 1946, the Huks had been forced by political repression to go underground, and its peasant members reorganized in the forests of Luzon to launch an armed resistance movement against the Philippine government.

Believing that the Philippines was not yet completely free from the grip of the United States, the Huks joined other nascent, nationalist, leftist-inspired movements in the Third World (like Ho Chi Minh's Viet Minh movement in Vietnam) in launching an organized insurgency against the Philippine republic. Between 1946 and 1950, they reorganized the *Hukbong Mapagpalaya ng Bayan* (HMB), or People's Liberation Army, which quickly grew in size, claiming at its peak roughly fifteen thousand armed guerrillas.[6] Supported by an even larger number of noncombatant, mostly peasant supporters, the Huks were able to capture villages, drive out landlords, and redistribute land among the tenants, while at the same time launching successful surprise attacks against the Philippine Constabulary.[7] By the beginning of the 1950s, the Philippine government, with the aid of U.S. military advisers, was pursuing an aggressive counterinsurgency campaign against the Huks, which entailed swift military action and a series of policies designed to win the "hearts and minds" of the population. By 1956, the Huks were in disarray, peasant support in the towns and *barrios* (villages) of Central Luzon had declined sharply, and the Huks were in a state of terminal decline. With the subsequent surrender of many leaders and rank-and-file members of the Huk movement, this phase of peasant revolution and communist insurgency came to an end.

The Huk Rebellion is considered by many historians and scholars to be the most successful resistance army in Asia during World War II, the most important peasant movement in Philippine history, and the first major challenge faced by the newly installed Republic of the Philippines. In the postwar global Cold War era, it became famous as the first major communist rebellion defeated by U.S. counterinsurgency operations. In the years after the Huk Rebellion, Philippine and U.S. policy makers and military personnel analyzed closely the different aspects of this counterinsurgency war, using its "success" as the model for future campaigns against left-wing insurgencies by the U.S. government.

But how truly successful was COIN in the Philippines? This essay aims to revisit the "success" of the U.S. counterinsurgency war against the Huks, focusing on the "people"—or, in the language of COIN strategists, the "enemy," the "civilian," the "population"—that were the targets of such campaigns. As most discussions of COIN endlessly reiterate, the most important principle of any successful counterinsurgency operation is winning the "hearts and minds" of the population, which is just as important as staging

successful military operations, if not more so. But who were these
people and how did they figure into the various discussions and debates on counterinsurgency? More specifically, I want to focus on
the women—both inside the Huk movement and among the civilian population—who were often depicted as the "targets" of COIN
operations, but whose voices and concerns were not sought out or
incorporated—and were often ignored—in counterinsurgency deliberations. Using my own work on the role of women in the Huk
Rebellion in the Philippines, I will focus in this essay on how notions about gender and sexuality shaped the counterinsurgency
campaigns launched against the Huks. In many ways, the successes and limitations of these COIN operations depended heavily
on the gendered assumptions—about appropriate male and female
roles, their different weaknesses, strengths, and limitations—
perpetuated by the political and military institutions of the Philippines and the United States.

ENGENDERING COUNTERINSURGENCY:
WHERE ARE THE WOMEN?

In 2008, Spencer Ackerman, a military affairs observer, wrote that
"while women are still underrepresented in the national-security
apparatus—and at the Pentagon specifically—counterinsurgency,
more than any other previous movement in defense circles, features
women not just as equal partners, but leaders." Defining counterinsurgency as "a method of warfare that emphasizes economy of force,
intimate knowledge of host populations and politico-economic incentives to win that population's allegiance," he described women as
"ideal counterinsurgents." Ackerman writes:

> In a series of interviews, leading women counterinsurgents,
> and some of their male colleagues, discussed how the un-
> conventional approach to military operations calls for skills
> in academic and military fields that have become open to
> women in recent decades. Others contend that counterin-
> surgency's impulse for collaborative leadership speaks to

women's "emotional IQ," in the words of one prominent
woman counterinsurgent. Another explanation has to do
with coincidence: the military's post-Vietnam outreach to
women has matured at the same time as counterinsurgency
became an unexpected national imperative.[8]

"It is not that women are 'better' at this stuff than men," according to
Janine Davidson, a former director in the Pentagon's Special Operations and Low-Intensity Conflict and Special Capabilities, "it is just
that the problems associated with populations involve non-military
skill sets and knowledge from fields where women have tradition-
ally been better represented than they have been in the military."[9]

The growing presence of women in defense and military circles
is a recent phenomenon, and many scholars and experts are quick to
point out that women still face enormous obstacles and that gender
parity in the military remains an elusive dream. But what is striking, according to Ackerman, is not only how many there are, but
"how many, if not most, of the most prominent women in defense
circles are counterinsurgents—even if most of those women are not
themselves combat veterans." The prominent role of women in current COIN circles and in COIN deliberations demonstrates the inextricable connection between gender and counterinsurgency. Such
debates are characterized by highly gendered assumptions about
women: that women's social, nonmilitary skills, their ability to negotiate and compromise, and their all-around image of passivity
(rather than aggression) make them naturally well suited to ensure
the success of COIN, where community building and reconciliation
are top priorities. In the battle for the "hearts," if not the minds, of
the civilian population, women have a natural advantage over their
male counterparts and counterinsurgents.

This sensitivity to gender has long been present in counterinsurgency strategy, although in the past, women were viewed principally
as the targets rather than the agents of COIN policies. Significantly,
in the joint U.S. and Philippine counterinsurgency campaign
against the Huks in the 1950s, women were completely absent from
defense circles. While they had enlisted in the U.S. Women's Army

Corps since 1943, it took another twenty years for women to enter the Women's Auxiliary Corps in the Philippines.[10] Women were marginalized in formal military circles through much of the early postwar period. Yet, discussions about military issues in general, and counterinsurgency in particular, were replete with notions about gender and sexuality and the role of women in Philippine society. Although not officially articulated, systematic efforts were advanced by both the U.S. and Philippine militaries that made women the central targets of counterinsurgency campaigns.

Between 1962 and 1963, the RAND Corporation, a private think tank, devoted two symposia to analyzing the success of U.S. counterinsurgency operations in the Philippines. Organizers hoped that the lessons learned from the war against the Huks could be replicated as the United States and other allied powers were drawn into a new counterinsurgency campaign in Vietnam.[11] The conferences included senior officers from various defense and military departments, including the air force and the army, and from various countries, including France, Great Britain, Australia, the United States, and the Philippines.[12] Not a single woman was present at the conference. But the conference itself and the book written soon after by Colonel Napolean Valeriano,[13] the leading counterinsurgency expert from the Philippine army, placed great emphasis on the role of women. Ideas about gender appeared in discussions on such topics as "knowing the enemy," the "civilian and targeted population," and the "propaganda and military campaigns." Counterinsurgency campaigns were framed as "unconventional warfare" precisely because of their emphasis on strategies intended to "win the hearts and minds" of the public, a public composed mostly of women.

In recent years, the relationship of gender and counterinsurgency has become an important research topic among social scientists and academics, and within military circles. A thesis written by Colonel Laura Loftus, for example, titled "Influencing the Forgotten Half of the Population in Counterinsurgency Operations," recognizes the role of women as peacemakers and peacekeepers, providing what she calls a "moderate voice" in both the public and private spheres, to help bring an end to armed conflict. As Loftus states, women are "hugely influential in forming the social networks that insurgents use for support." Indeed, without women's support, most armed movements would not be able to sustain themselves. But while the military often acknowledges women as victims of war, constituting 80–90 percent of civilian casualties, Loftus argues that it is time for the military to directly engage women, to understand their needs and interests and their influential role in society, and to use this knowledge in staging U.S. counterinsurgency campaigns.[14] This analysis reinforces highly conventional ideas about women by labeling them mainly as peacemakers and conciliators and also as people who care only about the private sphere—the home and children—and not about abstractions like justice and equality, which are seen as male obsessions and pregnant [sic] with violence.

These ideas have had an impact on U.S. COIN policy. In the current U.S. counterinsurgency campaign in Afghanistan, special units made up of women from the army and the marines called Female Engagement Teams (FETs) have been trained to work with Afghan women to engage in a range of missions, "from winning their hearts and minds" to "gathering intelligence." These FETs perform various functions: they deliver humanitarian aid, help out at health clinics, protect Pashtun women, and even "mediate between American and Afghan male egos." They are the face of American goodwill and soft, female power. Yet, as Ann Jones reports, these FETs often get no training and little resource support, and generally leave a "trail of good intentions and broken promises." As Jones writes, "it's one of the ironies of FETs that women soldiers, insufficiently trained to defend themselves, must still be escorted by men, just like Afghan women."[15]

U.S. military advisers also recognize the importance of targeting local Afghan women in counterinsurgency campaigns, as the military analyst Rikke Haugegaard argues of women:

- They build strong networks and conduct daily activities separated from the local men.
- They raise future generations and exercise strong influence in the family.

- They can generate their own income.
- Local women provide soldiers with important information about the local environment, including information about the Taliban, weapon stocks, etc.[16]

Nonetheless, and not surprisingly, Afghan women, the supposed beneficiaries of U.S. liberation, are often marginalized and treated instrumentally in COIN programs. As Jones writes, "American commanders, saddled with nation-building, doled out millions of dollars in discretionary funds intended for short-term humanitarian projects to build roads (which unescorted women can't use) and mosques (for men only) before anyone suggested that women perhaps should be consulted." Most often, women find themselves in a new form of imprisonment: being "locked up" by the men to protect them from the foreign military units that patrol everywhere. It is a strategy that is summed up in the title of one U.S. report: "Half-Hearted: Trying to Win Afghanistan Without Afghan Women."[17]

Some scholars explain the discrepancies between policy and practice of COIN by pointing out the specifically "gendered ways" that war against indigenous populations is "formulated, put in practice and experienced."[18] Laleh Khalili sees the gendering of counterinsurgency everywhere: in the way populations are targeted for violence, and for "nation-building"; in the ways soldiers use sexuality in dealing with locals; and in the way ideas about gender shape policy making. Counterinsurgency has become more "population-centric" and more sensitive to gender, and has been increasingly defined as a "feminized" form of warfare, in contrast to the mechanized, technologically advanced, and hypermasculine character of conventional and drone warfare. As Khalili remarks, "a gendered body becomes a necessary, indeed desired, accessory to war, serving the functions and interests of counterinsurgency—the softer, humanitarian tasks that are required to ensure the winning of hearts and minds—much more efficiently and effectively."[19]

And yet, this gendering of COIN policy does not necessarily mean a more empathetic view of women, or even a COIN strategy that is more community- and family-centered. While women are the effective targets of COIN, policies are still largely formulated by men, who insist that the way to "disengage" or "disarm" the enemy rests upon particularized and feminized priorities involving the family, children, and community. This feminization gives women (as both agents and receivers of COIN) a more central role, but, as we have seen in Afghanistan, still a subordinate one, in wars of conquest and occupation.

The simultaneous centrality and subordination of women also shaped the counterinsurgency war waged by the U.S. and Philippine governments more than five decades ago. The battle against the Huks marked an important turning point in the "engendering of war," as women and notions of gender and sexuality took center stage in COIN deliberations and operations. The role women played both inside and outside the Huk Rebellion remains instructive, and helps to deepen our understanding of the successes and limitations of COIN and its incorporation of women. How did women and notions of gender and sexuality shape the discussions, policies, and operations of the counterinsurgency war against the Huks?

THE BATTLE TO WIN HUK WOMEN'S HEARTS AND MINDS

Women are central to any understanding of the Huk Rebellion.[20] Recruited via familial and village networks, Huk women—most of them from peasant families, poorly educated and generally perceived as traditional and passive—joined the movement because of a variety of motivations: to be close to kin, to escape Japanese brutality, to continue their prewar political involvement, or to be part of a growing movement for national liberation. These women studied the tenets of Marxism, trained as soldiers and spies, and learned to use weapons. Occupying the full range of military roles, some of these Filipina revolutionaries attained formidable, even fearsome, reputations as aggressive fighters—hence their image as "Amazons" within the wider culture.[21] At its peak, about one in ten active guerrillas was a woman, numbering about one thousand to fifteen hundred active female Huk guerrillas, with thousands more women comprising a support network for the Huks in the villages.[22] Incorporating women into the military and political struggle waged by the Huks forced the male-dominated leadership of the PKP and the U.S.-sponsored Philippine government to confront new issues that were not part of their original political and military agendas.[23]

Women performed essential roles in the Huk movement as couriers, nurses, educators, propaganda workers, and even as combat soldiers. Many more were involved as peasant supporters in the *barrios* of Central and Southern Luzon, which were the major strongholds of the rebellion, performing mostly "domestic" duties such as cooking, washing, and housekeeping. The activities of these women, as either Huks or as supporters, were essential to the social basis of the Huk Rebellion. And for these women, participation in and support for the movement reinforced their sense of place and their connection to their families, their villages, and even to the nation.[24] Despite the absence of women in formal discussions about the Huk "insurgency," without women and their support there would not have been a rebellion in the first place. And without addressing issues that were important to women and issues of gender and sexuality, counterinsurgency operations would not have been effective. These were realities that both the Huks and the Philippine state and military understood very well.

In the three core wars that constituted the COIN campaigns against the Huks—the war against communities, the propaganda war, and psychological warfare—the Philippine military paid great attention to women, both inside and outside the movement. But inherent in the COIN strategies pursued by the Philippine state was a basic misunderstanding of women's role in the family and in the community. In the end, although women were used to weaken the movement, there were no serious efforts by government and military policy makers to incorporate their needs and interests into the COIN campaigns. Thus, from the perspective of women, COIN did not win hearts and minds, and even before the war ended, it had lost any real sense of legitimacy and purpose.

War Against Communities

In his 1962 book on counterinsurgency operations in the Philippines, Colonel Napolean Valeriano defined the guerrilla using Mao
Zedong's oft-quoted phrase, as one who "must move among the people as a fish moves in the sea." "This is the central, the essential, the
ineluctable characteristic of guerrilla warfare," Valeriano continues,
"without people, the guerrillas perish."[25] For him, the guerrilla, and
the Huk guerrilla in particular, was an "individual relying on the
support of the people, fighting the government . . . for an ideal not
otherwise attainable," and guerrilla warfare was characterized by
"maximum employment of deception, concealment, intelligence,
and improvisation."[26] Because guerrillas lacked logistical and combat capabilities, they relied almost totally on the "voluntary contributions" from the people, or the so-called masses.

Although guerrillas moved among the people and relied on
them for support, Valeriano distinguished carefully between the
guerrilla and the innocent, peace-loving village resident, whom he
regarded as a helpless victim, unable to resist the guerrillas' persuasive and coercive influence. Indeed, Valeriano believed it was vital
for the counterinsurgent to continually differentiate the guerrilla
from the innocent villager, although he realized that the embeddedness of the rebellion in village life made this task difficult—
even impossible. In his view, counterinsurgency operations aimed
to weed out the guerrilla from the village, and therefore to break
down communities and separate friends from the so-called enemy.
Breaking down village life was thus essential to counterinsurgency
operations and to the process of rehabilitating and reintegrating insurgent villages and villagers into a restored social order.

A gendered understanding of the Huk movement complicates
this rather narrow understanding of the roots of the rebellion.
Early on in the war, the Huk leadership recognized that the male-
dominated military alone could not win the war.[27] Despite the absence of a formal recruitment strategy, women quickly became an
important part of the national liberation movement.[28] And the recruitment and participation of women in the Huk Rebellion demonstrated how embedded the movement was in the villages of Central

and Southern Luzon. Just like the men, personal and extended family networks played a critical role in recruiting women to the Huk movement. Kinship relations, crucial to survival and security in Philippine rural societies, became even more important during the Japanese occupation, as families and neighbors provided mutual protection to the guerrillas against their perceived enemies, whether Japanese or Filipino collaborators, and provided vital support in the daily battle for survival. In the postwar period, the same networks of kin—close family, friends, and extended family—facilitated the recruitment of guerrillas to the HMB, and Huk guerrillas often found safe havens in the villages, where women provided them with much-needed logistical and material support.[29]

The female Huk courier Araceli Mallari echoed Valeriano's conception of the guerrilla in her reflections on the success of the Huks in mobilizing the villages of Central Luzon:

> In the towns, we tell [people] that the military cannot exist without the masses. It was like the fish in the water, parang isda at tubig iyan. Ang isda hindi mabubuhay kung wala sa tubig. Kaya, ang tubig ay ang masa, ang gerilya, ang militar ang isda. The fish will not survive if not in water. So, water pertains to the masses and the guerrillas are the fish. So, if you will not organize the masses, the guerrilla could not exist. Where will you hide? Who will feed you?[30]

As Mallari understood well, the bodies of water that sustained guerrillas were composed largely of peasant women, and these women were an indispensable part of the popular base of support for the Huks.

The Huk movement was therefore more than just an army; it was a movement embedded in the community, a fact that was enormously important to Huk men and women. Both men and women in the Huk movement abided by principles that were designed to break down the distinction and distance between the guerrillas and their peasant supporters. Villagers would feed guerrillas who helped them plant and grow their vegetables. They would hide guerrillas who vowed to stay away when danger was imminent. Preserving and encouraging the bond between Huk soldiers and the communities from which they came reflected the social logic of the Huk movement, but it became a major challenge to the government and military during the counterinsurgency war.

Interestingly, both the Huks and the practitioners of counterinsurgency used the "fish in the water" metaphor to explain Huk mobilization. But where Huks used the metaphor to explain the embeddedness of the movement, COIN experts used it to explain the dependence of the so-called guerrillas on so-called civilians, implicitly dividing the two and advocating that a wedge be driven between them. While the Huks saw the guerrillas and villagers as one and the same, COIN experts saw them as separate, and assumed that catching the fish would remove a source of contamination from the water.

This principle of separation and distinction legitimized the efforts of COIN operators to break up peasant communities. To the Philippine government and their American military advisers, it was not community solidarity and strong kinship relations but communist agitation that explained the success of the Huk movement and the threat it posed to the political order. According to them, the communists "undertook the organization of the restive agricultural workers in Central Luzon" by encouraging economic illusions and exploiting the "antagonistic attitudes" of peasants toward the government "to incite lawlessness and disorder."[31] Consistent with the paternalism of cold war ideology, the Philippine and U.S. governments pursued a policy designed to "unmask the Red monster that insidiously play [sic] on the gullibility of the masses."[32] Since the Huks were "Communists who sought only to overthrow democracy and the Philippine government," and "brainwash the poor peasantry" into thinking that their economic and social problems can be solved "through bloodshed, violence and revolution," the solution to the problem posed by the government was straightforward: repression and the defeat of the armed rebels.[33] While counterinsurgency experts had a basic understanding of the social connectedness that sustained the guerrilla movement, their solution was to divide communities and to pit close family and friends against one another. Such a solution reveals a masculinized conception of politics and community, in which both peasants and the guerrillas appear as free agents, easily manipulated and, in the end, acting only for themselves and their own personal interests. This atomistic and liberal conception of village life both underpinned official policy and was its logical goal.

A liberal masculine understanding of Huk support necessitated an equally masculine solution to the rebellion, a solution that found its embodiment in the person of Ramón Magsaysay. At the height of the rebellion in 1950, President Elpidio Quirino appointed Magsaysay, a congressman from Zambales, as his new secretary of national defense. Having been a guerrilla during World War II, Magsaysay had a definite plan for defeating the Huks, a standard COIN strategy that entailed not only strengthening the Philippine military but developing a political program that encouraged Huks to surrender and peasants to relinquish their support for the rebels. Magsaysay called the policy all-out force and all-out fellowship, and it aimed to "fight the active Huks with relentless military force but to give them all-out friendship when they have surrendered and proved their good faith by aiding the campaign against their former comrades."[34]

According to Walden Bello, the rapid political ascent of Magsaysay in the postwar period was part of a carefully orchestrated plan, conceived by the Philippine government in close collaboration with Colonel Edward G. Lansdale, an air force officer and Central Intelligence Agency (CIA) operative, who was the military adviser under the Joint U.S. Military Assistance Group (JUSMAG), and who personally directed the counterinsurgency war against the Huks. Bello argues that "the strategy that Lansdale put together cannot be separated from his personal background. He was not simply an agent of covert warfare and counterrevolution but apparently a 'true believer' in the export of U.S.-style democracy."[35] And it was Lansdale who perfected both a military and a political agenda aimed to win the war, an agenda premised on the principle of divide and rule, of exposing and isolating the guerrillas, and of threatening the local populace.[36]

The election of Magsaysay as president of the Philippines in 1954 further undercut the Huk movement and its support in Central and Southern Luzon. A self-styled populist who prided himself on his ability to connect with ordinary Filipinos, Magsaysay transformed the military into a more effective and less abusive institution, proclaiming the Armed Forces of the Philippines (AFP) and the Philippine Constabulary (PC) protectors of *barrio* people. Under his leadership, control of the AFP and PC was consolidated in the Department of National Defense, and eleven new battalion combat teams (BCTs) were created and trained in antiguerrilla warfare. He increased the number of well-trained soldiers stationed in Central Luzon, a measure he claimed was intended to protect innocent villagers from both Huk violence and landlord lawlessness, again ignoring the embeddedness of the Huks within their communities.[37] By focusing their military attacks on the Huks and pursuing a policy of coercion and conciliation in the *barrios*, these BCTs forced the Huks to retreat to their mountain bases, successfully cutting them off from their peasant supporters, and making the rebellion much more costly to the Huk movement. Between 1950 and 1955, the military claimed it had killed over 6,000 Huks, wounded nearly 2,000, captured 4,700, and forced almost 9,500 to surrender and accept an official amnesty.[38] Magsaysay's program of reform, which included improved infrastructure, the construction of health clinics, the creation of agrarian courts, and the provision of credit to small farmers, also appealed to Central Luzon peasants despite its often propagandist goals.

The best example of Magsaysay's rural reform program was the Economic Development Corps (EDCOR), which spent several million pesos and resettled 950 peasant families on land they were given in Lanao del Sur, Mindanao. Reinforcing the goal of breaking up communities, EDCOR allowed Huk rebels, especially those who voluntarily surrendered to the government, to uproot themselves from their homes and their communities in Central and Southern Luzon. It was a fitting piece in the elaborate construction of Magsaysay's image. According to Valeriano, EDCOR "was an example of Magsaysay's doctrine of all-out force or all-out friendship that effectively stole the thunder from the Huk propaganda cry of "land for the landless." [39] The choice of Mindanao was part of the elaborate plan. The Promised Land was in the far south, less settled and developed, and separated the guerrillas from any "possible Huk re-contacts." [40] Here the former guerrillas struggled to start their lives again with no linguistic training, and no support from kin and friends. Settlers were given only a modest amount of support to till the land and were not able to find jobs elsewhere in the area. The land given to these Huk rebels was also obtained by displacing poor residents of the area, including indigenous communities, and as a result, the Huk settlers were treated with hostility by the people of Mindanao. While government and military officials hailed this program as a success, most scholars regard EDCOR as a failure, and most of the former Huks quickly moved back to Central Luzon. Indeed, this program could probably claim only one major success: the breaking up of communities in both Central Luzon and the Lanao area in Mindanao.

The counterinsurgency war against the Huks was effectively a war against communities. As Colonel Valeriano stated, the purpose of COIN was not only to isolate the armed guerrillas but "actually to cause disruption and disaffection within guerrilla operations." [41] On one level, this strategy worked. As the guerrillas became more and more isolated, and as the military presence placed a serious strain on peasant support, the rebellion went into decline. But the Central Luzon communities suffered serious losses; families were torn apart by the counterinsurgency war; children were abandoned by their parents, who were killed, imprisoned, or forcibly relocated; and women, more often than not, were left to sustain their families by themselves. A gendered understanding of the rebellion—one that recognized not only the central role of women but the embeddedness of the movement in communities—would have provided a more nuanced and complex view of the Huks' strength. Rather than recognizing the value of strong communities, counterinsurgency operations aimed at destroying the bonds of community, a move that took decades to rehabilitate.

The Propaganda War

Another essential principle in counterinsurgency is the spread of powerful propaganda. Magsaysay was a master of propaganda, unleashing a well-conceived propaganda war against the Huks, again with the help of Lansdale, who was a former advertising executive and expert in "public relations and the manipulation of public opinion."[42] Magsaysay had at his disposal all forms of media communication, especially the press, which followed his every move and publicized his every word. Mainstream journalists heralded him as the hope of the nation, and as a strong, uncompromising, but compassionate anti-Communist crusader. Writers and authors gave him various titles: "the dynamic Huk conqueror," "an extraordinary man of faith," "a top friend of Asia and the U.S.," "the knight of the masses," and "a man of the people."[43] As the face of the new government, Magsaysay was both strong and tender, a man who embodied a rare form of Filipino masculinity. He always appeared regal—a gentle giant who stood more than six feet tall, with broad shoulders and a big smile—yet always possessed the common touch. Magsaysay was very physical, and as ready to give a strong slap on the back as a soft kiss on the cheek. While he exuded great confidence, he was never afraid to show his "soft" side, occasionally shedding tears in public. He was relentless in his fight against the Huks, but he also appeared sincere about encouraging the Huks to give up their arms with promises of amnesty and new lives in Mindanao. In all his speeches and press appearances, he bragged about the success of his counterinsurgency campaigns, especially in winning the hearts and minds of the people. A speech commemorating the fall of Bataan during World War II captures his style:

> By this policy of all-out force and all-out fellowship we are making good progress, we are fighting a winning war. But we cannot rest or relax as long as one armed Huk remains in the field or one scheming communist remains in his society. We must never let ourselves forget that a Huk until he changes his mind and his heart is not a Filipino but a traitorous agent of foreign aggression.[44]

Despite this tough exterior, Magsaysay never failed to show a compassionate side. For example, in a speech at the Army and Navy Club in the Philippines in 1952, he declared, "Not bullets but bread will hasten the solution of the Huk problem and a deep understanding of the lot of the masses will do wonders in restoring the rebels' faith in government." [45]

Government propaganda during the Huk Rebellion was gendered in many ways, and such gendering was all the more pertinent in the press appeal toward women—as Huks and as consumers. Throughout the rebellion, the press covered closely the exploits of female fighters in the movement. These female guerrillas were indiscriminately labeled *amasonas* (Amazons) in the Filipino vernacular, and their actions were followed with intense curiosity and scrutiny in the press—women warriors elicited awe and admiration, as well as fear and hostility. The portrayal of these women in popular newspapers and magazines was meant to represent a particular form of Filipina femininity that journalists hoped would be rejected by the reading public, and especially its female consumers.

Headlines in the postwar period that portrayed Huk women as hardened soldiers, distraught mothers, and communist organizers, as well as young, innocent, and pretty girls, capture the complex and contested representations of these women warriors. The depiction of Huk women was an important part of the government-backed propaganda war against the insurgents, and the government and press often acted in tandem to discredit Huk women. The press coverage of the Huk Amazons focused on three essential traits—female martial capacity, women's sexuality, and the issue of maternity.

The capture of Huk Amazons engaged in combat during the postwar period aroused great public interest. Journalists were obsessed with the appearance of Huk women and the contrast between their feminine appearance and their role as armed guerrillas. But fascination did not always translate into admiration. In the end, the government-controlled press was always critical of women who joined the Huks, and was generally unsympathetic and indifferent to their deaths at the hands of the Philippine military and Constabulary. This treatment was informed by a belief that female rebels, by virtue of their masculine, unwomanlike behavior, had forfeited any claim to respectable femininity, and deserved gruesome death, just like Huk men. Indeed, in order to justify violence against these women, the press cooperated with the state in depicting them as unnatural women. But despite its hostility to Huk women, the press was careful not to alienate them completely. After all, the real enemies were Huk men, and in the propaganda war it was vital to drive a wedge between Huk men and women, invite the women back into the fold of civilized society, and offer them the masculine protection of the Philippine state under Magsaysay.

This goal was most clear in the propaganda war's focus on issues of love and marriage. The government and the press portrayed Huk men as predatory communists and Huk women as innocent victims, a task made easier by the unorthodox sexual relations that characterized the Huk movement. During the late 1940s, the Huk movement was forced to deal with the "sex problem," when married men in the movement (and often in the Politburo) pursued relationships with young, single women in the forest camps, while their wives remained in the villages, often taking care of their families. This problem was addressed by the movement in a document called the "Revolutionary Solution of the Sex Problem (1950)," that permitted such relationships but only under certain conditions: that Huk men request the permission from their commanders to enter such relationships, that they disclose their status to both wife and lover, and that they settle with only one woman at the end of the rebellion. When journalists discovered this policy, they lost no time in using it to further discredit the Huks.

These "immoral relationships in the forest" fascinated the press, who sought to heighten the tensions within the movement by portraying Huk women as the sexual victims of predatory men. The press accused male Huk leaders of using their position to take advantage of women who were under their care and protection. "With lectures on party policy and a little flattery, coupled with these women's childlike simplicity and their hero-worship of their leaders," argued one writer, "high-ranking Huks had no trouble winning them over and conquering all resistance. The walls of modesty crumbled;

illicit relationships blossomed and became one of the great scandals of the Huk movement." This article traced the source of such scandal to the immorality of communist ideas, which encouraged "fornication in the forest," and "promiscuity in the party." "With no moral or religious principles to keep them away from evil," concluded a journalist, "the Huks fell headlong into the precipitous abyss of sex and grave moral disorder." [46]

The press knew how to take advantage of this "unfortunate" situation to win the propaganda war against the Huks. Stories of love-struck Huk women who had left the movement provided an ideal opportunity for the state to present itself as a "savior" who had "rescued" women from sex-starved, predatory communist men, restoring their femininity at the same time that it reinstalled them to their proper place in society. Most journalists played along, portraying communism as the enemy of femininity and domesticity, and praising female ex-guerrillas for "giving up the life of the hunted" and becoming dutiful wives. In this narrative of female redomestication, the Philippine military portrayed itself, and was portrayed by the press, as benevolent and sentimental, facilitating women's transition from rebels to wives and extending its paternalistic and protective care to all Huks, especially women and children.

Children also played a vital role in the counterinsurgency campaigns. In a 1962 symposium sponsored by RAND, military and government officials discussed how friendships with children—established through "the pocketfuls of candy," "playgrounds and youth centers, the officers' attendance at school games"—would aid the intelligence work of the counterinsurgents. Colonel Lansdale himself pointed out the "profound impression that American soldiers" made on the Filipino people simply by being kind to their children, feeding them sweets, and teaching them at school." [47] These actions, however, often led to a moral dilemma, even for the military, who wondered when the line between the benevolent, permissible use of children and their immoral exploitation should be crossed.

The sentimental attitudes of the state toward children appear often in the propaganda war against the Huks. While many journalists and reporters displayed sympathy toward Huk Amazons, especially those who fell in love with Huk men, this compassion vanished in stories about the children of the Huks. Indeed, the most serious charge leveled against female Huks was not that they were unnatural women, but that they were unnatural mothers. Newspaper reports of captured Amazons were often accompanied by stories of captured "Huklings," Huk children who were abandoned by their parents during military encounters, "rescued" by military authorities, and raised in military orphanages. In stories about the capture of Huk babies, the press and the authorities portrayed Huk Amazons as unfit mothers who waged war, had sex in the forest, got pregnant, and sacrificed their children to the goals of a communist revolution. These women had betrayed the nation and their duty as mothers by abandoning their children, who were now under the care of a benevolent state.[48] In the end, the only salvation for female Huks was to give up arms and embrace their natural roles as mothers in Philippine society. And their paternal state, with their paternal president, would be there to embrace them and welcome them home. Indeed, Magsaysay's policy of "all-out force and all-out friendship" reveals a father figure who could dispense punishment with as much ease as affection to his children. As José Veloso Abueva, the author of a political biography of Magsaysay, writes, "[H]is governmental outlook was familial and paternalistic. Like a good father, government was best to him which did most for the people, as quickly as possible, and with least waste."[49]

Psychological Warfare

Propaganda was only one aspect in the more general psychological war that the Philippine government and the military waged during their counterinsurgency campaigns against the Huks. An essential component of counterinsurgency is psychological warfare, which aims to break the morale of so-called dissidents, as well as elicit fear among their supporters. According to Walden Bello, "'psychological warfare' was one of Lansdale's specialties, and it ranged from 'dirty tricks' designed to confuse, disorient, and demoralize the Huks to public relations campaigns to win away their base and generate support for the government instead."[50] Just like the propaganda war, psychological warfare was gendered in many ways. The move to demoralize the Huks entailed the use of women and children as innocent, hapless victims caught in the middle of the war, and as agents who could bring dissidents back into the embrace of the family and society. The counterinsurgents used these gendered social relations in the many tactics of psychological warfare they employed against the Huks.

Some of the most potent weapons used by the Philippine government and military, in collaboration with the press and their American advisers, were the surrenders and gruesome deaths of Huk fighters. Here, women once again figured prominently. Most often, they were used by COIN agents to elicit guilt among the Huk men and to appeal to their sense of filial piety, as this story about the surrender of the Huk Supremo Luis Taruc demonstrates:

> The mother of Luis Taruc, the most respected of the Huk field commanders, made a tape-recorded appeal for him to surrender. This was broadcast over the radio repeatedly, primarily to show that this "hero" was actually a person who would not heed his mother. Taruc did surrender shortly afterward, and claimed that this appeal, which he had heard repeatedly, did have an effect on his actions.[51]

In his autobiography, Colonel Lansdale himself admitted his mastery of the techniques of psychological warfare.[52] One of the most effective tactics Lansdale employed was the so-called vampire death, as recounted by Bello:

> The body of the slain guerrilla was drained of its blood and puncture marks were made of its throat to make it appear like the victim of an *aswang* or vampire. It was then left on a trail. The trick apparently succeeded: prey to fears of the preternatural like so many other rural Filipinos, the guerrillas cleared the areas.[53]

In the Taruc case, the gendered nature of such appeals is inherent in the choice to use his mother as an agent of counterinsurgency.

But Lansdale's use of the *aswang*, a ubiquitous female figure in Philippine folktales, is more complex, reversing the discourse of victimization to men, away from the women. According to folktales, *aswangs* disguise themselves as young, incredibly seductive women during the day in order to attract unsuspecting men. But at night, they transform themselves into hideous creatures, whose winged upper bodies separate from their lower bodies in search of human blood. The use of the vampire was therefore not accidental in this psychological warfare. Here, women rather than men were depicted as predatory beings who use their bodies to deceive men. The use of the "vampire" also preyed on the insecurities of Huk men about their own masculinity. Choosing to become guerrillas, these men had abandoned their families and failed to provide security and support for their women and children, roles that were fundamental in Philippine society. Instead of being protectors and providers for women, they had exposed them to danger and placed them in harm's way. The vampire stories highlighted male vulnerability and female deviousness, further undermining a male sense of control within the Huk movement. The vampire tale, and "The Eye" leaflet, distributed among villagers to convey that they were constantly watched, were all part of an elaborate psywar campaign that aimed to break the Huks by generating fear and distrust in the Huk ranks.[54] No one could be trusted, not even women.

As long-suffering mothers or predatory vampires, women were central figures in the psychological warfare against the Huks. As Amazons or vampires, they were depicted as unnatural, bizarre, and deceitful women, who had to be controlled by men or rehabilitated by the state. And as love-struck guerrillas, or abandoned wives and mothers, women were portrayed as sympathetic creatures who followed their natural instincts to care for their families. In other words, different assumptions about women and gender were invoked depending on the Philippine state's intentions and strategies in conducting and winning the war. To sentimental and suffering women, the state revealed its own tender feelings and compassion, but to predatory and deceitful women, the state showed a firm hand.

In both cases, however, the paternalistic tendencies of the Philippine state and military were clearly enacted.

The appeal to family and traditional gender roles deployed by the Philippine and military authorities were all embodied in Magsaysay. As defense secretary and, later, president, Magsaysay exuded a persona that was both macho and paternal. Although he refused to back down or negotiate with the guerrillas, he also showed a humane side, was willing to forgive, and even posed as a father figure to Huk men who surrendered. Just as important, he was also something of a political celebrity who possessed a "showbiz" charm: tall, dark, and handsome, he possessed great popular charisma. Magsaysay's popular image reinforced dominant notions of masculinity in Philippine society: a macho man, who had a reputation as a ladies' man, he was extremely careful to cultivate an image as a loving and protective husband and a doting father that was deferential to familial and national authority. According to one leading counterinsurgent at that time, Magsaysay "was the champion of the masses, the great father and patriarchal figure of the nation, one who shows a deep and intimate understanding of the "people."[55] This larger-than-life image of Magsaysay as president, husband, and father was crucial to the government's psychological warfare against the Huks.

Such paternal imagery concealed the true nature of Magsaysay's political leadership. As Valeriano and Lansdale both attested, Magsaysay did not always adopt paternal policies toward the villagers of Central Luzon. According to Lansdale, Magsaysay became frustrated with the U.S. government when it began to shift its priorities to Korea in the early 1950s. And he was especially disappointed when the U.S government refused to give him napalm bombs, a weapon, Lansdale claimed, "Magsaysay very definitely desired to use against concentrations."[56]

Magsaysay however was only one part of the large and elaborate plan of winning the counterinsurgency war at all costs. As Bello further illustrates:

Psy-war [sic] also included the "planting" of false stories by contacts who were carefully cultivated in the mass media.

Anticommunist leaflets and films were also widely distributed. The selling of the land-resettlement program was
psy-war at its most sophisticated: a carefully crafted image
of plentiful land awaiting Huk surrenderees in the "virgin
land" of Mindanao was skillfully disseminated through the
media, and it achieved signal success in unsettling the Huk
mass base.[57]

The psychological warfare that Magsaysay and his agents waged
against the Huks helped to paralyze, demoralize, and deflate members of the Huk movement and erode its popular support. The tactics that were perfected during the Huk Rebellion were deployed
in innumerable and subsequent counterinsurgency wars by the
United States.

GENDER AND COUNTERINSURGENCY "SUCCESS"

In the counterinsurgency campaigns spawned during the Huk
Rebellion—the war against communities, the propaganda war, and
psychological warfare—women, as well as notions of gender and
sexuality, shaped COIN's discursive and strategic practices. Women,
children, and families, although not the direct targets of COIN, were
a central concern of policy makers and of the government and military officials responsible for the program to defeat the Huk insurgents. Indeed, the COIN campaign was shaped by their belief that
only by breaking down communities and families and promoting
traditional gender norms could they ensure COIN success. This did
not mean that the interests of peasant women concerned the agents
of COIN—far from it. It did not matter that female (and, to some
extent, male) involvement in the movement was directly related to
kinship ties and social networks. COIN required isolating the guerrillas from their supporters, and this involved dividing their communities and shattering the bonds of social solidarity and kinship
that played such a key role in village life.

In the COIN propaganda war against the Huks, women and notions of gender and sexuality shaped a developing national discourse

about appropriate male and female roles. Representations of Huk women also sent a strong message about the Huk men. Far from being the egalitarian crusaders they claimed, the Huk men were immoral predators who took advantage of young, innocent women and exploited them sexually. The psychological war against Huk rebels sought forcefully to remind Huk men of their roles as sons, husbands, and fathers, and to demonstrate the strong paternal hand of the state. By using women to lure men back into their families, where they belonged, or exposing them as deceitful and constant threats; by appealing to family values for Huk men to surrender and relocate to distant lands; and, most important, by promoting the career and image of Ramón Magsaysay as a strict yet loving and compassionate father, counterinsurgency operations ultimately broke the morale of the Huk rebels and led to the decline of the rebellion.

But what did these three "successful" COIN wars truly accomplish? Arguably, the COIN campaigns against communities served to further alienate villagers and peasants from the government. People stopped supporting the Huks out of fear and distrust toward the government, and toward one another, not because they were convinced of the state's benevolence and goodwill. And although both the propaganda and psychological wars foregrounded women, they did so only to pit them against their own families, reinforcing their passivity and contributing to their subordination. The complete absence of women in the conferences and deliberations in the aftermath of the rebellion indicates the lack of understanding of their essential roles and of the incorporation of their legacy in the male-dominated narratives of the revolt.

Predictably, the counterinsurgency campaign employed by the government was largely palliative, a strategy that attacked the symptoms of the sickness but not the sickness itself. Far from solving problems of inequality and social conflict in Central Luzon, counterinsurgency campaigns sought explicitly to increase social conflict, break down family and community life, shatter the collective morale of peasants in Central Luzon, and promote assumptions about gender that further victimized women and reinforced their inequality in society. The village strongholds of the Huks remained impoverished for decades, their residents traumatized by their post-war experiences. And while the Huks were defeated, the legitimacy of the government was constantly threatened by much stronger insurgencies led by the New People's Army (NPA), the MNLF (Moro National Liberation Front), and other dissident groups, all mobilizing support from villages much like those found in Central and Southern Luzon.

The failure to understand the social bases of rebellion, and the essential role of women in political struggles, explains much about the conduct of current counterinsurgency wars in the Philippines against the NPA and the Muslim insurgents in the south, as well as the U.S. COIN war in Afghanistan. In all these wars, women remain on the sidelines, their real views and desires ignored, while their bodies are used against their own families and communities to break the morale of guerrillas and their supporters. Far from "freeing women" from the godless, communist Huks or Islamic fundamentalists of the Taliban regime, counterinsurgency wars actually deploy highly conservative strategies toward gender and women that, in the end, exploit and marginalize women and reinforce masculine ideologies of conflict and power. More than sixty years later, the rhetoric and the reality of "winning the hearts and minds" of "civilian populations" in counterinsurgency wars still rings as hollow as true. This counterinsurgency war, premised on false assumptions about women and their central roles in the family, village, and society, is a war that will be forever unwinnable.

3

VIETNAM— UPROOTING THE REVOLUTION: COUNTERINSURGENCY IN VIETNAM

Hannah Gurman

"The legacy of Vietnam is unlikely to soon recede as an important influence on America's senior military. The frustrations of Vietnam are too deeply etched in the minds of those who now lead the services and the combatant commands. Caution has its virtues, of course. As will be noted, however, the lessons from which that caution springs are not without their flaws."

Major David Petraeus wrote these words in 1987, in his dissertation, "The American Military and the Lessons of Vietnam."[1] Two decades later, building on this argument for the revitalization of the U.S. military's counterinsurgency capacities, General Petraeus created the U.S. Army's Counterinsurgency (COIN) Center and oversaw the writing and publication of the much-celebrated 2006 counterinsurgency field manual. The guide became the basis of the new COIN doctrine and the conceptual blueprint for the wars in Iraq and Afghanistan under Petraeus's command. Repeating the old mantra of winning hearts and minds, but with a new twist, the post-9/11 proponents of counterinsurgency emphasized COIN's paradoxical nature: "Sometimes, the more force is used, the less effective it is," declares the 2006 COIN field manual (FM 3-24).[2]

The Vietnam War played an important though ambiguous role in the latest age of counterinsurgency. On the one hand, Petraeus and his supporters repeatedly dismissed analogies to counterinsurgency in Vietnam, arguing that "Afghanistan is not Vietnam. It's Afghanistan, just as "Iraq was not Vietnam. It was Iraq."[3] On the other hand, as part of an effort to incorporate the "successes" of past counterinsurgencies into the new COIN, they repeatedly invoked and incorporated into their manual and other literature 1960s counterinsurgency theory and specific programs from Vietnam.[4]

Thus, while ostensibly acknowledging the failure of counterinsurgency in Vietnam, the COINdinistas, as they became known, ignored the full extent of that failure and the underlying reasons for it. As the refusal to compare Iraq and Afghanistan to Vietnam suggests, these are not matters that U.S. military leaders or foreign policy makers like to discuss. To highlight them is to raise fundamental questions not only about the nature of U.S. counterinsurgency but about the broader motives and impact of U.S. military intervention.

THE LONG REVOLUTION AND LAND REFORM IN VIETNAM

In 1966, a Vietnamese farmer from the revolutionary stronghold of Hau Nghia Province in the Mekong Delta explained his motivation for joining the struggle against the U.S.-backed government:

> I was working as a laborer in a ricefield about a kilometer from my village when a VC cadre came and persuaded me to join the Front. . . . He said I would be working for the people and the nation, and thus for the liberation of the peasants from feudalism and feudal landlordism and the nation from American domination. Besides I would be given 2 hectares of land which I would then be able to farm as my own.[5]

Although the details of such individual stories vary, many accounts of the thousands who participated in the uprisings that swept the countryside of southern Vietnam over the course of the twentieth century echo the twin themes expressed by this farmer: freedom from foreign domination and the destruction of the feudal land tenure system.[6]

At the end of World War II, 80 percent of the population in southern Vietnam lived as tenant farmers, with 1 percent of the residents owning 44 percent of tillable rice land.[7] Land rents had increased over the previous four decades, while loans to poor farmers had decreased. These conditions worsened under the wartime Japanese occupation and one of the worst famines that Vietnam had ever seen, leaving large segments of the rural population destitute and hungry. An elderly man in My Thuy Phuong village recalled, "We got poorer every day. . . . There was no longer enough food."[8]

The redistribution of land played a key role in the postwar resistance against French colonialism. Through a campaign of cooperation with "enlightened" landlords and the assassination of those who resisted reform, the leaders of the anti-French Resistance redistributed large pieces of land to the rural populace. After the French defeat in 1954, the United States installed Ngo Dinh Diem, an ardent anticommunist and member of the conservative Catholic elite, as president of South Vietnam. Diem showed little interest in meaningful reform. Cadres in the National Liberation Front (NLF), the political organization of the uprisings—whose members included northerners who had resettled in the south after 1954, hoping to gain power through democratic elections—were instructed to "turn every issue into land terms."[9] Membership in the Front grew rapidly, drawing not just men, but also women and youth, who sought greater social as well as material equality. As one Front supporter in My Thuy Phuong put it, "We knew that everyone would not be rich under the Liberation policy, but we hoped that life would be better."[10]

This movement fueled the unrest that the United States confronted in the next phase of the war, the anti-American Resistance, known in the United States as the Vietnam War. The Resistance brought various segments of the population together under the broad banner of social and political revolution. While no single factor explains the appeal of the NLF, the historian David Elliott argues that NLF recruits were typically motivated by a combination of self-interest and idealism.[11] When he joined the NLF in 1964, the man from Hau Nghia Province considered himself a revolutionary, participating in a "people's war" against an unjust government. According to U.S. military and government officials, however, he was a communist insurgent who threatened the existence of a noncommunist South Vietnam.

The United States justified its intervention in Vietnam as an effort to save the Vietnamese people, Asia, and the world from the evils of communism. Though the theme of political freedom dominated the public rhetoric, geostrategic and economic imperatives also played a role in this rationale. Several internal reports from the 1950s stressed the need to maintain Western-oriented economic markets in Asia, lest the Japanese become dependent on trade with China and the Soviet Union, compromising U.S. efforts to make Japan a "bulwark of stability" and "workshop" of capitalist democracy in Asia.[12]

The United States did not sign the 1954 Geneva Accords, which granted Vietnam independence and made provisions for free elections to be held two years later. In 1956, the Eisenhower administration supported the cancellation of these elections by the Diem regime, knowing the communists had the popular advantage. Rather than admit the local, regional, and national roots of the rebellion, the Cold Warriors reframed it, casting the NLF as "internal aggressors" and North Vietnam's president Ho Chi Minh as an extension of Chinese and Soviet power. Elected in the wake of McCarthyism and fearing the perception that he was weak in the fight against communism, President Kennedy actively advanced this framework, although he experimented with different approaches to the problem. After the botched Bay of Pigs invasion in 1961, he presided over international negotiations that neutralized Laos in 1962. For reasons that continue to stoke confusion and debate among historians, Kennedy adopted a more aggressive approach toward Vietnam, which became a symbolic centerpiece in the Cold War, the place where the United States would demonstrate its ability to counter communism. At this point, whether U.S. policy makers really believed or simply manufactured the idea of a communist threat in Vietnam largely ceased to matter. Either way, they were going to fight it.[13]

The mission to counter the insurgency raised fundamental

questions about the war in Vietnam and about "people's war" more generally, which proponents of counterinsurgency failed to address adequately. How can one government justify its support of another in the name of democracy when a significant segment of the local population is justifiably opposed to its unelected government? More fundamentally, how can a powerful state that is waging a war on behalf of its own geopolitical and economic interests really listen to or protect the very people who are preventing it from achieving its geostrategic goals?

The refusal to acknowledge—let alone answer—these questions reflected the willful blindness of the U.S. war effort and contributed to the grim realities of counterinsurgency on the ground in Vietnam. In addition to costing the lives of fifty-eight thousand American soldiers and at least three million Vietnamese people, counterinsurgency campaigns in Vietnam displaced millions more.[14] Instead of engaging in meaningful land reform, the effort to defeat the insurgency forcibly removed the rural population from the land on which they lived.

CAMELOT AND COUNTERINSURGENCY

The United States has a long history of fighting insurgencies, dating back to the Indian Wars of the nineteenth century and the suppression of rebels in the Philippines following the Spanish-American War at the beginning of the twentieth. But it was not until the Kennedy administration that the practice of counterinsurgency was systematically theorized and made a centerpiece of foreign policy. Kennedy had a developing interest in counterinsurgency, shaped in part by his 1951 congressional visit to Vietnam and his readings of Mao Zedong and Che Guevara. Ivy League social scientists, including the MIT economist Walt Rostow, who later became Kennedy's Deputy Special Assistant for National Security Affairs, also pored over this body of literature for keys to countering "people's revolutions." At his first National Security Council meeting in January 1961, the president turned to his advisers and asked, "What are we doing about guerrilla warfare?"[15]

In the ensuing months, the U.S. foreign policy establishment became a virtual university of counterinsurgency. The president gave speeches on unconventional war and counterinsurgency (terms he used interchangeably) and established a White House interagency task force to make recommendations and oversee the institutionalization of counterinsurgency. The group laid the groundwork for the training and instruction of military and civilian officials in the history and tactics of counterinsurgency. Each person who completed the six-week training course at the Foreign Service Institute (FSI) was invited to the White House to meet directly with the president.[16]

Rostow and others regarded communist subversion in the developing world as a "disease of the transition to modernization." The only reason communists were winning in undeveloped regions like Vietnam, they argued, was that the West had failed to offer the people an alternative vision. In its earliest and most idealistic versions, counterinsurgency was envisioned as the embodiment of this alternative. In *On Guerrilla Warfare* (1937), Mao had directed the guerrilla to "move amongst the people as a fish swims in the sea." Through development and other civic programs, counterinsurgency would similarly aim to integrate officials of the South Vietnamese government (GVN) and their U.S. advisers into the fabric of rural life to implement the very reforms that drew people to the revolution. The United States would thus work with the government of South Vietnam to best the insurgents at their own game, thereby wining the loyalty of the contested population.[17]

In reality, a people's war could not be mirrored and outdone so easily, if at all.[18] The conditions that drew different segments of the population to the Front were the product of decades of social and political strife. Moreover, government officials and bureaucrats with whom the Americans had partnered were largely responsible for the creation and maintenance of these very conditions. The NLF and its supporters perceived the United States as the new colonial power, which had aligned itself with the Vietnamese government at the expense of the Vietnamese people.[19]

It is not surprising, then, that counterinsurgency in Vietnam involved a heavy measure of coercion, as evident even in the metaphors of counterinsurgency planners. When it became clear that they would not be welcome as fellow fish in the sea, U.S. and South Vietnamese officials turned their focus to "draining the swamp." Over the course of the war, the rural countryside of South Vietnam was incrementally depopulated, first as a result of civic-military programs and later in the course of aerial bombardment and combat operations on the ground. This dislocation of the rural populace served to erode the social fabric of rural South Vietnam, affecting the lives of ordinary civilians on all sides of the conflict.

EARLY COUNTERINSURGENCY PROGRAMS:
FROM AGROVILLES TO NEW LIFE VILLAGES

Though counterinsurgency would not become the touchstone of U.S. strategy until the early 1960s, the tactics of counterinsurgency had been used before in Vietnam. From the beginning, Diem made defeating the NLF a priority. His brother, Nhu, and his close associate, Tram Kim Tuyen, directed intelligence and security to carry out anticommunist repression. Continuing in various forms throughout the war, the system had "buy-in" from officials at every level of government—the low-level police officers who demanded bribes at security checkpoints, the military officers who served as smugglers and middlemen in the expanding opium trade, the high officials who got kickbacks from their subordinates, and the politicians who received payment for voting for the "right" way.[20]

At the same time, using the vast sums of aid pouring in from the United States, the Diem government initiated a highly publicized counterinsurgency program aimed at winning the loyalty of the rural populace. Although these programs typically employed the carrot and stick approach, the emphasis tended heavily toward coercion and the threat of force. Half-hearted attempts to address long-standing social and economic grievances were overshadowed by more concerted efforts to corral the population into government-controlled areas.

Land reform ostensibly constituted a central aspect of the early counterinsurgency effort. However, Diem's program, which began in 1955, failed to tackle the problem in earnest. It redistributed pockets of land to wealthy and middle peasants but did not reach the poorest, those most likely to support the revolution. In 1960, 15 percent of the population still owned 75 percent of the land in South Vietnam.[21] At the same time, Diem implemented aggressive police and military measures to rid rural villages of communism. The Anti-Communist Denunciation Campaign of this period claimed to target leaders of the revolution but resulted in the arrests of thousands of low-level Front supporters. In 1959, the government announced Decree 10/59, under which suspected insurgents were charged with treason, paraded before a military tribunal, and subject to heavy sentences, including death. These draconian measures, which touched the lives of virtually every resident in the contested villages of rural Vietnam, further fueled hostility toward the Diem government and its allies. In this period, the revolution accelerated at a pace that took the Communist Party of South Vietnam—and even Hanoi—by surprise.[22]

To curb this momentum, Diem implemented a new program that moved entire populations from their villages and resettled them in secure areas. Diem's U.S.-sponsored construction program, which began in July 1959, aimed to separate "the people" from the "insurgency." In addition to building a fence to keep insurgents out, it would build a whole new society within. The constructed villages, or agrovilles, would model a modern way of life. By 1960, the government had constructed twenty-three agrovilles, each with several thousand residents.[23]

Though its rhetoric focused on people-centered development, in action, the agroville program consisted mainly of coercive security measures. Village residents were told to abandon their homes, stirring anger and resistance. As one Front defector would later explain, "A piece of property in the village, however big or small it was, represents the results of hard work and savings through many generations, and the villagers were very reluctant to leave it behind for an unknown future."[24] In the face of resistance, efforts to persuade people that their lives would be better in agrovilles were coupled with threats of force. Residents had no choice but to move. Once relocated, they often had to supply their own food and were forced to build the agrovilles themselves. One agroville had space for only a quarter of the workers that built it. Promised compensation often came too little, too late, or not at all.[25]

In 1961, a frustrated Diem hired Robert Thompson, a British military officer and counterinsurgency expert, as his resident counterinsurgency adviser. In the 1950s, Thompson had helped to design the counterinsurgency campaigns in Malaya. The communist insurgency in Malaya grew out of the anti-Japanese resistance during World War II. With little help from British forces, which abandoned Malaya after the fall of Singapore, the Malayan Communist Party (MCP), most of whose members were of Chinese descent, played a key role in resisting the Japanese occupation. This strengthened their position after the war, a period that was also marked by severe economic hardship and increasing labor unrest that threatened stability and British rule. After issuing a state-wide "emergency" in 1950, which turned Malaya into a virtual police state, General Harold Briggs and his successor, Gerald Templer, designed and implemented counterinsurgency campaigns that resettled five hundred thousand squatters and six hundred thousand laborers into "secure" villages, part of a population control campaign that included mass deportation, information and food control, and collective punishment of whole villages.[26]

Diem admired the "success" of this campaign and sought to replicate it in Vietnam. Integrating elements of COIN in Malaya into his own plan, he created the Strategic Hamlet Program. The program employed a "clear, hold, build" strategy (the term and derivation of this strategy would surface again in Iraq and Afghanistan) in which troops "separated" insurgents from villages, secured the village, and developed the area. These secure zones were sometimes envisioned as "oil spots" (another term that was used in Iraq and Afghanistan), which would gradually spread throughout the country.

As with the British in Malaya, the overarching goal was to extend government control to the rural countryside. Although Vietnamese officials and their U.S. advisers made gestures toward social, economic, and political reform within the hamlets, the program was fundamentally an elaborate security system designed to separate people from the guerrillas. As with the agroville program, however, the Strategic Hamlet Program embodied the central contradictions of counterinsurgency in Vietnam: the population was being protected from an insurgency that many supported. Moreover, the U.S.-supported government protecting them was the same government whose corruption and contempt for rural villagers had fueled unrest in the first place.

The practice of protecting the people involved various forms of coercion that coupled vague incentives with much clearer threats. Faced with the prospect of arrest or worse, people in contested areas had little choice but to relocate. In many instances, their homes and belongings were burned. As in the agroville program, the relocated population was forced to build the hamlets at their own cost. They had to provide the bamboo for the barbed-wire fences that surrounded the hamlets, dig the ditches that surrounded these fences, and construct the earthen mounds that encircled them. The area immediately outside the village was cleared to create a buffer zone between the insurgents and the residents. Alarm and bell systems alerted residents of communist attacks. Surrounding fields were declared free-fire zones in which any villager was considered fair game.[27]

A leaflet prepared by a U.S. psychological operation advertising the Strategic Hamlet Program gives a sense of how counterinsurgency forces attempted to control the population. The leaflet depicts people happily residing inside the hamlet. Two smiling residents stand close to the surrounding fence. One holds a hoe while the other waves his hand. The caption at the top says, "Building up strategic hamlets in the Republic to realize true peace and to bring joy and tranquility to every family." Additional text on the back of the pamphlet contrasts this idyllic life with communist North Vietnam, where "people are always herded to work in labor camps and die in thick forests." But not all in the picture is idyllic. Just a few yards away, outside the fence, another man trembles in fear as a government soldier points the end of his rifle directly at the man's abdomen. The image sent a double message, one in which the government assures the people protection from the "bad guys" outside the wire and another in which, outside the wire, the government soldier—pointing his weapon at an unarmed man—is seemingly the "bad guy."

This double entendre unwittingly highlights the irony of countering a broad-based insurgency like the one in South Vietnam: in the name of protection, the people inside were being protected against the threat of their own potential disloyalty.[28]

Despite its fundamental contradictions, the Strategic Hamlet Program accelerated at breakneck speed. In October 1961, the South Vietnamese government reported that three thousand hamlets had been completed. The following September, official reports stated that 4,322,034 people, or 33.9 percent of the population, were living in strategic hamlets. By July 1963, 7,200 hamlets had been completed, housing a total of 8,737,000.[29]

The numbers, however, were deceptive. They did not reflect the most important measure—government loyalty. As with the agrovilles, strategic hamlets backfired, further fueling dissatisfaction with the Diem government. Members of the U.S. embassy reported, "To villagers near the old capital of Hue in Thua Thien province, for example, the strategic hamlets were more accurately described as 'small concentration camps.'"[30]

What Kennedy and his advisers called counterinsurgency, the leaders of the NLF called "special war," which they combated through a combination of military and political campaigns. In 1962, the Communist Party published a booklet condemning the Strategic Hamlet Program. The revolutionary apparatus called for villagers to "resist the program and destroy hamlets wherever they exist." As one pamphlet proclaimed, "The enemies build the hamlets; we destroy them until they abandon the project."[31] In cooperation with residents, the Front destroyed strategic hamlets in revolutionary strongholds throughout the south. In July 1964, only thirty out of over two hundred strategic hamlets in Long An were reported to be under government control. Half the remaining hamlets were destroyed by NLF forces or their occupants. Only fourteen hundred of 8,500 strategic hamlets built in southern Vietnam survived through the next year.[32]

At the end of 1962, party leaders concluded that the NLF and not the Diem government had succeeded in "winning hearts and minds." One tradesman in My Thuy Phuong village later recalled of the period, "There were so many people here who supported the communists, that sometimes I had the idea everybody supported that side." In the revolutionary stronghold of My Thuy Phuong, roughly 75 percent of the province actively supported the Front in these years. With some notable exceptions, the 3–5 percent that supported the GVN represented the same segment of the population that controlled land and wealth during French rule.[33]

Meanwhile, struggles among competing factions of the governing elite came to a head on November 2, 1963, when Diem and his brother were assassinated in a U.S.-supported military coup, followed by Kennedy's assassination just three weeks later, effectively ending the Strategic Hamlet Program. Despite the Kennedy administration's investment in counterinsurgency, 1961–63 proved to be a high-water mark for popular support of the revolution.[34]

THE GREAT SOCIETY IN VIETNAM?

By early 1964, the revolutionary forces held sway in large areas of South Vietnam. In March, the South Vietnamese government estimated that the Front controlled 50 percent of the land in twenty-two of forty-four provinces. Overall, it controlled an estimated 30 percent of the land and 15 percent of the population. This period also marked a rise in tensions between the policies of the revolutionary forces and the populace supporting them. Up to this point, the NLF had relied heavily on a spirit of volunteerism. Following Diem's assassination, the communist regime in Hanoi opted to intensify and militarize the struggle. The Front began to levy taxes and conscript soldiers, policies that over time strained popular support. In contested villages, cadres punished individuals suspected of disloyalty, and snipers fired into and around government-controlled areas, to undermine the security benefit of siding with official authorities. These coercive measures contributed to some military gains, but in the long run, they could not sustain the revolution, whose success since the 1930s had depended on a spirit of political and social activism that distinguished it from the official authorities and their U.S. backers.[35]

Some historians argue that the NLF's employment of coercive tactics created an opportunity for the South Vietnamese government. However, at the local, provincial, and national levels, the Saigon government did little to enact a viable alternative to the colonial form of governance in South Vietnam. With U.S. support, Diem's successors continued governmental attempts to control and subdue the rural populace rather than implement real political and economic reform.[36]

As president, Lyndon Johnson echoed his predecessor's awareness that the conflict in Vietnam was fundamentally political. "So we must be ready to fight in Vietnam," said LBJ during a May 1965 dinner party speech in Texas. "But the ultimate victory will depend upon the hearts and minds of the people who actually live out there." Johnson portrayed Vietnam as another venue for the Great Society, his ambitious social program that extended and updated the New Deal. Just as the Tennessee Valley Authority had brought modern infrastructure and electricity to rural parts of the United States, so would counterinsurgency modernize and electrify the Mekong Delta. The hearts and minds of the Vietnamese people, it was assumed, would follow the path of modernity. Local elections would supply the infrastructure for grassroots democracy, both instilling and cementing the people's trust in their government.[37]

This lofty vision was deeply problematic. It projected the American social landscape onto Vietnam, took for granted the Vietnamese government's commitment to rural development, and assumed an inherent link between development and democracy. But more immediately, it ignored the ways in which the very practice of counterinsurgency undermined its lofty vision.

On the ground, civil counterinsurgency programs replicated the coercive practices of earlier programs. New Life Hamlets, which replaced Strategic Hamlets, were, like their predecessors, more prison than home.[38] The Civilian Action Program (CAP), implemented in 1965, brought U.S. advisers into direct contact with the Vietnamese people. Locals initially welcomed U.S. forces into many of these areas, in part because they seemed to treat the residents with kindness and generosity. As one villager in My Thuy Phuong explained, U.S. soldiers "gave children candies, cookies, and clothes" and "old people cigarettes." However, these individual acts of trust building were frequently offset by larger acts of destruction: "Out in the fields amphibious vehicles have destroyed all the rice plants." In contested areas, U.S. forces employed "harassment and interdiction" ("H and I"), in which bullets were randomly fired into contested villages.[39]

In addition to casting light on the psychological stresses placed on the civilians caught up in these operations (not to mention the soldiers who carried them out), such scenarios illuminate the schizophrenic nature of counterinsurgency in Vietnam. Policy makers idealized counterinsurgency as a campaign of persuasion, but persuasive tactics were typically employed alongside or as part of campaigns of force and violence. The tendency for the carrot to become a stick was predictable if not inevitable, given the centrality of armed security forces in carrying out counterinsurgency on the ground. Other factors were the geostrategic and historical frameworks that aligned the United States and the South Vietnamese government against social and political agitation in southern Vietnam. Thus, it is hardly surprising that counterinsurgency programs of this period destroyed more than they built and bore little resemblance to the vision of "winning hearts and minds" that LBJ advertised to the American people.

DRAINING THE SWAMP: EMPTYING THE COUNTRYSIDE IN THE BIG-UNIT WAR

When LBJ gave his "hearts and minds" speech he had already approved a campaign of massive aerial bombardment in Vietnam. Over the course of the war, more than a million tons of ordnance saturated South Vietnam. In contrast to the fraught decision to inaugurate a "precision" bombing campaign in the north, policy makers engaged in substantially less debate over the decision to inaugurate an area bombing campaign in the south.[40] Counterinsurgency in Vietnam had always been violent. The escalation of the "big-unit" military war expanded the scope and scale of this violence, devastating the countryside and uprooting large portions of the rural population.

The Communist Party had declared 1965 the "year of the big change," which was to be a decisive push toward victory. It did turn out to be a year of big change, but not in the sense the revolution intended. The change of biggest consequence came from America's decision to escalate military operations. From this point forward, the big-unit war would dominate the situation on the ground in southern Vietnam.[41]

Frustrated with the enemy's ability to escape more targeted tactical bombs in the south, General William Westmoreland, the commander of Military Assistance Command Vietnam (MACV), received authorization to deploy B-52 bombers for "saturation attacks against target areas known to include VC [Viet Cong]-occupied installations and facilities for which precise target data to permit pinpoint bombing attacks was not available." Flying at altitudes of twenty-five to thirty thousand feet, the pilots of these area bombing missions could not see the villages they were targeting. When pressed to consider whether they might be killing innocent people, one pilot said, "If we are killing anybody down there with our bombs, I have to think we were bombing the enemy and not civilians."[42]

In his memoir of the war, NLF member Truong Nhu Tang describes what B-52 raids felt like on the ground: "[T]he sonic roar of the B-52 explosions tore eardrums, leaving many of the jungle dwellers permanently deaf. From a kilometer, the shock waves knocked their victims senseless. Any hit within a half-kilometer would collapse the walls of an unreinforced bunker, burying alive the people cowering inside. Seen up close, the bomb craters were gigantic—thirty feet across and nearly as deep." As the bombing campaigns escalated, the Front's casualty reports became increasingly generic. Instead of recording how many died, some accounts simply noted that many died. In interviews with U.S. personnel, Front defectors reported that bombing raids killed more women, children, and elderly than they did revolutionary forces. Using Soviet intelligence trawlers and local radars, Front cadres and soldiers sometimes had advance warning of B-52 attacks, giving them just enough time to burrow into their bunkers or escape along emergency trails. Tang's memoir describes the experience of returning to a village just hours after a B-52 attack: "It was as if an enormous scythe had swept through the jungle, felling the giant teaks and go trees like grass in the way, shredding them into billions of scattered splinters."[43]

In addition to inflicting heavy civilian casualties, the bombing of southern Vietnam increasingly restricted the civilian population's freedom of movement. Most people's response to the aerial assault was to run. But as David Hunt writes, "In the logic of counterinsurgency, running was a mortal sin." Civilians began to adapt their daily patterns of movement to lessen the risk of being targeted by the bombs. As one former Front supporter explained, since aerial bombs focused on population clusters, villagers "didn't dare to farm in groups." In the field, farmers wore white clothes, the color of the wealthy, rather than the traditional black costume worn by the laboring classes: "While working, if we see aircraft drop smoke grenades, everybody has to put on his white clothes at once and then walk slowly (no running) toward a nearby GVN outpost."[44]

Agent Orange and other toxic defoliants were sprayed from airplanes to strip the environment bare. Incendiary bombs dropped napalm on villages suspected of VC sympathy, creating massive smoke clouds that forced residents to come out of their hiding places and causing severe, often fatal burns that literally melted the skin away. When white phosphorus ("Willie Peter") was added to the napalm, the effects were even more severe. As one U.S. pilot explained, "The original product wasn't so hot—if the gooks were quick they could scrape it off . . . now it sticks like shit to a blanket . . . And one drop is enough, it'll keep on burning right down to the bone so they die anyway from phosphorous poisoning."[45]

Attempting to escape the aerial onslaught, residents increasingly abandoned their homes in the shady tree-lined areas, which were considered insurgent hideouts, and set up temporary huts in the middle of the rice fields under the scorching sun. When that no longer worked, they relocated to live near government checkpoints and roads, which were less likely to be bombed. As the bombing escalated, the people were confined to smaller and smaller pieces of land. For villagers accustomed to living in tightly knit clusters, life in the middle of rice paddies and on the edge of hamlets was lonely and isolated.[46]

Thousands had no choice but to leave the village altogether. "Draining the swamp," a phrase also used by the British military in Malaya, became a central aim of combat operations—in the paradoxical rationale of counterinsurgency, the only way to "save" the people from the insurgency.[47] Westmoreland explained the logic of this strategy without a hint of irony: "So sympathetic were some of the people to the VC," he said, "that the only way to establish control short of constant combat operations among the people was to remove the people and destroy the village. That done, operations to find the enemy could be conducted without fear of civilian casualties."[48]

According to official estimates (which counted only the number of people receiving government assistance), between 1964 and 1965, 510,000 people were forced to relocate as a result of the war. That number nearly doubled in 1966 and reached 1.2 million the following year. In a 1967 report, Undersecretary of State Nicholas Katzenbach recommended an additional intensification of this effort: "We should stimulate a greater refugee flow through psychological inducements to further decrease the enemy's manpower base."[49]

Describing how the production of refugees came to dominate the landscape and overwhelm the Vietnamese security forces, Douglas Valentine writes, "The VCI fish were submerged in the sea of refugees that was rolling like a tidal wave over South Vietnam." Most of the refugees were women and children who subsisted on meager rice rations and lived in squalid camps that lacked sanitation. Because the camps were located far from arable land and labor markets, economic opportunities were slim. Underresourced schools functioned as holding zones for children. A 1966 RAND study reported favorably on these developments: "The effects of the departure of large numbers of villagers for GVN areas are beginning to be felt."[50]

Four decades later, proponents of counterinsurgency in Iraq and Afghanistan argued that the escalation of the military war displaced what might have been a successful counterinsurgency strategy. But this distinction fails to account for the continuities between the big-unit war and ostensibly more political programs. Both wars used force and coercion to dislocate the population and dismantle the social structure of the countryside. The big-unit war did so in a more technology-driven, aerial—and ultimately more lethal—fashion.[51]

Even as it escalated the military war, the Johnson administration once again attempted to demonstrate its commitment to the "other war." In April 1966, at a conference in Honolulu, Johnson took steps to unify this effort. "Pacification," a term the French used to describe their military campaign to suppress colonial liberation movements, increasingly supplanted the use of the term "counterinsurgency." In the ensuing months, Johnson moved to consolidate civilian and military pacification efforts into one office under the umbrella of military command. The office of Civilian Operations and Revolutionary Development Support (CORDS) was created in 1967 and headed by Robert "Blowtorch" Komer, a trusted White House adviser with a reputation within the bureaucracy for sparing no enemies.[52]

As the vastly more resourced big-unit war increasingly dominated the lives of the civilian population, official pacification operations took on an especially confusing and sinister quality. One program deployed the standard intimidation tactics of counterinsurgency against the backdrop of an American-style Fourth of July barbecue. In these "County Fair" operations, U.S. units cordoned off a village, and ARVN units entered it. The ARVN checked the men for identification cards, interrogated them about their affiliations with the enemy, and arrested any suspects, while the rest of the residents received medical services and political education from civil affairs teams composed of American and South Vietnamese personnel. In the afternoon, there was a lottery, a lunch, and a band to entertain the locals. Then, almost as quickly as they entered, the soldiers departed to another area, leaving the residents to make sense of what had happened. Locals found the experience bewildering. One man in Hau Nghia province asked, "How would you feel if a bunch of burly foreigners invaded your hamlet, took away your men, and played weird foreign music to 'entertain' you?"[53]

Other civic programs with a more long-term outlook often confused and alienated the rural population in deeper and more lasting ways. Agricultural development programs, for example, typically introduced a new more expensive strain of "miracle rice," which required heavy doses of fertilizers and pesticides. As one destitute resident of My Thuy Phuong explained, "We watched the program carefully and saw the rich men get richer and the poor men stay just the same." In addition to fueling class resentment, these programs bred resentment against the government: "The only ones helped by the Self-Development programs were the government followers, not the people." Elections, which were state-sponsored acts of political theater, similarly benefited local elites. The government established the slate, using bribes and intimidation to ensure the victory of its candidate. When asked by an American researcher to comment on elections, one student in My Thuy Phoung said, "Don't ask me about the elections. That's the government activity that we hate most of all." In Vietnam, as later in Iraq and Afghanistan, disdain for the corrupt nature of elections belied supposed progress in counterinsurgency.[54]

A U.S. internal report from the period observed "an everwidening gap of distrust, distaste, and disillusionment between the people and the GVN."[55] Such candid remarks stand as momentary flickers of insight into the deeper social and political conflicts of Vietnamese society fueled and exacerbated by the war.

THE MYTH OF ACCELERATED PACIFICATION: 1968–72

Although counterinsurgency programs did little to gain the support of the civilian population, the big-unit war made it increasingly difficult for the Front to maintain the support and resources it needed to survive. In 1968, the Tet offensive targeted urban centers.

Simultaneous uprisings in rural areas were perceived as a sign of the Front's strength and resiliency, forcing the United States to revise its strategy once again. In March, Johnson announced that he would not run for re-election, and in June he installed General Creighton Abrams to replace Westmoreland as the war's top military commander. Unlike his predecessor, who focused on the big-unit war, Abrams believed in counterinsurgency. He called pacification "the gut issue of the Vietnamese" and directed his subordinates to integrate military operations and pacification, to conduct big-unit war and pacification operations as "one war." Together with his new civilian deputy, William Colby, formerly head of CIA efforts in Vietnam, Abrams implemented what became known as the Accelerated Pacification Campaign (APC).[56]

Accelerated pacification has been heavily mythologized by latter-day COINdinistas. According to the version told by Petraeus and the authors of the COIN field manual, Abrams's pacification efforts successfully turned around what had been a losing war. The key ingredient in accelerated pacification, they argue, was the people. Thus, the authors of the 2006 COIN field manual explain that the accelerated pacification programs gave "keen attention" to "the ultimate objective of serving the needs of the local populace." By 1972, the manual claims, "Pacification had largely uprooted the insurgency from among the South Vietnamese population." According to this analysis, the defeat of South Vietnam in 1975 resulted entirely from the North's military victory after the United States abandoned Vietnam due to lack of domestic support for the war effort.[57]

This version of counterinsurgency history was easily sold to the White House in 2006. Struggling to come up with a new strategy in Iraq, the George W. Bush administration latched on to counter-insurgency as a more grassroots political approach in which the United States would reach out to ex-Ba'athist and other "insurgent" groups in an effort to stabilize the country. However, in Vietnam (as in Iraq), the line between the military and the political war was never as clear as the terminology and bureaucratic structures suggest. It became increasingly blurry under Abrams's "one war" approach, which the Nixon administration intensified in its efforts to ramp up the war and maximize its position at the negotiating table before exiting Vietnam.

Accelerated pacification included some of the most brutal campaigns of the entire war. As many critics have argued, the police and intelligence program was little more than an "assassination campaign." Developed out of earlier programs run by the CIA under Colby's direction, and informed by the Malaya model as well as the selective terror tactics of the VC, the goal was to "neutralize" high-level party members and cadres through an intelligence network that extended its tentacles into every level of the targeted community. The program, dubbed "Phoenix" in English, comes from the Vietnamese "Phung Hoang," meaning "all-seeing bird." Teams of Vietnamese and American officers established quotas of "VC" to be neutralized. One Navy SEAL officer who worked with the program explained that informants from the VC as well as government supporters were merely turning over internal enemies: "They would feed information through us and other intelligence sources to the CIA and set up a target that maybe wasn't a Viet Cong. . . . It was absolute chaos out there." Many of those targeted had, at best, loose ties to the Front. Some were shot immediately, before any questions were asked. Members of local security forces originally under CIA command killed thousands, including AWOL soldiers and political dissidents. In cases where NLF ties could not be proven, the assassins created them ex post facto.[58]

Upon their arrest, many suspects were taken for interrogation to detention centers, where they were tortured by CIA-trained National Police. "Despite the fact that brutal interrogation is strongly criticized by moralists," wrote one student of CIA torture training in a 1971 paper, "its importance must not be denied if we want to have order and security in daily life." Police interrogation teams included rank-and-file mafia members and run-of-the-mill criminals whose tactics included water torture, electric shock to the genitals and nipples, gang rape, and summary executions. After touring three detention centers, John Paul Vann, Deputy Director of CORDS, noted, "Any detainees not previously VC or VC sympathizers would almost assuredly become so after this period of incarceration." Conviction and sentencing procedures were riddled with corruption. Bribery and personal favors were used to negotiate lighter sentences. Detainees with enough money to pay the interrogators, or who could prove that they were the friend or relative of a government official, had a good chance of being let go without any sentence at all.[59]

Phoenix was an elaborate numbers game in which U.S. officials used statistics to demonstrate "progress." According to official data, the number of communists central to the logistical workings of the revolution shrank from 84,000 in 1968 to 56,000 in February 1972. However, 50 percent of the 28,000 "neutralized communists" were killed in military operations and another 30 percent defected through other channels. One internal report conceded that only half of the Viet Cong captured or killed were even party members. Ultimately, the program was as ineffective as it was brutal.[60]

Under Westmoreland's command, the stated goal of military operations had been to engage conventional forces in relatively unpopulated areas. Under Abrams, military operations increasingly focused on the densely populated areas of the delta. Operation Speedy Express, carried out by the Ninth Division in the Mekong Delta, exemplifies the bloody nature of "population-centric" pacification. The operation's commander, Julian Ewell, nicknamed "the butcher of the delta," demonstrated a particular obsession with "body count" as a measure of progress in the war. Most of the casualties were inflicted by air. Members of the Ninth Division would hover over a farmer in helicopter gunships, wait for him to run, and shoot him down. Meanwhile, U.S. troops on the ground used civilians to set off booby traps.[61]

The carnage prompted one sergeant to write an anonymous letter to Westmoreland and, later, two other top generals, in which he described how the brigade commander, Ira "Jim" Hunt, who also served as Ewell's chief of staff, "used to holler and curse over the radio and talk about the goddamn gooks and tell the gunships to shoot the sonofabitches, this is a free fire zone." The sergeant reported that together, the four battalions in the area were killing forty to fifty people a day, or twelve hundred to fifteen hundred a month. "If I am only ten percent right, that means 120–150 month, or a

My Lai a month for over a year." The division itself reported 10,883 "VC" killed, but only nine hundred weapons were recovered.[62] One adviser who served in the delta during Speedy Express underscored the implications of this disparity in a 1970 internal report: "The percentage of Viet Cong killed by support assets is roughly equal to the percentage of Viet Cong in the population. That is, if 8 percent of the population [of] an area is VC about 8 percent of the people we kill are VC." According to a document produced in December 1969 by the Vietnamese revolutionaries, the operation had slaughtered "mostly old folks, women, and children." In June 1969, the Ninth Division received an official award for humanitarianism. Following a half-hearted internal investigation, the sergeant's letter was buried in a dusty archive.[63]

Accelerated pacification resulted in heavy civilian casualties and the physical devastation of whole villages. As the Vietnamese report noted, Speedy Express destroyed "thousands of houses" and "hundreds of hectares of fields and orchards." With their villages no longer habitable, the survivors of these "mopping up" operations often had no choice but to move into government-controlled areas. A battalion commander in the Ninth Division noted that this was deliberate. Ewell, he explained, wanted to "drain the Delta before the Delta pulled the plug on him."[64]

Like My Lai, Speedy Express was part of a systematic program of destruction. In 1970, the Department of Defense acknowledged the destruction of a half million acres, or 10 percent, of arable land in South Vietnam. "Whether by accident or design," notes Elliott, "[pacification] worked by making life in non GVN areas unlivable for civilians."[65] Rural depopulation continued apace throughout 1969. The Russell Beach/Bold Mariner operation in Quang Ngai, the same province where U.S. troops committed the My Lai massacre, displaced twelve thousand people, 40 percent of the area's entire population. In mid-1969, the region had over two hundred thousand refugees.[66]

Official reports cited the influx of people into government-controlled zones as evidence of progress. Though the numbers suggested a significant increase in security between 1969 and early 1972, the gains resulted largely from forced relocation. People who entered these areas "voluntarily" were not running toward the government but away from the bombing and shelling. Life inside government-controlled areas reproduced the problems of counter-insurgency programs past. Secure areas were police zones in which officials controlled every aspect of daily life. As in earlier programs, villagers had meager rations and limited freedom of movement. Warned not to venture outside the secure area, they were subject to corruption and abuse inside.[67]

Government control did not necessarily translate into loyalty. Especially in revolutionary strongholds, it served as a reminder of why many had joined the Front. As one U.S. refugee adviser argued, "When the relocated people are then left without adequate assistance from the GVN, then their enmity increases. . . . This is a good recipe for losing the war."[68]

In 1973, when the United States signed the Paris Peace accords and formally withdrew from the fighting, support for the Front once again rose. In My Thuy Phuong, formally rated as relatively secure, as much as 70 percent of the population supported the revolution. This story and others like it challenge the myth of pacification perpetuated by more recent proponents of counterinsurgency. A more convincing argument about the war's end goes something like this: "The North Vietnamese tanks rolling into Saigon on 30 April 1975 sealed a victory that the Southern insurgents had won more than a decade before." These are the words of Richard Ahern, a CIA operative during the war. COIN gurus invoke him as one of the leading experts on counterinsurgency in Vietnam.[69]

LAND REFORM IN AN EMPTIED LAND

COINdinistas have a tendency to find success in failure. President Nguyen Van Thieu's Land-to-the-Tiller program was one of the last counterinsurgency operations highlighted by American COIN proponents before the U.S. exit from Vietnam. It was also one of the most paradoxical. The program redistributed land to poor villagers throughout the south. U.S. officials and commentators praised

Land to the Tiller, arguing that it "increased stability in the South" and predicting that if the program continued, the South Vietnamese government would "win in its competitive struggle with the Viet Cong on the land issue." This optimism omitted the larger social and political contexts of the war in South Vietnam. For decades, the Front had led the way in the attempt to redistribute land to the rural poor. In many cases, Land to the Tiller's efforts merely duplicated and thus confirmed land reforms that had already been carried out. The program was a classic example of too little, too late that characterized the government's shallow approach to reform.[70]

The massive depopulation of the rural areas brought about by the war constituted an even more basic barrier to the program's success. Many of the liberated areas had more land than people to cultivate it. Between 1960 and 1970, the population living in the South Vietnamese countryside had declined from 80 to 70 percent. Of them, only 35 percent worked primarily as laborers. The draining of the swamp had rendered land—and thus Land to the Tiller—increasingly moot. By 1974, according to official estimates, the war had displaced 11,147,000 people. Two million of these had moved from rural areas into Saigon and other cities, where women survived through prostitution, and children and preteens sold drugs to U.S. soldiers. The journalist Michael Herr described being in Saigon these days like "sitting inside the petals of a poisonous flower, the poison history, fucked in its root no matter how far back you wanted to run your trace."[71]

Focusing on the return of American G.I.s and stories of anticommunist refugees escaping Vietnam, U.S. media outlets routinely ignored the crisis of internal displacement in Vietnam. The omission frustrated Ngô Vĩnh Long, who had left Vietnam in 1964 and became the first Vietnamese student to attend Harvard and an important voice in the antiwar movement. As a co-author of a response to a magazine article about defoliation in Vietnam, he wrote, "People from the countryside are being driven into the cities and 'refugee' camps where they can be more easily controlled. We are witnessing not only the deliberate destruction of the environment but the deliberate destruction of a society."[72]

Though Long and his colleagues did not use the word "counter-insurgency," their letter aptly characterized the counterinsurgency campaigns in South Vietnam, revealing, among other things, the twisted response of counterinsurgency to the land claims that fueled the revolution. From Strategic Hamlets to Speedy Express, counterinsurgency operations in Vietnam removed the rural poor from the land with increasing lethality. By the end of the war, pacification had not just uprooted the insurgency from among the South Vietnamese population, as the COIN field manual claims. It had physically as well as socially and psychologically uprooted huge swaths of the rural population on all sides of the conflict—whose best interests were supposed to be the driving force of the counterinsurgency campaign. It is hard to envision an alternative to this outcome that does not reinvent the history and politics of Vietnam and of the Cold War in Asia.

REMEMBERING TO FORGET THE LESSONS OF VIETNAM

The claim that Afghanistan is not Iraq is not Vietnam is ostensibly an argument for paying attention to the specific context of a conflict. Preoccupied with curing the military of its Vietnam War syndrome, Petraeus's study of Vietnam did not, however, reflect on the local, national, and international historical context that contributed to the grisly realities of counterinsurgency in Vietnam. This shortsighted-ness continued in Iraq and Afghanistan where military and civilian advocates of counterinsurgency brushed historical and political context aside when such frameworks threatened to reveal fundamental rifts between stated U.S. goals and the varied interests of the Iraqi and Afghan populations whose support they were courting. While it is important to distinguish between Vietnam, Iraq, and Afghanistan, these conflicts are nonetheless connected by the shared mental frameworks that U.S. policy makers applied to them. In Iraq and Afghanistan, as in Vietnam, U.S. advocates of COIN similarly dismissed the local, national, and international histories whose reverberations could lead to questions about the fundamental promise of U.S. counterinsurgency.

For the commander of the U.S. wars in Iraq and Afghanistan, the key point to remember about Vietnam was to forget it. As he became the guru of counterinsurgency, David Petraeus avoided thinking too hard about the shadow that Vietnam potentially cast over the U.S. counterinsurgency campaigns in Iraq and Afghanistan. In an October 2009 interview on *NBC Nightly News*, Brian Williams asked Petraeus how often he thinks about Vietnam in planning the wars in Iraq and Afghanistan. "Very little," he said. "In fact, one of the biggest lessons out of the work that I did on my dissertation is making sure that you're not a prisoner of the most significant lessons that you learn." Two months later, in his speech announcing the decision to commit thirty thousand additional troops to the war in Afghanistan, President Obama spoke directly against "those who suggest that Afghanistan is another Vietnam," dismissing once and for all the notion that Vietnam might hold any lessons for the current conflict and opening yet another chapter in the sorry story of COIN.[73]

4

EL SALVADOR—
THE CREATION OF THE INTERNAL ENEMY:
PONDERING THE LEGACIES OF U.S.
ANTICOMMUNISM, COUNTERINSURGENCY,
AND AUTHORITARIANISM IN
EL SALVADOR (1952–81)

Joaquín M. Chávez

During the official commemorations of the twentieth anniversary of the peace accords that put an end to the civil war in El Salvador (1980–1992), held in January 2012, President Mauricio Funes visited El Mozote, a hamlet in the eastern department of Morazán, to pay tribute to the victims of one of the worst mass killings perpetrated by members of the Salvadoran army during the war. In December 1981, the Atlacatl Battalion, a U.S.-trained counterinsurgency unit led by Colonel Domingo Monterrosa, systematically murdered some nine hundred civilians, mostly children, women, and elderly people at El Mozote.[1] In an unprecedented event, a visibly emotional Funes asked the relatives of the victims of the El Mozote Massacre—as the episode is widely known—forgiveness on behalf of the Salvadoran state. Moreover, Funes ordered the military to refrain from publicly honoring the memory of Colonel Monterrosa or other military officers accused of perpetrating human rights violations during the war.[2] Not surprisingly, a group of right-wing politicians and retired military officers openly rejected Funes's apology and called Monterrosa and other commanders of the Atlacatl Battalion war heroes.[3] Despite the significance of President Funes's gesture, it is striking that he ignored the obvious connection between the El Mozote

Massacre and the legacies of U.S. counterinsurgency in El Salvador. After all, the Atlacatl Battalion, Colonel Monterrosa, and numerous state agents accused of perpetrating mass killings during the civil war were scions of U.S. counterinsurgency. However, Funes's silence was not unique. Probably due to the restrictions of its mandate, the Truth Commission Report (TCR) on El Salvador issued in 1993, which is generally considered the most credible account of the human rights violations committed in El Salvador during the civil war, also omits substantial references to the impact of U.S. counterinsurgency in the conflict.[4]

The origins of the civil war in El Salvador are virtually unintelligible without a careful examination of the reverberations of U.S. Cold War anticommunism and counterinsurgency in that country during the three decades that preceded the conflict. This focus does not preclude the relevance of other internal dynamics that led to the war, such as the history of the oligarchic military regimes that ruled the country between 1932 and 1979, but it highlights the devastating ramifications of the convergence between the longstanding antidemocratic and genocidal trajectory of the Salvadoran elites and U.S. anticommunism and counterinsurgency on Salvadoran society and politics.[5] The extent and the characteristics of state terror in El Salvador between 1950 and 1980 have not been sufficiently studied. During that time, state agents systematically murdered, imprisoned, tortured, and "disappeared" thousands of activists and intellectuals in the context of the U.S. national security doctrine adopted by the oligarchic military regimes. The confluence between the authoritarian and repressive tradition of the Salvadoran elites and U.S. Cold War anticommunism, especially its counterinsurgent incarnation, not only undermined the prospect of democratization in the decades leading to the conflict, it radicalized university intellectuals who founded insurgent organizations in the early 1970s. Moreover, the oligarchic military regime framed the leaders of the teachers' union, peasant organizations, and progressive Catholic priests as the "internal enemy" in an effort to justify state repression against the emerging social movements, a counterinsurgency policy that motivated many activists to join or support the insurgency. In this vein, counterinsurgency helped to transform the broad-based pro-democracy movements of the 1960s and 1970s into one of the most potent insurgencies in the modern history of Latin America. During the 1960s, the oligarchic military regime, in effect, fought a counterinsurgency war against a nonexistent insurgency. It carried out an undeclared war against public intellectuals, trade unionists, peasant leaders, teachers, Catholic priests, and laypeople, as well as political activists who advocated democratic reforms, including free elections, freedom of expression, labor rights, and agrarian reform. In the early 1970s, radicalized university intellectuals (mostly Catholic intellectuals) and dissidents of the Communist Party of El Salvador (PCS) founded several urban insurgent organizations. As state repression mounted during that decade, peasant leaders, teachers, Catholic priests, and other activists joined the insurgency in growing numbers. In 1980, the various insurgent organizations united to found the Farabundo Martí National Liberation Front (FMLN), which became the most powerful political and military movement in the country's history. During the 1980s, the war between the Salvadoran government and the insurgent FMLN was arguably one of the most devastating modern conflicts in Latin America. It dominated international headlines, claimed the lives of seventy thousand civilians and tens of thousands of soldiers and guerrilla combatants, generated half a million refugees, destroyed the infrastructure of the country, and became the focus of U.S. political, military, and diplomatic efforts. Peace negotiations brokered by the UN settled the twelve-year conflict and opened up the first sustained democratic period in Salvadoran history.

U.S. pundits, counterinsurgency experts, and politicians have often hailed the "success story" of U.S. counterinsurgency in El Salvador. Although they offer slightly different versions of the nature of this purported success, they often point out that it prevented an imminent victory of the insurgent FMLN by promoting democratic reforms, particularly free elections. U.S. counterinsurgency, the story goes, also transformed the repressive and archaic Salvadoran army into a professional military institution that defeated the insurgency. El Salvador was frequently cited as a model for the U.S.

counterinsurgent effort in Iraq, and some former U.S. military advisers in El Salvador were deployed to that country to help train Iraqis for counterinsurgency.[6] In fact, the FMLN was never defeated politically or militarily, as it became a party to the peace accords that set the basis for the most important political reform in the country's history and recently became the governing party of El Salvador.

More important, however, the apologists for U.S. counterinsurgency in El Salvador often ignore the dire consequences that it had on Salvadoran society, especially the thousands of civilian victims generated by the U.S.-sponsored COIN apparatus. Human rights groups, artists, and members of civil society organizations in El Salvador have resisted attempts to erase or trivialize the magnitude of the genocidal campaign that the Salvadoran state carried out against civilians in the 1970s and 1980s. The images of El Salvador in the center of this book show the ways in which relatives and friends of the victims honor their memory. These include the image of the hands of the Salvadoran performer Patricia Morales pointing at the names of Iride del Carmen Marasso Beltrán de Burgos, a Chilean activist who resided in El Salvador, and Carlos Manuel Serrano Merino, a Salvadoran activist, who were victims of the state terror in 1980. State forces disappeared Marasso Beltrán in Guatemala and Serrano Merino in El Salvador. Another image shows a picture of Patricia Emilie Cuellar, a Salvadoran activist disappeared by the Salvadoran security forces in 1982. While the apologists for U.S. counterinsurgency in El Salvador silence the consequences these policies had and arguably have on Salvadoran society (in other words, the destruction of the country's social fabric and the psychosocial impacts that the political repression carried out by the state forces in the 1970s and 1980s had on various generations of Salvadorans), the relatives and friends of the victims of state terror constantly remind us about this tragic period in the country's history.[7] In the remainder of this chapter, I will examine key moments in the history of U.S. Cold War anticommunism, counterinsurgency, and Salvadoran authoritarianism during the three decades that preceded the war, and its multiple reverberations in Salvadoran politics and society.

PREVENTING DEMOCRATIZATION: THE ANTICOMMUNIST
CRACKDOWNS OF 1952, 1960, AND 1961

The Salvadoran poet José Roberto Cea was born in the town of Izalco, the epicenter of the 1932 indigenous peasant uprising and subsequent mass killings perpetrated by state forces that claimed the lives of nearly thirty thousand people in the western region of the country, an episode known as *La Matanza* (The Killings).[8] Cea grew up listening to stories of the massacre told by survivors of 1932, many of whom were his relatives and neighbors. In 1952, Cea moved to San Salvador and witnessed the first anticommunist crackdown ordered by President Oscar Osorio (1950–56) against union leaders, students, public intellectuals, and artists that same year.[9] Lieutenant Colonel Osorio had come to power through the "1948 Revolution" that deposed General Salvador Castaneda Castro, himself a successor to the military dictatorship of General Maximiliano Hernández Martínez (1932–44). In essence, it was a coup conducted by a group of military officers influenced by the populism of Juan Domingo Perón in Argentina and the experience of the Revolutionary Institutional Party (PRI) in Mexico. Osorio promoted the modernization of El Salvador in the context of the U.S. Cold War anticommunism of the early 1950s. He substantially expanded the country's infrastructure and created the rudiments of a welfare state, as well as cultural institutions, that left an important imprint on Salvadoran society. At the same time, U.S. anticommunism also motivated Osorio to relentlessly persecute trade union leaders, intellectuals, students, and politicians who advocated civilian rule and democratic reforms. Osorio's 1952 crackdown targeted hundreds of political opponents, including the biologist Celestino Castro; the labor leaders Salvador Cayetano Carpio and his wife, Tula Alvarenga; as well as student leaders such as the editors of the student newspaper *La Opinión Estudiantil*.[10] Cea recalled that the crackdown of 1952 revived his fear that another *Matanza* might be imminent:

> I came from Izalco and had the fear of 1932, I was born seven years after the 1932 massacre, but I had the fear of the

killings of 1932 and 1944. My fear was great, having a book with a red cover in 1952 was considered a crime.[11]

In his monograph *El Salvador*, the poet Roque Dalton, a contemporary of Cea, described the 1952 crackdown:

The repression against the people reached its maximum level with the crimes of 1952. During that year hundreds of labor and student leaders, patriots, and members of democratic parties were incarcerated, tortured, sent to exile, and in some cases assassinated. During those long and cruel days, incredible crimes were committed against the people. Beloved labor leaders were tortured in front of their children and wives, and the latter were raped in front of their tied husbands at the police dungeons.[12]

Salvador Cayetano Carpio, one of the labor leaders that Osorio's police captured along with his wife, Tula Alvarenga, wrote a well-known memoir called *Kidnapped and Hooded in a Country of the Free World*.[13] Carpio described in excruciating detail the medieval torture techniques he and his wife endured at the police headquarters in San Salvador, including the infamous *capucha* (the hood), a technique in which an interrogator placed a rubber hood over his victim's head and gradually tightened it until the victim nearly suffocated. Reportedly, two police torturers inflicted the hood on Carpio himself. According to Carpio, the political prisoners also endured lashes and mutilations, and were severely beaten.[14] The chief investigator of the National Police, Major José Alberto "El Chele" Medrano, along with Police Commander Roque Antonio Canales and other well-known police officers, is said to have supervised the torture of hundreds of political prisoners.[15] Carpio viewed the 1952 repression as part of the anticommunist crackdowns perpetrated by U.S.-sponsored regimes against trade unions, student movements, and opposition parties throughout Latin America. He claimed that Medrano and other police officers who carried out the repression were trained by "U.S. police technicians" in "the cruelest methods of terror and police persecution against the popular sectors."[16] He also wrote that police engaged in a systematic campaign of assassinations during the Osorio administration that targeted not only political opponents but also common criminals.[17] Like Carpio, Roque Dalton stated that the police murdered hundreds of thieves in San Salvador during the 1952 crackdown. Dalton claimed that the policeman José Urías Orantes "personally killed more than three hundred unfortunate criminals whose bodies were thrown into the Lempa River."[18]

Osorio sent hundreds of political opponents into exile and offered many intellectuals, whom he considered potentially threatening to his regime, scholarships to study abroad. For instance, he gave members of an influential literary group known as the Committed Generation—such as the playwright Waldo Chávez Velasco, who at the time was a member of the Communist Party, and the essayist Ítalo López Vallecillos—scholarships to study in Bologna and Spain.[19] The dismantling of the emerging opposition movement that resulted from the 1952 crackdown enabled Osorio to focus on his modernization plan and to present his regime as a model of political stability in the midst of the increasingly turbulent situation in the Caribbean basin. Osorio even managed to secretly support the 1954 CIA coup against the democratically elected president Jacobo Árbenz in Guatemala while pretending to embrace a neutral position vis-à-vis the Guatemalan crisis.[20] Osorio's anticommunist crackdown of 1952 was consistent with U.S. Cold War policies in Latin America in the aftermath of World War II, which aimed at undermining communist influence in labor unions and dismantling left-wing opposition parties and movements in an effort to consolidate ideological and political control of the state and U.S. hegemony in the region. U.S. diplomats, military attachés, intelligence officers, and labor leaders affiliated with the American Federation of Labor (AFL) played different roles in monitoring and fighting what they deemed communist activities in Latin America.[21]

The second crackdown against the pro-democracy movements occurred in 1960 during the government of President José María Lemus (1956–60), and it was mainly fueled by U.S. efforts to halt the growing influence of the Cuban Revolution in Central America.

Lemus, a protégé of President Osorio, rose to power in 1956. At the outset of his presidency, Lemus allowed the return of exiles and abolished the "Law in Defense of Democratic and Constitutional Order," which sanctioned Osorio's anticommunist crackdown in 1952, creating in fact a political opening that enabled the reorganization of the trade unions, student movements, and other sectors of the opposition.[22] Lemus governed El Salvador during a period of declining prosperity as coffee prices plunged in the international markets, forcing an economic restructuring that had particularly negative consequences for the poor. But more important, the changing political landscape in Latin America posed new challenges to Lemus. The ousting of the Venezuelan dictator Marcos Pérez Jiménez in January 1958 and the Cuban Revolution of January 1959 inspired a new wave of mobilization in El Salvador. The recently formed Revolutionary Party of April and May (PRAM) and the National Front of Civic Orientation (FNOC) defied Lemus's authoritarian regime.[23] At that time, Lemus and the Revolutionary Party of Democratic Unification (PRUD), the official party, showed a renewed determination to prevent the spread of "Cuban-inspired subversion" in El Salvador.[24]

In the aftermath of the 1954 CIA coup against President Árbenz in Guatemala, U.S. pundits and policy elites revived the specter of communist expansion in Central America and the Caribbean.[25] For example, the confrontation between Lemus and the opposition in El Salvador in 1960, which involved a sector of the university community, was intertwined with U.S. efforts to limit the impact of the Cuban Revolution. At that time, the Eisenhower administration showed a rising concern over Lemus's inability to fight "communism" in El Salvador, and it pressured the Salvadoran president to curtail the opposition movement against his regime, particularly at the National University.

In the late 1950s, El Salvador seemed to be a relatively stable nation amid the increasingly volatile situation in the Caribbean basin. In this context, the Lemus government became a showcase for U.S. foreign policy in Latin America. In 1958, State Department officials prepared a "full state visit" for Lemus, partly to show that U.S.–Latin American relations were not in such dire straits as the rough reception Vice President Richard Nixon had received during a recent visit to Caracas might have suggested.[26] State Department officials concocted an elaborate state visit for Lemus, but privately they harbored concerns about Lemus's apparent laxity in fighting "communism" in El Salvador.[27]

Thorsten Kalijarvi, the U.S. ambassador in El Salvador, also expressed his dissatisfaction with Lemus's efforts "to combat communism in El Salvador." "The Ambassador reports that two years of efforts by the Embassy and the OAS [the Organization of American States] of suggesting the Government of El Salvador methods of combating communism have not been very fruitful," reads a memo written by a State Department analyst in preparation for Lemus's state visit to the United States in March 1959. State Department officials thought it necessary to raise Lemus's apparent lack of resolve or skill to combat communism in El Salvador as a central issue during his visit.[28]

U.S. labor officers also expressed concern about what they considered Lemus's lack of resolve to crack down on union leaders and other members of the opposition whom they labeled communists. Serafino Romualdi, the international representative of the Inter-American Regional Organization of Workers (ORIT), and Andrew McClellan, the Latin American representative of the International Federation of Food and Drink Workers, told Ambassador Kalijarvi in March 1959 that the activities of trade unionists affiliated with the General Confederation of Salvadoran Workers (CGTS) and student groups at the University of El Salvador against Lemus were part of a Cuban conspiracy to implant "Castro-type" regimes in Central America.[29]

In June 1960, Lemus reportedly told C. Allan Stewart, a State Department official, and Donald P. Downs, the chargé d'affairs at the U.S. embassy in San Salvador, that he had uncovered a plot against his government, supported by Cuba, that was orchestrated by Salvadoran opposition leaders based in Costa Rica. He allegedly announced to Stewart and Downs his intention to crack down on the opposition movement operating at the University of El Salvador.[30] In July 1960, he declared PRAM illegal, a decision that sparked widespread mobilization in San Salvador led by the FNOC.[31] In the following days, Lemus jailed and sent into exile members of the university community, including the student leaders Shafik Hándal and José Vides, as well as the writer Manlio Argueta.[32] In a recent interview, Argueta recalled that the Salvadoran and Guatemalan military closely collaborated in the repression against the pro-democracy movements in both countries. Argueta, Hándal, Vides, and other political prisoners of the Lemus government were transported by the Guatemalan military to a town near the Mexican border, where they were held for several weeks.[33] But despite the initial crackdown, mass demonstrations against Lemus continued in San Salvador in August 1960. On September 2, Lemus ordered a full-scale attack against the university. The attack was swift and brutal. Members of the National Police and National Guard entered the campus, beating to death Mauricio Esquivel Salguero, a university student and employee, and seriously injuring hundreds of students, workers, and faculty. Napoleón Rodríguez Ruiz, rector of the university, and other university officials were also severely beaten and incarcerated. The policemen and guardsmen who entered the university campus reportedly raped several students. The state forces severely damaged the university facilities during the raid. After the attack, the university closed down its activities and did not reopen until after Lemus's downfall.[34]

Ambassador Kalijarvi offered Lemus advice and U.S. military aid to deal with the political unrest.[35] He also encouraged Lemus to harden his position against the demonstrators. The U.S. ambassador asked Lemus why "the student organization AGEUS had not been disbanded," to which Lemus replied that this action would be futile since there were a number of "illegal organizations such as the PRAM and the CGTS" that were also active. Kalijarvi criticized Lemus for exiling members of the opposition, arguing that this was indeed a useless tactic, and he advised Lemus to create legislation to incarcerate "agitators" for a period of "one to ten years." Lemus replied that Salvadoran law did not allow punishment of this kind and that only military tribunals could impose this type of sentence. This last option, both men agreed, would only further the government's authoritarian image. Kalijarvi reported that Lemus seemed indecisive on how to handle future demonstrations. However, Lemus showed interest in learning "how to handle tear gas and techniques for the use of other means to control mobs." Kalijarvi reported that he bluntly asked Lemus: "What do you want?" "Do you want arms?" Lemus supposedly responded, "Yes I have already asked for arms." Kalijarvi further asked Lemus, "Do you want the U.S. army?" Lemus responded "no."[36]

On October 26, 1960, Lemus was ousted by an unlikely alliance between a group of military officers loyal to Osorio and university intellectuals who advocated the democratization of the country. The Civic-Military Junta that replaced Lemus embraced a democratization program that included free elections, the demilitarization of society, the creation of political parties, and an independent foreign policy. The junta's democratization program and its refusal to break diplomatic relations with Cuba apparently motivated the Eisenhower administration to support a reactionary coup conducted by a group of high-ranking military officers and lawyers closely associated with the Salvadoran elites, which was sanctioned by the Kennedy administration on January 25, 1961. On that day, members of the National Guard massacred dozens of demonstrators in San Salvador while they marched along Avenida España.[37] According to several witnesses to these events, members of the U.S. military mission in El Salvador played a key role in the organization of the bloody coup. Héctor Dada, a founder of the Christian Democratic Party (PDC), maintained that the authorship of the coup was distinctly "North American." "The coup aimed at avoiding the Cuban influence. That coup was conducted by a gringo Colonel," Dada said.[38] Víctor Valle, a scholar at the University of El Salvador during the 1960s, told a similar story.[39] Fabio Castillo, a medical doctor and former rector of the University of El Salvador, testified before the U.S. Congress in 1976 that "members of the U.S. Military Mission openly intensified their invitation to conspiracy and rebellion" against the junta and that "members of the U.S. Military Mission were at the San Carlos Headquarters on the day of the coup."[40] Dada blamed Eisenhower, not Kennedy, for ousting the reformist junta. For him, it is clear that the Kennedy administration only rubber-stamped the coup. "Kennedy took over on January 20 [1961] and the coup happened on

January 25 [1961]," recalled Dada. He remembered (inaccurately) that the coup coincided with the Bay of Pigs invasion.[41] But in fact, the coup followed Eisenhower's decision to break diplomatic relations with Cuba in early January 1961.[42]

In the aftermath of the coup of January 1961, communist intellectuals and leaders of social movements formed the United Front of Revolutionary Action (FUAR), a militant organization that constituted the left's first attempt to carry out armed struggle in El Salvador since *La Matanza* of 1932. The creation of the FUAR in 1961 was the left's response to the mounting state repression during the Lemus regime and the ousting of the short-lived reformist Civic-Military Junta that replaced him. Although FUAR was demobilized in 1963 by Salvador Cayetano Carpio (the labor and communist leader influenced by the Soviet policy of "peaceful coexistence" with the U.S., who was a target of Osorio's crackdown in 1952), it left an enduring legacy among activists who continued debating the formation of insurgent groups in the 1960s and 1970s.

The events of 1960 and 1961, with their international and internal dimensions, significantly altered the political awareness and political culture of left-wing activists and intellectuals in El Salvador. After these episodes, they viewed the U.S. government as a crucial internal actor in Salvadoran politics. Unlike the crises of the military regimes of the 1940s and 1950s that were largely resolved through intra-elite negotiations, the revamping of the military regimes, and the creation of new official parties, U.S. participation in Salvadoran affairs became ubiquitous after 1959, a situation that in turn reinforced the left-wing activists' revolutionary nationalism. Left-wing intellectuals like Fabio Castillo and Víctor Valle shared the perception that the U.S. military mission in San Salvador orchestrated the 1961 coup. Moreover, the leaders of FUAR deemed the 1961 coup the start of a new "colonization" under President Kennedy's Alliance for Progress, which purportedly aimed at transforming El Salvador into a "second Puerto Rico" or a "new U.S. colony" in Central America.[43]

Lemus's despotic government and the failed reformist experiment of the Civic-Military Junta, which ended in the bloody coup of January 1961, during the intensification of U.S. hostilities against the Cuban Revolution, marked the beginning of a discussion on armed struggle among left-wing intellectuals and activists in the 1960s. By this logic, the events of 1960 and 1961 can be seen as the starting point of the insurgent and counterinsurgent politics that characterized El Salvador in the subsequent three decades.

COUNTERINSURGENCY WITHOUT INSURGENCY

U.S. counterinsurgency doctrine in the early 1960s defined the term "enemy" in the "broadest possible terms."[44] In 1962 the U.S. Joint Chiefs of Staff characterized "insurgency" as a condition of "illegal opposition to an existing government" that could range from passive resistance, illegal strike action or demonstrations, to large scale guerrilla operations, but fell short of civil war."[45] In other words, this definition virtually conflated the pro-democracy movements (opposition parties, trade unions, and social movements that advocated democratic reforms) and the guerrilla organizations that emerged across Latin America during that decade into a single analytical category.[46] Since the early 1960s, U.S. advisers supported the creation of a massive counterinsurgency apparatus in El Salvador at a time when no armed insurgency had yet emerged in the country. This apparatus systematically persecuted activists, public intellectuals, and members of independent political parties, as well as priests and laypeople associated with the progressive sector of the Catholic Church. In doing so, the counterinsurgency created "an internal enemy" as radicalized activists and intellectuals joined or supported the armed insurgent groups founded at the end of that decade.

The history of counterinsurgency proper in El Salvador starts with the creation of the Civic-Military Directorate that replaced the reformist Civic-Military Junta in January 1961, the foundation of the Party of National Conciliation (PCN), the new official party, and the subsequent election of Colonel Julio Rivera as president of the Republic in an uncompetitive election held in April 1962. In the eighteen months that followed the January 1961 coup, the oligarchic military regime was reorganized under U.S. tutelage to fit the Alliance for Progress model of governance, which featured economic modernization, industrialization, political reforms, and the refurbishing of the national security apparatus under the guidelines of U.S. counterinsurgency.[47] The Civic-Military Directorate constituted by Rivera, another colonel, and three civilians took over power and declared martial law in January 1961.[48] In an attempt to create a reformist image for the new government, the leaders of the coup initially asked the Christian Democrats to become the new official party, a proposal that was rejected by the majority of PDC leaders. However, a conservative faction of the PDC left the party and joined former members of the PRUD (Lemus's official party) to form the PCN, the new official party.[49] The Directorate called for the election of a constitutional assembly for December 17, 1961. While only the PCN and an obscure right-wing party participated in the election, the Directorate labeled the event "the country's first clean election since 1930."[50] Rivera resigned from the Directorate in September. In January 1962, "the Constitutional Assembly revised the 1950 constitution, gave itself the status of a national assembly, and scheduled a presidential election for April [1962]."[51] Not surprisingly, Rivera ran as the PCN candidate and won the presidency in a noncompetitive election. However, to avoid Lemus's fate, he embarked on a series of political reforms, most notably the establishment of proportional representation in the National Assembly, on the advice of Murat Williams, Kennedy's ambassador in El Salvador.[52]

The Rivera government (1962–67) fully embodied the Alliance for Progress counterinsurgency model. Héctor Dada labeled it "the ideal Alliance for Progress regime" in that it combined an "intensely modernizing platform but before anything else, national security." Furthermore Dada recalled that the Rivera government implemented "a reform of agrarian property, of defense of the interests of workers, in short, [the] Alliance for Progress [model]."[53] Domingo Santacruz, a former member of FUAR, deemed Rivera's decision to tolerate the electoral participation of opposition parties and to establish a new system of proportional representation at the National Assembly a maneuver aimed at countering the influence of the Cuban Revolution through a limited political opening. However, according to Santacruz, Rivera closed down alternatives for the much-needed socioeconomic reforms and focused solely on the creation of the Central American Common Market, hoping that it would stimulate employment and the growth of the internal market as an alternative to the impending social crisis.[54]

Rivera fully implemented the U.S. counterinsurgency program, which included the restructuring of the country's public security, military, and intelligence apparatus, as well as the integration of the Central American armies and security agencies. Under Rivera's government, the army and the security forces received U.S. training in counterinsurgency warfare and repression of mass demonstrations.[55] The United States trained 1,971 Salvadoran military officers between 1950 and 1979. During this period, hundreds of Salvadoran officers received specialized counterinsurgency training.[56] The Nationalist Democratic Organization (ORDEN), a paramilitary anticommunist organization and intelligence-gathering network, which also doubled as a structure used by the official party to intimidate voters and rig elections, was also founded in 1965 by Colonel José Alberto "Chele" Medrano of the Salvadoran army, with the support of U.S. Green Berets.[57] U.S. advisers helped the Salvadoran regime create an extensive intelligence apparatus that comprised specialized army and public security units, as well as thousands of civilian informants, to counter a purported "communist threat" at a time "when no significant organized leftist opposition to the government existed."[58] In addition, an assortment of paramilitary clandestine groups started operating under the protection of the Rivera government.[59] The Salvadoran military also played an active role in the Central American Defense Council (CONDECA), a body that integrated the command structures of the Central American armies.

The 1960s was a period of rapid growth of social movements and opposition parties in El Salvador. By 1967, left-of-center and left-wing parties like the Christian Democrats and the Party of Renovative Action (PAR), respectively, had become significant electoral forces in San Salvador and other major cities and towns. But more significantly, the tensions between the trade unions and the government of President Rivera grew during a labor conflict at ACERO, a steel factory in Zacatecoluca, owned by Antonio and Mauricio

Borgonovo, two prominent members of the Salvadoran elites. The ACERO job action escalated into a national strike in 1967 supported by roughly thirty thousand workers. Amid the conflict, Salvador Cayetano Carpio, at the time the Secretary-General of the PCS, believed that the workers' militant spirit was so high that they were willing to shed their blood in defense of their cause. Carpio wrote: "[T]he proletarian army [is] ready to defend its rights, ready to shed its blood [to defend] its right to strike." Carpio deemed the strike a resounding victory for the workers at ACERO, who showed a remarkable level of unity and solidarity despite the government repression of the trade unionists. He also considered the state anticommunist discourse ineffectual in its attempt to deter the revolutionary mobilization of workers.[60]

The mobilization of teachers affiliated with the National Association of Salvadoran Educators (ANDES) in 1968 and 1971 constituted pivotal moments in the conflict between the social movements and the government of President Fidel Sánchez Hernández (1967–72), the successor to President Rivera. The two-month teachers' strike in 1968 became the first major confrontation between the emerging teachers' union and the Sánchez Hernández government. Striking teachers camped outside the new building of the Ministry of Education at a place they called "the plaza of the teachers' dignity." The plaza became a symbolic space where teachers, workers, students, and vendors from local markets gathered every day for "58 days" to denounce the "humiliation[s], the selling of [teacher's] degrees" and other practices linked to "the partisan politics" that dominated the profession.[61] The 1968 strike was largely resolved through negotiations between the striking teachers and the education minister; however, the Sánchez Hernández government severely cracked down on ANDES affiliates during the teachers' national strike in July and August 1971, when state agencies that had been created in the context of U.S. counterinsurgency—such as the National Center of Information (CNI), a psychological operations center, and the ORDEN paramilitaries—played major roles in the repression of teachers and their supporters. The teachers' mobilizations of 1971 anticipated the open confrontations between the social movements and the oligarchic military regime during the rest of that decade. During the strike, public security forces and ORDEN paramilitaries conducted a violent campaign against the teachers and their supporters. While the striking teachers were constantly vilified in the official press, paramilitaries and other state agents stoned, machine-gunned, and burned ANDES affiliates' homes. They also killed, tortured, and "disappeared" several teachers and other activists. ORDEN paramilitaries, members of the National Guard, and other state agents severely beat teachers who occupied public schools in Santa Tecla, Cojutepeque, Santa Ana, and other cities and towns. But despite the attacks, the striking teachers and their supporters gathered at schools across the country for fifty-three days.[62]

The state's response to the strike epitomized "the making of the internal enemy." It was a carefully orchestrated effort of the Salvadoran state and the official media to equate social activism with communist subversion and terrorism so as to legitimize the repression. In the 1960s, the pro-government newspapers featured a vaguely anticommunist discourse, but by the early 1970s they had begun to label specific individuals communist agitators.[63] More to the point, the state anticommunist discourse incarnated in the political personas of Mélida Anaya Montes, José Mario López, and other leaders of ANDES, as well as in the members of an obscure guerrilla cell made up of university intellectuals who kidnapped and murdered the industrialist Ernesto Regalado Dueñas, the heir of the wealthiest Salvadoran family, which government officials labeled "El Grupo" (the Group).[64] Anaya Montes in particular was the focus of the government's propaganda campaign against ANDES, spearheaded by the CNI, which was run by the former left-wing intellectual Waldo Chávez Velasco, under the authority of President Sánchez Hernández. The CNI, in a series of anonymous publications that appeared in *La Prensa Gráfica*, a pro-government newspaper, during the teachers' strike described Anaya Montes, who held a doctorate in education and was professor at the University of El Salvador, as a perfidious and childless agitator who manipulated well-intentioned but naive teachers on behalf of the emerging guerrilla groups. The publications, seeking to portray the striking teachers as irresponsible individuals who undermined the purported exemplary work ethic of traditional teachers and attempted to divide the movement, emphasized that leaders of ANDES, like Anaya Montes and López, were in fact privileged union bosses who would not be affected by the salary cuts and other penalties. The consequences of the repression of the teachers' union were far-reaching. After the crackdown, leaders of the teachers' movement, particularly Mélida Anaya Montes and José Mario López, seriously pondered armed struggle as the only viable way to oust the authoritarian regime. Numerous rank-and-file teachers also joined the insurgency after these events.[65] University students equated the state repression of the teachers' movement and their allies in 1971 with President José María Lemus's crackdown on the university in 1960. They called the state officials in charge of the repression and of the psychological operations against ANDES "the followers of Lemus."[66]

Mélida Anaya Montes has argued that the state's repression of the teachers' movement in 1971 was fueled mainly by U.S. counterinsurgency efforts, which aimed at preventing the emergence of guerrilla organizations by cracking down on the growing social movements. She also made reference to the increasing tensions between the social movements and the PCS. While the teachers' union, peasant organizations, and other social movements that constituted the rising New Left favored more radical forms of mobilization, such as strikes, occupations of public buildings, and mass demonstrations, the PCS, which she termed "the traditional left," focused on electoral politics despite the mounting state repression.

> The Salvadoran state in the last years has entered the phase of framing the solid popular movements within the [U.S.] special warfare strategy an anti-guerrilla measure [sic]. This is the origin of every punitive measure that sometimes seems exaggerated and inexplicable (to crack down on demonstrations, to imprison, to torture to obtain declarations). Its essential objective is to destroy every germ of the guerrillas before they develop and to destroy every possible popular support that generally comes from sectors radicalized in

concrete struggles and not in "study circles." That is why the massive popular movements are seen with singular antipathy by the government and with distrust and rivalry by the traditional left. In El Salvador methods of counterinsurgency proper are being applied before there is really an offensive of revolutionary groups willing to use arms as a method of struggle to conquer political power. The preventative aspect of the government's measures motivate them to attempt the destruction of any peaceful popular movement that is independent of the government and the traditional left. ANDES is a peaceful association, and the government knows it better than anybody else, but it is considered dangerous due to its strict independence . . .[67]

In her memoir of the 1971 teachers' strike, Anaya Montes wrote that the teachers were totally unprepared psychologically, politically, and logistically to face the crackdown.

Such an element [the repression] had been used in El Salvador against workers and peasants in the past, but not with teachers. The reason is very simple: teachers had never combated [the regime]. During the 1968 strike [the government] pressured [the teachers] in other ways, that is why perhaps [they] had the audacity to rise up again. . . . [In 1971] the government [was] willing to give [them] an exemplary lesson."[68]

In the aftermath of the strike, Anaya Montes publicly advocated the use of revolutionary violence and faulted the PCS for its unwillingness to initiate the armed struggle against the authoritarian regime.[69] In her distinctive rhetorical style, she wrote a vignette that illustrates this point. When members of the National Police laid siege to the Teacher's House during the 1971 strike, Anaya Montes purportedly asked the leaders of ANDES who met at the site if anyone had at least a "shaving blade" to defend themselves, to which "they responded in unison, no." "I only had a 30 centimeter pin attached to my dress. Outside there were thirty machine guns pointing at the

Teacher's House. We [the leaders of ANDES] continued our discussion. We had words they had weapons," Anaya concluded.[70] Carlos López, a former member of ANDES, recalled that the 1971 strike became a turning point in the radicalization of the teachers' movement. After the event, many teachers started labeling the government, the security forces, and the army "the enemy." López recalled that while some teachers joined the official party to preserve their job stability, he and other ANDES affiliates joined the insurgency.[71]

RURAL COUNTERINSURGENCY AND INSURGENCY IN CHALATENANGO

Massacres perpetrated by state forces against peasant communities, university students, and other social movements escalated after 1971, largely as a result of the further militarization of the country after the war between El Salvador and Honduras in 1969, which virtually destroyed the Central American Common Market, severely weakening the Salvadoran economy. After the 1969 war, the Salvadoran elites responded with brutal force to the growing demands of political democracy and socioeconomic reforms articulated by the emerging social movements, progressive sectors of the Catholic Church, and the opposition parties. I illustrate this trend by analyzing the massacre at La Cayetana, a mass killing perpetrated by members of the National Guard in San Vicente, and the roles that ORDEN paramilitaries played in the intensification of rural conflicts in Chalatenango, a northern department in El Salvador, in the early 1970s.

The sheer savagery of the state repression against the nascent peasant movement in San Vicente in 1974 produced shock waves among peasant communities across El Salvador. In fact, the massacre at La Cayetana in November of that year motivated peasant leaders in Chalatenango and San Vicente to form the Union of Rural Workers (UTC), a potent peasant movement that played an important role in the political history of El Salvador in the 1970s. Peasant activists affiliated with the UTC who survived the repression of the 1970s constituted the backbone of the insurgent army that emerged in San Vicente and Chalatenango in the early 1980s. According to David

Rodríguez, who was then a diocesan priest working in Tecoluca, a town near the site of the massacre, a group of landless peasants from La Cayetana, a hamlet in the San Vicente volcano, formed a "pro-lease committee" in an effort to rent land for the cultivation of corn and beans. After the Ministry of Agriculture failed to support the peasants' demand to conduct negotiations with the local landowners, they organized a land occupation near La Cayetana. The next day, pro-government newspapers accused priests of "being the agitators of peasants and responsible for that usurpation." On July 25, 1974, unidentified individuals gunned down the leader of the pro-lease committee, and on November 29, "three trucks loaded with National Guards" entered La Cayetana, "shooting" at the inhabitants of the hamlet. Subsequently, they captured the participants in the land occupation and moved them to the *ermita* (the local chapel). At the chapel, the guardsmen "stripped [peasants] of their clothes leaving them in their underwear facing down on the floor and then they danced on top of them singing . . . Alleluia, Alleluia! They cursed and insulted [the peasants], then they tied them up with ropes and took them to the trucks to transport them . . ." As the guardsmen were leaving the hamlet they encountered a group of workers (men and women) who attempted to escape the site. "Six of them took refuge in a thatched house [nearby]. . . . There [the guardsmen] shot them. . . . Then they destroyed their faces with machetes . . . put [the bodies] in sacks and moved them away in a truck. . . . Two days later [those] who had been captured reappeared after having been tortured. [The guardsmen] threatened them not to continue working at [the previously occupied] land and warned them not to visit the parish. . . . A few days later the bodies of the six [people who were summarily] executed [by the guardsmen] appeared thrown in the streets near Tecoluca, destroyed by dogs . . ."[72] In the aftermath of the murders perpetrated by the state forces at La Cayetana, peasant leaders from San Vicente led by Rafael Barrera met their peers from Chalatenango to create a new peasant organization they eventually called the UTC.[73]

As in the hamlets near the town of Aguilares studied by the anthropologist Carlos R. Cabarrús in the 1970s, the peasant communities in northeast Chalatenango grew deeply divided between those who supported the emerging peasant movement and those who joined ORDEN. Peasants affiliated with ORDEN, along with members of the National Guard, engaged in a terror campaign against members of the emerging peasant organizations, who often were their close relatives and neighbors. The Salvadoran military had armed ORDEN paramilitaries with weapons after the conflict between El Salvador and Honduras in 1969 and gave them leeway to repress individuals linked to the peasant movement and their families. In this sense, counterinsurgency intensified local conflicts in towns and hamlets across Chalatenango, which ultimately escalated into a civil war among peasant communities in the area. Previous political affiliations of the local peasant leaders and kinship relations informed the antagonism between peasants affiliated with the emerging UTC and members of ORDEN. For instance, in the case of La Ceiba, a hamlet near the town of Las Vueltas, most members of the Mejía family joined the UTC, following the leadership of Justo Mejía, a former Christian Democratic activist and a volunteer teacher of a Catholic education program called the Radio Schools. Most male members of the García and Cartagena families joined ORDEN, following the leadership of Pedro Zamora (aka Pedro Cartagena), who was previously affiliated with the PCN, the official party. Chinda Zamora, a sister-in-law of Justo Mejía, who joined the UTC, blamed Pedro Zamora, the local leader of ORDEN (who was also her relative), for the killing of many residents in the area.[74] Guadalupe Mejía, a former resident of La Ceiba, also branded Pedro Zamora *un oreja* (a snitch) who constantly reported the whereabouts of Justo Mejía to the National Guard despite the fact that they were close relatives and neighbors.[75] Hilda Mejía, a former resident of La Ceiba, commented that the acute polarization of the community there, which occurred between 1974 and 1980, turned into a "very ugly melée" (*un revoltijo bien feo*), meaning that the growing paramilitary repression of the members of the UTC and the ensuing violent responses of the latter against the members of ORDEN generated numerous fatalities among closely related families.[76]

After the war between El Salvador and Honduras in 1969, members of the *patrullas cantonales* (paramilitaries under the direct jurisdiction of the army) and ORDEN underwent intense anticommunist indoctrination through their contacts with local military commanders and other members of the security apparatus. However, these organizations were far from monolithic. In fact, several founders of the UTC, including Justo Mejía and José "Santos" Martínez, at one time served in the *patrullas cantonales*, and active members of ORDEN secretly collaborated with the peasant movement.[77] These shifts from collaboration to resistance suggest that although subaltern groups play an active role in the functioning of state domination, their loyalty to community-based organizations such as the UTC often remains strong, despite their multiple associations with the state repressive apparatus.[78]

The formation of the first armed peasant organizations, called "self-defense groups," which operated under the authority of the UTC leaders in the area, started in 1975. Facundo Guardado, José "Santos" Martínez, and Justo Mejía, three leaders of the UTC, played key roles in forming these groups. Martínez and Mejía were older community leaders and former paramilitary commanders who had ample experience organizing local paramilitary forces (army reserves).[79] Mejía was also forcibly mobilized by the Salvadoran army during the war between El Salvador and Honduras in 1969 and probably had combat experience.[80] Guardado, on the other hand, was a young peasant leader who had participated in the foundation of rural cooperatives in his native town, Arcatao. Guardado argued that his decision to form the UTC and the armed peasant groups was mainly influenced by the mounting state repression against the peasant, student, and teacher movements. In particular, Guardado mentioned that the massacre perpetrated by state forces against a student demonstration in downtown San Salvador on July 30, 1975, which resulted in dozens of civilian victims, rang an "alarm bell" among the peasant leaders.

> We [the peasant leaders in Chalatenango] took the decision to form the UTC in 1974 as a response to the killings [perpetrated by state forces] in León de Piedra and La Cayetana [San Vicente]. . . . Then [the] July 30 [massacre against students

in San Salvador in 1975] was an alarm bell [*un campanazo*] for us, they [the state forces] had decided to crack down on us. But if one thinks about it, in those years it was not yet a policy of systematic extermination but rather a repressive policy aimed at impeding the strength of the [popular] movements. When they [the government of President Arturo A. Molina, 1972–77] realized that the movements were strong, they reacted in a virulent manner closing [political spaces] and eliminating the leadership. It was a deliberate policy. They killed 401 teachers in the 1970s. The same happened with the rest of [the popular organizations]. In the case of the peasant leaders, I don't think there was a national list [of people whom the state planned to eliminate], so to speak, but it was clear to us that they had a policy of identifying the regional leaders. The [repressive] actions were clearly planned. They were not casual. They pointed at one person and then they killed her. They killed the leaders. The idea was to strike at the head [of the movement]. Also the ORDEN paramilitaries [in Chalatenango] roamed heavily armed. They looked at you in the face and fired their guns in the air with total impunity. The affair was getting more and more complicated.[81]

In addition to the self-defense groups controlled by the peasant leaders, the Popular Liberation Forces FPL-Farabundo Martí, an insurgent organization founded in 1970, which operated in Chalatenango, also formed clandestine peasant militias in the area. Some of the more politicized peasant leaders became militia leaders and combatants. The militias' main role was to provide security for peasant demonstrations in rural and urban areas and to conduct propaganda operations and minor attacks against state forces.[82] Although in theory the FPL conceived the militias as a force separate from the self-defense groups, in practice they intermingled and performed similar functions in Chalatenango. However, the self-defense groups expanded at a much faster pace than the militias. Most of the combatants who first joined the guerrilla army in 1980 were former members of the self-defense groups and militias.[83]

While the peasant insurgency expanded in Chalatenango and elsewhere in the country, the oligarchic military regime, for the second time during that decade, rigged the presidential election results in 1977. (The first electoral fraud took place in March 1972.) However, this time, the state forces also massacred opposition activists who protested the electoral fraud in downtown San Salvador on the night of February 28, 1977. Facundo Guardado remembered that his hopes for a political settlement of the country's growing conflict waned after he walked near the site of the massacre in downtown San Salvador at dawn and saw a group of firemen hosing off the blood of the victims of the repression.[84]

THE SECOND *MATANZA*

Between 1977 and 1983, the oligarchic military regime conducted a terror campaign against vast sectors of Salvadoran society, which is comparable only to the 1932 massacre. I call this campaign the Second *Matanza*. It included mass killings, summary executions, disappearances, torture, rapes, and other human rights violations perpetrated by state forces and armed illegal groups that operated under state protection, known as "death squads," against social and political activists; Catholic priests, nuns, and laypeople; public intellectuals; teachers; journalists; artists; and ordinary people accused of collaborating with the insurgency. No fewer than thirty thousand civilians were victims of the repression that took place in this period. To this day, no comprehensive study of the characteristics of this state terror and the roles that U.S. counterinsurgency played in it has emerged.[85] A former RAND Corporation analyst acknowledged the magnitude of these killings and claimed that the purported success of U.S. counterinsurgency in El Salvador "was based on 40,000 political murders."[86] It is apparent that despite its initial hesitation to provide military and security aid to the intensely repressive government of President Carlos H. Romero (1977–79), the Carter administration financed the Salvadoran army and public security forces during this period. After 1981, the Reagan administration escalated the levels of military aid to the Salvadoran government during the civil war. I will now briefly discuss events that took place in the initial period of the Second *Matanza*, during the government of President Romero, as well as the reaction of the Catholic hierarchy against the state repression during the rule of Archbishop Oscar A. Romero (1977–80).

The fraudulent election of President Romero in 1977 inaugurated one of the most violent periods in Salvadoran history. President Romero's two-year rule was characterized by brutal repression against social movements, opposition parties, and members of the Catholic Church. It featured mounting death squad activity, massive military operations in rural areas, massacres, torture, disappearances, imprisonments, and the summary executions of activists and ordinary citizens. The terror was sanctioned by the Law of Defense and Guarantee of Public Order approved by the National Assembly in November 1977 and was matched by intense state propaganda.[87] During one of the most notorious episodes of this period, public security forces massacred scores of demonstrators at the National Cathedral on May 8, 1979, and at the Venezuelan embassy later that month, who protested the disappearance of Facundo Guardado and other leaders of the Popular Revolutionary Bloc (BPR), the largest coalition of social movements in the 1970s.

The crackdowns at the cathedral and the embassy generated a potent militant reaction in San Salvador and other major cities, which included strikes and sabotage, as well as multiple guerrilla attacks against state forces. The Sandinista victory against the Somoza dictatorship in Nicaragua on July 19, 1979, further strengthened the left-wing offensive against the government as the guerrilla groups, now closely allied with massive social movements, attempted to topple President Romero. As the confrontation between the government and the opposition escalated, President Romero made a last-ditch attempt to foment "national unity," calling for the formation of a "National Forum." Romero's initiative amid the generalized state repression did not go far. Most political parties and social organizations rejected his proposal and instead formed the Popular Forum in September 1979, which aimed at ousting Romero to "stop the [imminent civil] war." Although the opposition parties and several popular organizations joined the Popular Forum, some movements (such as the BPR) that were closely allied with the insurgency re-jected it as the "validation of an eventual coup that would promote a 'Romerismo without Romero.'"[88] In fact, on October 15 of that same year, a group of military officers which called itself the Mili-tary Youth, in collaboration with the Jesuits at the Central American University (UCA) and other sectors of the opposition, overthrew Romero in a final attempt to avert a civil war.

Archbishop Oscar A. Romero, the newly appointed head of the Catholic Church, defended the social movements' rights. From his appointment in January 22, 1977, until his assassination at the hand of a right-wing death squad on March 24, 1980, Romero openly con-demned the growing state terror. The relations between the state and the Church reached a breaking point after National Guards-men assassinated Rutilio Grande, a Jesuit priest working in Aguil-ares and El Paisnal in March 1977. On May 11 of that year, the death squads murdered Alfonso Navarro, another Catholic priest in San Salvador. The conflict between the Catholic Church and the gov-ernment of President Romero reached an "unsustainable point in August 1979" when state agents murdered Alirio Napoleón Macías, another Catholic priest, in San Esteban Catarina.[89] The polariza-tion within the Catholic Church also intensified in the late 1970s. Conservative Catholic bishops who constituted the majority in the Episcopal Council condemned the peasant organizations and called on priests and laymen not to collaborate with them.[90] In turn, Arch-bishop Romero and Bishop Arturo Rivera y Damas, the auxiliary bishop of San Salvador, issued a joint Pastoral Letter called "The Church and the Popular Organizations," in which they defended on theological grounds the popular organizations' social and political rights. In the letter, the bishops also condemned the growing vio-lence perpetrated by ORDEN paramilitaries against the members of the peasant organizations:

> In order to overcome misery, some [peasants] are seduced by
> the advantages that the pro-government organizations offer
> them; in exchange for these, they are used in various repres-
> sive activities, which often include denouncing, terrorizing,

capturing, and in some cases and circumstances killing their own fellow peasants.[91]

The bishops' letter also offered a detailed analysis of the violence that prevailed in El Salvador in the late 1970s. They readily condemned state and "seditious or terrorist" violence (in other words, insurgent violence) but also acknowledged that the escalation of state repression motivated members of the popular organizations to engage in what they termed "spontaneous violence." The bishops argued that the constant state attacks against the "demands, demonstrations, just strikes," and other forms of popular mobilizations motivated activists to engage in improvised and ultimately ineffective forms of self-defense. They also stated that the Catholic Church doctrine sanctioned the use of "violence in legitimate defense," suggesting that the social movements were in fact exercising their right to self-defense vis-à-vis implacable state violence.[92]

> The Church permits violence in legitimate defense under the following conditions: a) the defense should not exceed the degree of the unjust aggression (for instance if it is enough to use the hands it is not licit to shoot the aggressor); b) to engage in proportionate violence after exhausting all possible peaceful means; c) that the violent defense does not bring as a consequence a worse evil than the one against which it is defending: for example, more violence, more injustice.[93]

Despite the Catholic bishops' attempts to stop the cycle of political violence, the intensification of state repression in the late 1970s and the ensuing insurgent response generated a full-scale civil war in 1980.

THE EL MOZOTE AND EL SUMPUL MASSACRES: EPITOMES OF RATIONAL CHOICE COUNTERINSURGENCY

On May 14, 1980, the Salvadoran army—with the complicity of the Honduran military—massacred approximately six hundred civilians at the Aradas de Yurique, on the banks of El Sumpul River in Chalatenango. The Salvadoran troops that carried out the massacre gathered in Las Vueltas, San José Las Flores, and Ojos de Agua, and moved toward Las Aradas, forcing thousands of displaced peasants as well as a few peasant insurgents in the area to move toward the Sumpul River. They trapped hundreds of men, women, and children on the banks of the river. When people crossed the Sumpul River into Honduran territory, the Honduran army units and paramilitaries turned them back to the Salvadoran army. Many people drowned while swimming in the river's turbulent waters. Ester Arteaga, a survivor of the massacre, remembered that she and three other young women who hid near the river witnessed how the Salvadoran soldiers "killed many people." [94]

> Some ran from here to there, others tried crossing the river. They never imagined that the Honduran army would be waiting for them there. The Salvadoran soldiers separated people, two women, two men, and two children. They pulled people by the hair and put them face down over the rocky terrain [el pedrero] and shot them. Some drowned, and the soldiers shot at those who started swimming. [95]

Like Ester Arteaga, many survivors of the massacres perpetrated by the Salvadoran military before and during the civil war have testified over the years that the soldiers systematically murdered the civilians they suspected of collaborating with the insurgency. Massacres like El Sumpul, El Mozote, and many other similar mass killings perpetrated by the Salvadoran military at that time show a pattern that suggests that these events were part of an elaborate strategy of mass extermination. [96] In my view, this pattern illustrates the practice of what Ron Robin called "rational choice" counterinsurgency. [97] Rational choice counterinsurgency constituted a break with the so-called behavioralist counterinsurgency theories applied in Vietnam in the 1950s and early 1960s, which aimed at "winning hearts and minds." These theories promoted the defection of peasant collaborators of the insurgency by offering them material or symbolic benefits, chiefly access to land and state protection. In contrast, rational choice counterinsurgency deems that basic cost-benefit logic ultimately determines human behavior. In this vein, the main objective of the counterinsurgent forces is to alter the behavior of insurgent sympathizers by elevating the cost of engaging in such conduct to unbearable levels. According to Robin, the rational choice counterinsurgency paradigm was originally developed at the RAND Corporation during a critical juncture of the Vietnam War.[98] Robin summarized the logic of rational choice counterinsurgency:

> Rand's counterinsurgency experts proposed defeating in-surgents by modifying the behavior of peasant supporters through a harsh coercive campaign of counterterror. Rand advisors argued that forceful, suppressive measures would lead Vietnamese peasants to a rational calculation of the costs and benefits of continuing support of insurgency. Ac-cording to this theory, the embattled yet calculating peasant would ultimately choose to abandon, if not actively resist, rebel forces. Despite the controversial nature of this model, and even though the Rand reports did not offer solid his-torical examples or empirical evidence to sustain this re-furbished image of the enemy, the military accepted these recommendations with breathtaking alacrity.[99]

Obviously, the state forces in El Salvador did not attempt to "win the hearts and minds" of the peasant communities living in the ar-eas of conflict by exterminating thousands of unarmed civilians. Instead, they aimed at raising the cost of their purported collabora-tion with the insurgents to indeed unbearable levels. To put it more bluntly, they attempted to terrorize people into submission. By this logic, El Salvador's civil war arguably became a laboratory for the emerging rational choice counterinsurgency paradigm.

Why, then, did rational choice counterinsurgency fail to demo-bilize the supporters of the insurgency? Although a comprehensive response to this question goes beyond the scope of this chapter, Elis-abeth Jean Wood's study on peasant collaborators of the Salvadoran insurgency offers important clues to answer this query. Based on her ethnographic research in several regions of El Salvador, Wood argues that a set of moral incentives and specific notions of historical change (for example, the making of "a history [peasants] perceive as more *just*") and agency shaped the collective mobilization of peasants during the civil war. Wood coined the term "pleasure in agency" to define the peasants' sense of "self-determination, autonomy, self-esteem, and pride that come from the successful assertion of intention" during the civil war.[100] In so doing, Wood questions the fundamental premise and ensuing effectiveness of the rational choice counterinsurgency paradigm—the idea that the motives of human behavior can be reduced to a basic cost-benefit rationale and that, ultimately, state terror creates perverse incentives (such as facing brutal death at the hands of state agents), which can successfully demobilize the supporters of the insurgency.

The El Sumpul, El Mozote, and other similar massacres constituted the tragic pinnacle of the convergence of U.S. anticommunism, counterinsurgency, and the repressive trajectory of the Salvadoran state during the Cold War. Here, I have discussed key moments of this process. The social movements and the opposition parties of the 1950s, 1960s, and 1970s articulated basic democratic demands such as free and fair elections, the existence of independent political parties, freedom of expression, freedom of the press, labor rights, agrarian reform, and so forth. The oligarchic military regime tenaciously fought the pro-democracy movements, drawing on U.S. Cold War anticommunism and counterinsurgency. The paradox is, of course, that the United States forged a solid alliance with one of the most antidemocratic and repressive regimes in Latin America in the name of freedom and democracy. Looking back, counterinsurgency not only failed to contain the insurgency, it helped to transform the broad-based pro-democracy movements of the 1960s and 1970s into one of the most potent insurgencies in the modern history of Latin America, namely, the FMLN.

Police talking to an old Malayan who may have information about the communists in the area, April 23, 1949. *Bert Hardy/Picture Post/Getty Images*

Police standing over bodies of slain Communists in Malaya, while wives try to identify them. *Jack Birns/ Time Life Pictures/ Getty Images*

A member of a Malayan Home Guard mans a checkpoint on the edge of a town. Such checkpoints allowed the authorities to search vehicles and intercept food and supplies being smuggled out to the Communist terrorists. *Imperial War Museum, London*

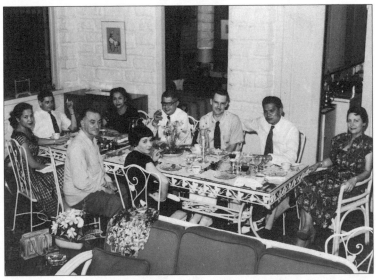

In this rare photo, Magsaysay (second from right) is seen relaxing with American friends, including Edward Lansdale (to his right) and David Sternberg (at the head of the table), a journalist and alleged CIA operative. *Courtesy of American Historical Collection, Rizal Library, Ateneo de Manila University*

Magsaysay always attracted the press and throngs of people in his public appearances. He was a media darling and political celebrity. *Courtesy of Pardo de Tavera Collection, Rizal Library, Ateneo de Manila University*

Leonora Hipas, a Huk Amazon, is shown here in full military gear with her husband after their arrest. Reproducing masculinized images of women Huks is an important component in the government's propaganda war. *Manila Times,* October 7, 1954. *Courtesy of Pardo de Tavera Collection, Rizal Library, Ateneo de Manila*

Photographs of abandoned Huk children in military orphanages, such as this one, frequently appeared in newspapers and magazines as the government launched a propaganda campaign aimed at Huk women to leave the "life of the hunted" and reunite with their families. *Philippines Free Press*, early 1950s. *Courtesy of Pardo de Tavera Collection, Rizal Library, Ateneo de Manila University*

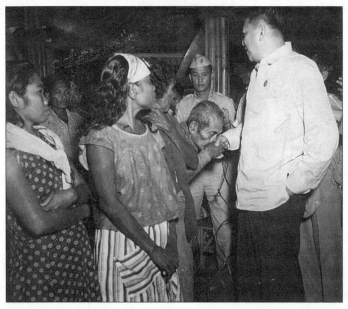

In this photograph, Aurelio Victorio, an indigenous peasant, kisses the hand of Magsaysay on his birthday, a telling portrait of a paternal president who blesses and at the same time receives the blessing of his "children." *Manila Times*, September 1, 1954. *Courtesy of Pardo de Tavera Collection, Rizal Library, Ateneo de Manila University*

Magsaysay visited Camp Olivas to "chat" with wives of notorious Huk commanders. Displaying both presidential power and paternal authority, Magsaysay talks intimately with the Huk Amazons Flor, Rebecca, Luningning, Luz, and others to welcome them back into the "folds of society," August 31, 1954. *Courtesy of Pardo de Tavera Collection, Rizal Library, Ateneo de Manila University*

Sample leaflet prepared by Vietnamese in 1963 depicting happy Vietnamese citizens ridiculing a frightened Viet Cong who faces an armed Vietnamese soldier outside the wire of a strategic hamlet. The text says, "Building up strategic hamlets in the Republic to realize true peace and to bring joy and tranquility to every family." *Leaflet Catalog Psywar Training courtesy of Herb Friedman*

Vietnamese woman and children and an American military adviser sit amid ruins of village in South Vietnam that was burned by government troops because it was thought to have been a Viet Cong stronghold, 1963. *AP Photo, Library of Congress, Prints & Photographs Division, LC-USZ62-128851*

The Uprooted: Operation Sunrise in South Vietnam. Photograph shows men driving ox carts in preparation for moving people from an isolated village to a more secure location in Binh Duong province, 1962. *UPI, Library of Congress, Prints & Photographs Division, LC-DIG-ppmsca-09181*

CAN BINH VIỆT CỘNG
ĐÂY LA DÂU HIỆU CỦA THÂN CHẾT!

CÒN TIẾP TỤC CHIẾN ĐẤU CHỐNG LẠI CHÁNH NGHỈA QUỐC
GIA, CÁC BẠN CHẮC CHẮN SẼ BỊ CHẾT THỀ THẢM NHƯ THỀ
NÀY !!   246-362

The leaflet reads: "Viet Cong! This is a sign of death! Continue your struggle against the National Cause and you will surely die a mournful death like this!"

FRONT

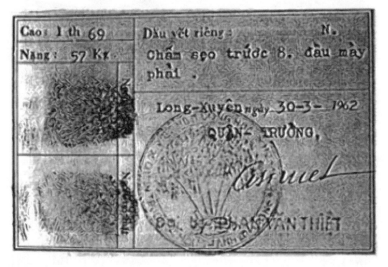

BACK

Identity cards, which all Vietnamese eighteen years of age or older must carry on their persons at all times. *Courtesy of USAID*

Training Advisor Brooks D. Anderson illustrating hand-to-hand combat tactics to N. P. instructor and trainees. Anderson died on duty in Saigon in May 1966.

Training Advisor Thomas P. Isbell illustrating use of the "sawed off" 12 guage shotgun to N. P. firearms instructor

U.S. training advisers in Vietnam. *Courtesy of USAID*

Pointing at the name IRIDE DEL CARMEN MAZARO BELBRON DE BURGOS at the Memorial of the Civilian Victims of Human Rights Violations in San Salvador. Iride del Carmen Marasso Beltrán de Burgos's name is actually misspelled on the monument, according to her husband, J. Burgos (personal communication with the author, September 25, 2012). *Photo by Saúl Romero, courtesy of Patricia Morales, San Salvador, 2011*

Pointing at the name of Carlos Manuel Serrano Merino at the Memorial of the Civilian Victims of Human Rights Violations in San Salvador. *Photo by Saúl Romero, courtesy of Patricia Morales, San Salvador, 2011*

Altar honoring the memory of Patricia Emilie Cuellar created by her relatives and friends, titled "Thousand Roses to Paty Cuellar" at the Memorial of the Civilian Victims of Human Rights Violations in San Salvador. *Photo by Julio López, courtesy of Julio López, San Salvador, 2012*

Picture of the civilian victims of the crackdown at the National Cathedral in San Salvador on May 8, 1979, circulated by the BPR at that time. *Courtesy of the "P. Florentino Idoate, S.J." Library of the Central American University "José Simeón Cañas"*

Poster circulated by the BPR in May 1979. The caption reads: "Stop the Repression Against the People!—Committee for the Freedom of Political Prisoners of the BPR." *Courtesy of the "P. Florentino Idoate, S.J." Library of the Central American University "José Simeón Cañas"*

Car bomb outside the Green Zone, Iraq, 2005. *Courtesy of David Enders*

Outside Abu Ghraib prison, Iraq, 2003. *Courtesy of David Enders*

Martyrs' cemetery in Fallujah, Iraq, 2004. *Courtesy of David Enders*

Nawar Ismail, pictured with her children, left the Shiite-minority city of Haswa, Iraq, after her parents, husband, and siblings were killed. She was living in Chikook in April 2006. *Courtesy of David Enders*

Sheik Abbas al-Zubaidy and followers on the grounds of Sharoodi Mosque in Baghdad following a car bomb attack, April 2006. *Courtesy of David Enders*

U.S. troops lead an Iraqi prisoner from the Iraqi Criminal Court, summer 2004. *Courtesy of David Enders*

Inside the Zabul village nearest an IED blast, an Afghan police officer questions a suspect in the bombing. The police officer punched and kicked the young man, until he ran away and escaped through an orchard. *Courtesy of Ben Brody/GlobalPost*

The villagers near Combat Outpost Baylough, in Zabul Province, Afghanistan, are caught in the middle of almost weekly battles between U.S. soldiers and Taliban. *Courtesy of Ben Brody/GlobalPost*

A young resident of Lakokhel, near Kandahar City, Afghanistan, stares at American troops in his village, July 21, 2010. The soldiers are likely the first foreigners he has ever seen. *Courtesy of Ben Brody/GlobalPost*

A man prepares grapes for drying in a Kandahar barn, July 21, 2010. *Courtesy of Ben Brody/Global Post*

Under a tangle of razor wire and hung from a blast wall, the 10th Mountain Division's Spartan Brigade asks itself an existential question. *Courtesy of Ben Brody/GlobalPost*

An Afghan interpreter hired by the U.S. Army buys candy for local children at a rural gas station in Zabul Province, Afghanistan, August 3, 2010. *Courtesy of Ben Brody/GlobalPost*

5

IRAQ, PART I—
COUNTERINSURGENCY IN IRAQ

Rick Rowley

April 9, 2003
Around the world, television screens flicker in unison with im-
ages from one of Siddoun Street's minor traffic circles. Newscast-
ers breathlessly narrate the fall of Baghdad as their colleagues
crowd Firdos Square's centerpiece—a 20-foot-high statue of
Saddam Hussein. Marine Corporal Edward Chin looks down
into a thicket of camera lenses and covers Saddam's face with an
American flag. An M-88 recovery vehicle pulls the statue off its
pedestal, and dozens of Iraqis swarm the metallic corpse, beating
its head with their shoes. Journalists paint a scene of cathartic
resolution capping their three-week drama of invasion coverage.
They are standing less than 100 feet from their hotel rooms.

The story of the United States in Iraq is full of moments like this—
moments that pretend to crystallize the occupation's truth in a single frame. A fallen statue in Firdos Square and a nation joyful in its
liberation. A hooded prisoner at Abu Ghraib and a cruel, cynical occupier. Mercenaries strung up on a bridge in Fallujah, and a violent
nationalist insurgency. A bombed shrine in Samarra and a brutal
civil war. But occupation and resistance in Iraq were never static,
and their outcomes were never certain.

The United States did not have one fixed counterinsurgency
strategy. It was repeatedly forced to reinvent the goals, strategy, and

justification for its presence in Iraq. And the Iraqi resistance grew, fragmented, and transformed itself alongside the occupation it opposed. America began its occupation of Iraq unprepared for any kind of organized resistance, and in the end it was Iraq's brutal civil war that finally broke the insurgency's back.

At the time of this writing, it is nine years after the statue fell in Firdos Square. Iraq lies in ruins, with hundreds of thousands of dead and millions of refugees. But in those halcyon early days of April 2003, this tragedy had not yet been written. Saddam had disappeared, and his images were being ripped from the capital. For the invasion's authors in Washington, all that remained was a triumphant denouement. But sooner than anyone expected, America's television victory would violently collide with a reality outside camera range.

THE NEW IRAQ

L. Paul Bremer III liked to wear combat boots as a martial counterpoint to his cufflinks and pocket square—a combination that matched the daring spirit of his mission, no doubt. But he looked exactly like what he was—a wealthy Republican ideologue with no Iraq experience, drafted from the corporate world to run a country of over 30 million people. Bremer embodied the American occupation: as arrogant as he was out of touch with reality. The plan he had been sent to implement was simple: erase everything. Raze the institutions of the old Iraq and a new nation would be born from its ruins. Bremer ruled by decree, and his infamous "100 Orders" disbanded the four-hundred-thousand-member Iraqi armed forces, dismantled all of the institutions of the state, radically privatized the economy, and installed a group of expatriate Iraqis with no local support in positions of power.[1]

Given an $18 billion budget and authority over Iraq's massive oil revenues, Bremer's billions and the army of foreign contractors that flooded into the country failed to replace the state he had dismantled.[2] Thousands of newly unemployed Iraqi soldiers protested the dissolution of the army.[3] Oil workers protested the privatization of state industries.[4] Ordinary Iraqis across the country protested the lack of electricity, water, health care, education, security, and jobs. They marched in demonstrations that Western commentators reminded the world would have been illegal under Saddam Hussein.

The Western commentators were right. After decades of war and dictatorship, an Iraqi civil society was struggling to be born. In the first days of the occupation, independent newspapers were launched, Iraqi nongovernmental organizations (NGOs) opened their doors, and everyone from oil workers to doctors tried to organize unions. Iraqis, emerging from a stifling dictatorship, sought to exercise their newfound freedoms of speech and assembly, and—time and again—they were shot down in the street.

April 15, 2003, Mosul: 10 protesters killed[5]
April 29, 2003, Fallujah: 13 protesters killed[6]
April 30, 2003, Fallujah: 2 protesters killed[7]
June 18, 2003, Baghdad: 2 protesters killed[8]
June 24, 2003, Basra: 4 protesters killed[9]
August 10, 2003, Basra: 1 protester killed[10]
August 13, 2003, Baghdad: 1 protester killed[11]
October 4, 2003, Baghdad: 1 protester killed[12]
October 4, 2003, Basra: 1 protester killed[13]
December 31, 2003, Kirkuk: 2 protesters killed[14]

Cloistered inside the cavernous marble-clad halls of the old Republican Palace, Bremer continued his work. He rewrote Iraq's laws and held countless upbeat press conferences, seemingly undeterred by the country on the other side of what became known as the Green Zone. His administration arrested Iraqi and Arab journalists, shut down newspapers that "encouraged attacks on Coalition Forces,"[15] maintained Saddam-era laws banning unions, arrested clerics who preached against the occupation, and presided over a military crackdown on street protests. "Iraq is open for business!" Bremer announced to a room full of reporters, as he signed into law the most radical and unpopular set of economic reforms in modern Iraqi history.[16] At some point during that first long year of occupation, Iraqi civil society suffocated and the resistance began.

THE RESISTANCE: MADINAT AL-THAWRA, REVOLUTION CITY

The camera zooms and pans erratically. It is 1998; Friday prayers are being held under the open sky; rows of brazen men wearing leather jackets and carrying folding-stock Kalashnikovs; Mohammed Sadiq al Sadr, white-bearded in the year before they kill him. His voice is heavy with the weight of so many martyrs. "Thawra. Thawra. Thawra." Ten thousand tongues roll the word back—deep, round, and hard. In a year, hundreds of the people in this video will be dead. In a decade, recordings of these speeches will be sold in markets across Baghdad.

Years later, on another Friday under the open sky, the tar softens in the cracked streets. A young cleric wearing a black turban directs traffic near the market, but the streets around the "Martyr al-Sadr's Office" are all closed down. Abu Zeinab abandons his car and makes his way on foot.

Saddam had feared Abu Zeinab and his neighbors. He had outlawed their prayer services, and there are no large mosques here where they can assemble. Under the old regime, Abu Zeinab had never been particularly devout, but now he comes out every Friday. Prayers here are political rallies and celebrations of communal survival.

By the time Abu Zeinab arrives, the street is paved with twenty thousand prayer rugs. Men sit shoulder to shoulder, their ranks stretching into the distance. The imam's white cloak billows in the breeze—a sign that he has prepared himself for martyrdom. "Protest has become a losing card. Yesterday we fought Saddam. Today we fight the Americans."

Before American tanks crossed the Tigris, Baghdad's Saddam City neighborhood had already been renamed Sadr City, but residents still remember its original name—Madinat al-Thawra, Revolution City. With 2 to 3 million mostly poor, mostly Shiite residents, it is home to nearly half of Baghdad's population. And no neighborhood suffered under Saddam the way Sadr City suffered. The enclave was a hotbed of Communist resistance to the Ba'ath Party coup in 1968, and it was the urban epicenter of Shiite rebellions against Saddam Hussein's regime that were brutally suppressed.[17]

When the beloved Shiite cleric Mohammed Sadiq al Sadr was assassinated in 1999, the resistance he led went underground. For years, his sole surviving son, Moqtada, was protected and raised by al Sadr's closest followers, who kept holding their Friday services in secret. The neighborhood paid a heavy price for its resistance. It is difficult to find a home in Sadr City without framed pictures on its walls of brothers and sons who disappeared into Saddam's Abu Ghraib prison.

In the first months of the U.S. occupation, Baghdad spiraled into chaos. The state disappeared, and most neighborhoods lacked the social cohesion to organize for their own survival. Schools, offices, museums, and even hospitals were stripped bare by looters. The Sadrists—now led by Moqtada—emerged from a decade underground as a well-organized movement deeply rooted in their community and with broad popular support.

The Sadrists quickly brought order to Baghdad's Shiite slums. In the absence of a functioning state, they did everything, including running courts, providing security, directing traffic, and restoring trash collection. They quickly became the unchallenged representatives of Iraq's rebellious Shiite underclass, and that made them a threat to Bremer's newly formed Iraqi Governing Council. There simply was no place for the Sadrists in Bremer's "New Iraq."

MOQTADA AL SADR

The Iraqi Governing Council (IGC) was more an aspirational title than an accurate political description. Its hand-picked leaders neither lived in Iraq at the time of the invasion nor wielded actual governing power. The council's leadership was drawn from the ranks of the privileged expatriate community. They had spent Saddam's rule living in comfortable exile while the Sadrists had stayed and suffered with the Iraqi people. For around half of Baghdad's population, the Sadrists were the only functioning government, but in countless PowerPoint slides, projected on the walls of countless heavily curtained conference rooms, the unelected and unpopular IGC was the country's only legitimate political body. When one of Bremer's own councilors warned him of the support the Sadrists enjoyed in the street, Bremer angrily responded that he "didn't care a damn about the underclass and what they [the Sadrists] represented."[18] Bremer excluded the Sadrists from the IGC and waited for an opportunity to crush the movement.

After Moqtada published an editorial praising the September 11 terrorist attacks, Bremer made his move. On March 28, 2004, he closed down the Sadrist newspaper, *al-Hawza*, on the grounds that it was fomenting violence.[19] On April 3, the U.S. proconsul increased the pressure, ordering the arrests of dozens of Sadrist leaders.[20] The next day, the Shiite insurgency began. Thousands of Sadrists flooded the streets, led by their black-clad militia, the Mehdi Army. They quickly occupied Kut, Kufa, Najaf, Sadr City, parts of Nasseriyah, and dozens of smaller towns. Overnight, the United States lost control of southern Iraq.[21]

The Americans put out an arrest warrant for Moqtada al Sadr, who responded with a defiant call to arms. "Make your enemy afraid, for it is impossible to remain quiet about their moral offenses. . . . I beg you not to resort to demonstrations, for they have become nothing but burned paper. It is necessary to resort to other measures, which you take in your own provinces."[22] His call was answered in Baghdad and across the Shiite south, but by that time, the insurgency in western Iraq was already well under way.

FALLUJAH

The wind off the desert is full of Anbar's sand, as fine as talcum powder. It clings to beards and eyelashes and leaves a stale taste in the back of the mouth. Land smears into sky without a seam, and the city's one hundred minarets are slowly swallowed by the storm.

Gates twist off their hinges. Doors and furniture splinter. There are angry, incomprehensible screams from a woman in dark glasses. Her son's face is ground into the dirt with a combat boot. One thousand of Fallujah's sons and fathers disappear behind concrete walls.

The shops remain shuttered, the fields are untended, and a knot of women gathers at the gate, begging for a word, a charge, a sentence, a sign of life.

Fallujah—"The City of Mosques"—lies on the banks of the Euphrates, ringed by green, canal-fed farms and date palm groves that fade into the vastness of the desert. The city accepted the American invasion without resistance. Residents quickly organized their own governing council and security patrols to prevent the looting and chaos that scarred so many other Iraqi cities. After early protests in which more than a dozen civilians were killed, U.S. troops struck a deal with Fallujah's council and moved into a resort outside the city limits that the Americans named Forward Operating Base Dreamland.[23] Fallujah's most prominent cleric, Sheikh Abdullah Janabi, urged residents not to attack the Americans but to give them six months to finish their work and leave the city. "When this period is finished, the patience of Muslims will run out and jihad will be declared," he warned in a sermon.[24] It was July 9, 2003. At the time, Janabi's name was unknown in the West.

Fallujah's governing council negotiated with local U.S. commanders, demanding that they confine their operations to inside the city limits. The 82nd Airborne Division dramatically decreased the U.S. troop presence on Fallujah's streets, and Major General Charles Swannack boasted of a 60 percent decline in violence midway through his deployment. "We're on a glide-path towards success," he told reporters on November 18, 2003.[25] Paul Bremer was livid. A self-governing city may have looked like a success to the commanding officer in charge of U.S. troops there, but it was incompatible with the "New Iraq" being imagined by Bremer's team inside the

Green Zone. When the newly formed Iraqi Police and Iraqi National Guard were dispatched to extend the writ of the IGC to Fallujah, trouble began immediately.

Fallujah's governing council refused to accept the authority of the young Iraqi Police recruits brought in to administer the city. Residents regularly clashed with the Iraqi Police. The 82nd responded with lightning raids and spot patrols but kept their incursions into the city under forty-five minutes. If they stayed any longer, they routinely came under attack. Paul Bremer recalls in his memoir complaining to the U.S. military command: "The 82nd isn't realistic, The situation is *not* going improve until we clean out Fallujah." In the spring of 2004, the marines replaced the 82nd in Fallujah, and Bremer eagerly anticipated the more aggressive approach he hoped they would take.[26]

MUQAWAMA SHARIF: THE HONORABLE RESISTANCE

"Ladies and Gentlemen . . ." Paul Bremer scans the room full of reporters, pausing for dramatic effect. "We got him." Bremer struggles to suppress a triumphant grin as he lets the whistling and applause die down. "This is a great day in Iraq's history. . . . With the arrest of Saddam Hussein, there is a new opportunity for the members of the former regime—whether military or civilian—to end their bitter opposition."

The giant flat screens flanking the lectern light up with images of the haggard former dictator. There is an uncomfortable intimacy to the footage; the soldier's latex-gloved hands firmly grip Saddam's head. Saddam passively surrenders himself to the inspection, allowing the soldier to pick through his hair and beard in search of lice. It is December 14, 2003, and after months of press conferences chronicling America's progress against the last Saddamist hold-outs, Bremer delivers a perfect television ending. A humbled Saddam Hussein is in the hands of the U.S. Army, and the "former regime elements" will now surely abandon their lost cause.

"Iraq's future—your future—has never been more full of hope," Bremer says to the Iraqi people, but his real audience is in America. To Iraqis living outside the Green Zone, Bremer's sunny optimism seemed unbearably cruel.

One hundred thirty-nine American troops and uncounted thousands of Iraqis had died by the time "major combat operations" officially ended on May 1, 2003. But as the year wore on, both Iraqis and Americans kept dying. By year's end, U.S. fatalities had risen to 486 (Iraqi deaths remained uncounted).[27] More Americans had already been killed occupying Iraq than had died in the invasion, but in countless upbeat press conferences, Paul Bremer refused to recognize that the insurgency even existed. In the American narrative, there were no insurgents, only "former regime elements" (FREs) and so there was no counterinsurgency campaign, just a mopping-up operation. With Saddam's capture, that narrative came to an end.

THE FIRST BATTLE OF FALLUJAH: VIGILANT RESOLVE

The first marine was killed on patrol in Fallujah the day before U.S. forces officially took command of the city on March 20, 2004. The marines immediately began aggressive operations that routinely ended in firefights. In the first week and a half, seven marines were killed, along with dozens of insurgents and civilians. Calling cards were left scattered around the city with an ominous warning: "You can't escape and you can't hide . . . the coalition will find you and bring you to justice."[28]

Fallujah boiled with anger. The marines were reentering the city at the same time that stories of abuse and torture at Abu Ghraib prison had begun to circulate in the press. Thousands of Fallujans had sons, brothers, and fathers in American detention centers and were humiliated and outraged at the treatment their families were being subjected to. Rocket and mortar attacks, roadside bombs, and ambushes became daily occurrences for the marines.[29]

When four American mercenaries in unarmored vehicles

blundered into a traffic jam in downtown Fallujah on March 31, 2004, the violence that ensued was entirely predictable. The four private security contractors from the American firm Blackwater were killed and dragged through the street. Two of their bodies were hung from a bridge over the Euphrates.[30] In response, the marines launched an all-out attack to "pacify" the city, and across Iraq, a growing but diffuse resistance suddenly crystallized into a full-blown nationalist insurgency.[31]

On April 4, two thousand marines surrounded Fallujah, beginning Operation Vigilant Resolve.[32] After pounding the city with air strikes, marines moved in with tanks and air support. They sealed the roads, shut down the hospitals, bombed mosques (which they claimed sheltered insurgents), and slowly pushed into the city. A favorite American tactic was to set up a sniper position and then blast anti-Muslim taunts and heavy-metal music through loudspeakers.[33] They would lure enraged Fallujans into the open and kill them from their fortified positions. A typical marine sniper had thirty-one kills during the battle.[34] Operation Vigilant Resolve was meant to bring "overwhelming force" to bear to wipe out Fallujah's "former regime elements" once and for all.[35] But the United States was no longer fighting elements of the former regime. Instead, it faced a broad-based popular insurgency that was far more powerful than it had anticipated. Graffiti appeared on the city walls: "Long live the *al-muqawama al-sharifa*" (Long live the honorable resistance).[36]

As the marines attacked the city, a dozen insurgent groups emerged to block their advance. They were organized around different affiliations—some tribal, some ideological, some neighborhood based—but quickly began to coordinate their fight. They divided Fallujah into areas of operation, with each group defending its own sector.[37] The insurgents faced overwhelming firepower from American artillery, attack jets, and AC-130 gunships, but they quickly blunted the American assault.[38]

Sheikh Abdullah Janabi, who had been named overall leader of Fallujah's Mujahideen Council, spoke on behalf of the city's insurgents. Janabi and Iraq's Association of Muslim Scholars, to which he belonged, were Sunni nationalists. They were religious scholars seeking to represent Iraq's Sunni minority, but they articulated insurgency politically as the defense of Iraq and its people against foreign invaders. In their political platforms and communiqués, Janabi and the AMS appealed to the human right to self-defense and the national right to self-determination.[39] They called on all Iraqis to unite in a national resistance and saw the Shiite Mehdi Army as an important ally.[40]

SADR CITY SUPPORTS FALLUJAH, FALLUJAH SUPPORTS NAJAF

Hussein's eyes, still open, stare down from the poster. He lies by his white horse on the hill at Karbala. On the opposite wall, Abbas gazes up at the sky as the river slips through his fingers. A line of men wraps around the mosque under the ruthless Sadr City sun. They wait their turn to donate blood for Fallujah's wounded.

Flags of red, black, and green are draped from the walls of the Sadrist mosque. The imam maintains a calm, measured tone amid the chaos around him. Dozens of trucks, cars, and buses are being loaded with food, medical supplies, and people. "The American occupation united Sunni and Shia in a way they never were under Saddam."

By the spring of 2004, the United States was fighting two full-scale offensives. In the west, U.S. troops were bogged down in Fallujah, and in the south, they struggled to retake Najaf, and capture or kill Moqtada al Sadr.[41] The Sadrists organized a humanitarian aid convoy to break the siege of Fallujah,[42] and Mehdi Army fighters infiltrated the military blockade to join the city's resistance.[43] At the same time, weapons and fighters from Fallujah were smuggled into Najaf to bolster the Sadrist defenses.[44] In both cities, the United States suffered humiliating setbacks against an increasingly unified national insurgency.

In Fallujah, by May 2004, the marines had suffered twenty-six dead and over ninety wounded.[45] They managed to occupy only a small fraction of the city, but the civilian toll was tremendous. The widespread use of air strikes and artillery flattened buildings and caused hundreds of civilian casualties. With hospitals closed by the siege, wounded Fallujans bled to death in their homes from what would have been treatable injuries. They buried their dead in a soccer field that was renamed "Martyr's Cemetery."[46] Eight hundred Fallujans—mostly civilians—were killed,[47] but the resistance only grew stronger. As the insurgency spread to Mosul, Ramadi, and smaller cities across Anbar Province, the United States was forced to call off the offensive.[48] Paul Bremer announced a unilateral cease-fire, and a month later the city was under the complete control of Abdullah Janabi's Mujahideen Council.[49]

In Najaf, the Mehdi Army continued to hold out, controlling the city center, while Moqtada remained a free man. In Bremer's world, the Sadrist insurgency remained incomprehensible. He continued to treat it as a momentary aberration of lawlessness, a dark anachronism that would disappear in the bright light of the New Iraq. He refused to negotiate with the Sadrists and demanded nothing less than their unconditional surrender or military destruction. To Bremer, the Sadrists were common criminals, but in the end they would far outlive his own relevance to Iraqi politics.[50]

BREMER'S ESCAPE

June 28, 2004
Fountains choke with dust, pigeons nest in palace rafters, and rows of squat air-conditioned containers are crowded around the monumental architecture on the west bank of the Tigris. Inside the convention center, eighteen-year-old public affairs officers rush to find whatever journalists are nearby. "An important announcement. Press conference in fifteen minutes."

Paul Bremer loves press conferences, and he is good at them, but he has been slipping in recent months. He seems sleep deprived, and even fainted in front of reporters earlier this year. The room fills in front of an empty lectern, but Bremer never appears. Instead, the flat screens light up.

Paul Bremer is poorly framed next to Iraqi Prime Minister Ayad Alawi, an air-conditioning vent over his shoulder. He bends awkwardly over a bound document and stumbles as he reads, "We welcome Iraq's steps to take its place of equality and honor among the free nations of the world." By the time the video begins to play, Bremer, fearing an attack on the ceremony, is already twenty thousand feet in the air, fleeing the country. Iraq is declared a sovereign nation two days ahead of schedule. Eight Iraqis die in fighting during the country's two "bonus days of sovereignty."

During the first year of occupation, the United States had ignored, stifled, and violently repressed protests from Iraqi civil society, and when an armed insurgency began, the Americans refused to recognize its existence. The United States did not have a counterinsurgency strategy because it refused to believe that an insurgency existed. Bremer and the Bush administration he served were so invested in their image of a "New Iraq" that they could not understand the insurgents as anything other than Saddamist "dead-enders." At the time of Bremer's escape from Baghdad, the Iraqi insurgency had the initiative, and the U.S. occupation would be forced to change its course.

THE SALVADOR OPTION

The camera sits clumsily on its tripod. A row of men sits under unforgiving fluorescent light—faces bruised, eyes hollowed by fatigue. Behind them hangs a crudely made banner with a military insignia bearing the image of a wolf. "Your name?" "Mohammad Samir Mohammad Ramadhan . . ." His confession begins in a voice full of exhausted surrender. It's nine o'clock, and Iraq's state broadcaster is airing the country's most famous television show—Terror in the Grip of Justice.

The show's host and creator, Abdul Walid, barks questions from behind the camera, and his humiliated prisoners confess to everything. They are terrorists. They are violators of Islam. With enough prompting, they even admit to homosexuality.

Abdul Walid began his career fighting alongside Iran's Revolutionary Guard. But he has now joined forces with the Americans against Sunni insurgents, marking the emergence of America's new counterinsurgency strategy.

After its failures in Fallujah and Najaf, the United States finally acknowledged that it was fighting against an insurgency and that it was losing. By the summer of 2004, the contours of America's first real counterinsurgency strategy had begun to emerge. Bremer was replaced by John Negroponte, who had built his career first during America's brutal counterinsurgency effort in Vietnam and then in the Central American dirty wars of the 1980s. He joined a growing number of veterans of America's many Latin American interventions, and Defense Department officials leaked to the press that a new plan was on the table—it became known as "The Salvador Option."[51]

The objectives of the new approach were never publicly acknowledged. New U.S. policies and carefully worded Defense Department leaks, however, hinted at familiar counterinsurgency tactics: exploit the Sunni/Shia division within the insurgency, put an "Iraqi face" on the occupation by building indigenous proxy forces, and attack the insurgency's civilian support base. "We have to find a way to take the offensive against the insurgents," one unnamed military source told *Newsweek*. "Right now, we are playing defense. And we are losing." "The Sunni population is paying no price for the support it is giving to the terrorists," an anonymous source continued. "From their point of view, it is cost-free. We have to change that equation."[52]

The United States had once imagined a New Iraq run by secular, pro-American Iraqi expats. But in Paul Bremer's final days in office, America had already begun to tilt toward the most sectarian Shiite religious parties. Chief among them were the Dawa Party and the Supreme Council for the Islamic Revolution in Iraq (SCIRI), which had both been based in Tehran until the U.S. invasion. They had been Iranian proxies in Iraqi politics for years but now shared many of America's interests. Perhaps their most valuable asset to the

Americans was SCIRI's thirty-thousand-member militia—the Badr Brigade—which was armed and trained by the Iranian Revolutionary Guard.[53] One of Bremer's final edicts, Order 91, incorporated the entire Badr Brigade into Iraq's military.[54] America's erstwhile secular allies in the Iraqi Governing Council protested impotently as the Badr Brigade effectively became the core of Iraq's new security services.[55]

Under Bremer, the United States had inadvertently united Sunnis and Shiites in a nationalist insurgency. After Bremer's departure, U.S. forces rapidly deescalated their attack on the Shiite Mehdi Army, while at the same time increasing pressure on Sunni insurgents in Fallujah. A cease-fire was reached in which all of the Mehdi Army fighters in Najaf were allowed to go free, and the attempts to capture Moqtada al Sadr were abandoned.[56] The United States put the most sectarian Shiite religious parties in control of the government and the army, called off attacks on Shiite insurgents, and would now focus on fighting the insurgency in Sunni areas.

Sunni Islamists inside Iraq and around the region reacted with alarm. To them, it looked as if Iraq had been handed over to sectarian Shiites under the influence of their historic enemy, Iran. The influx of foreign fighters and money—especially from Saudi Arabia—increased dramatically,[57] and the face of the Iraqi resistance began to change.[58]

THE FOREIGNERS ARRIVE IN FALLUJAH

Sheik Ritha'a's modest home, shaded by a stand of date palms, sits near the canal that waters his family's fields. He has the calloused hands of a farmer, like all of his neighbors, and he chain-smokes Turkish Marlboros between sips of tea. "When the Americans first entered, they said they were peaceful people, and that this country would not be destroyed. And our tribal sheikhs let them in. They told them, 'You have come to remove Iraq's leader. Do that and leave.' But they never left. . . . We became an occupied country. When the Americans didn't leave, the jihad began."

"Soon Arabs from other countries began to come. . . . We thought they were good mujahideen. We welcomed them, fed them, cared for them when they were injured . . . Lebanese, Saudis, Kuwaitis, Jordanians . . ."

Abdullah Janabi remained in control of Fallujah's Mujahideen Council, and he continued to call for Sunni and Shiite unity within a nationalist insurgency, but his authority was increasingly challenged. Omar Hadid, a Fallujah native who claimed to have fought in Afghanistan, represented a growing countertendency within the Mujahideen Council. While Janabi couched the struggle in more nationalist terms, Hadid saw the defense of Fallujah as part of the global defense of Sunni Islam against Western aggression.[59]

To Hadid, and many fundamentalist Sunni fighters from around the region, the U.S. occupation was beginning to take on a sectarian character. They considered the Shiite parties that ran the government Iranian puppets and the Shiite-dominated military Iranian proxies.[60] As sectarian Sunni fighters and money flooded into Iraq, car bombs and suicide attacks aimed at Shiite politicians and police began to rise.[61] In Fallujah, Omar Hadid formed an alliance with a well-connected Jordanian, who linked Hadid to a pipeline of Saudi cash and foreign fighters. The ranks of Hadid's mujahideen group, the Black Flag Brigade, swelled to around fifteen hundred, and they took over responsibility for defending one of Fallujah's most important front-line neighborhoods. As the power and prominence of Hadid and the foreign fighters grew, they began to challenge Abdullah Janabi's leadership. They saw Janabi's nationalism as too secular and narrow, and they wanted no part of an alliance with the Shiites in the Mehdi Army, whom they regarded as apostates.[62]

THE BREAKDOWN OF THE NATIONALIST RESISTANCE

A scorched tank tread is still nailed to a lamp post, and the walls recall April's slogans: "Vietnam Street—Here We Will Bury the Americans." But the mood on the street in Sadr City has changed.

A glass cup clinks against a saucer, and Abu Zeinab sips the sweet, hot tea. A group of friends discusses the day's speeches in an improvised outdoor diwan, or advisory council, shaded by tarps.

"When Fallujah rose, all of Iraq rose with her. . . . We gave our blood and we housed her refugees. But now, everything has changed."

In Baghdad, the intercommunal goodwill of April 2004 evaporated in a relentless summer of car bombs and suicide attacks by Sunni extremists. For the Sadrists, the final blow came on June 15, when a convoy of trucks from Baghdad was stopped at an insurgent checkpoint in Fallujah. Seven Shiite truck drivers were accused of being spies and were beheaded on the spot. Thousands of Sadr City residents protested, demanding that Abdullah Janabi atone for the crime. But while Janabi condemned the killings, he admitted he had no control over some elements within the insurgency. "It is unthinkable that I would be involved in such a crime," Janabi said. "There were some killings but I absolutely do not know the identity of the authors of the crime." [63]

Sunni-Shiite solidarity was collapsing, but the Sadrist leadership still officially called for support of the Sunni insurgency. In spite of rising sectarian anger, Sunni groups like the Association of Muslim Scholars remained the only available political allies for nationalists like the Sadrists. The U.S. occupation had put in power the most sectarian elements of the Shiite ruling class, represented by the Supreme Council and Dawa Party. The Shiite ruling class held the Sadrists and their constituency in complete contempt, and the two groups' political parties had irreconcilable visions for the country's future. [64] SCIRI and Dawa wanted to split Iraq into a loose federation, and they dreamed of a Shiite region with Najaf as its capital and the vast majority of Iraq's oil resources inside its borders. [65]

The Sadrists came into increasing conflict with Sunni insurgents, but they remained militantly nationalist and steadfast in their opposition to any subdivision of Iraq. They continued to voice their support for the Sunni insurgency, but there would be no more blood drives in Sadr City for the people of Fallujah, and Mehdi Army fighters would never again rush to aid in the city's defense.

THE RISE OF ABU MUSAB AL-ZARQAWI

The influx of Saudi money and foreign fighters from across the region fed a sectarian current within the Sunni insurgency, but it remained a minority position. The Iraqi nationalist Association of Muslim Scholars was still seen as the public representative of the Sunni insurgency, but Omar Hadid's Jordanian ally—a little-known figure named Abu Musab al-Zarqawi—would soon change all that. Zarqawi's acts of spectacular brutality and his skillful use of the media quickly made him the face of Iraq's insurgency in the eyes of the world.

Zarqawi chose to make his first public appearance on May 11, 2004, on an insurgent website in a video with the opening title, "Abu Musab al-Zarqawi slaughters an American."[66] In the video, Nicholas Berg, a U.S. military contractor in Iraq, is shackled on the floor, wearing an orange jumpsuit that had become a symbol of U.S. military prisons in Guantánamo Bay and Iraq. A masked man behind Berg reads a statement denouncing the torture of Iraqis at Abu Ghraib. Berg is then held down, screaming, while they decapitate him with a knife.[67]

At the time, Zarqawi was wanted for attacks in Jordan but was a marginal figure inside of Iraq.[68] The execution of Nicholas Berg instantly catapulted him into the media spotlight. The United States was eager to publicly portray the insurgency as led by foreign extremists and made Zarqawi Iraq's most wanted insurgent. The U.S. government put a $25 million bounty on his head and retroactively identified him as the mastermind behind virtually every major terrorist attack in Iraq.[69] The hunt for Zarqawi replaced the hunt for Saddam Hussein as a central public goal of the U.S. campaign. The American attention was useful to Zarqawi, who quickly rose to prominence within the insurgency, and his prominence was useful to the Americans, who would use it to justify their bloodiest military operation of the war.[70]

THE SECOND BATTLE OF FALLUJAH: PHANTOM FURY

By September 2004, U.S. officials were leaking to the press that their highest priority in Iraq was the capture of Abu Musab al-Zarqawi, who was said to be operating out of Fallujah.[71] In October, as the U.S. military ramped up its bombing campaign and massed considerable forces for an all-out assault on the city, Zarqawi renamed his group Al Qaeda in Iraq. With its new name, Zarqawi's group became a lightning rod for Iraqi and international opinion. Inside Fallujah, Zarqawi was technically under the orders of Omar Hadid, who was theoretically under the orders of Abdullah Janabi and the Mujahideen Council,[72] but to the rest of the world, the Second Battle of Fallujah would be a fight between the United States and Al Qaeda in Iraq.

The U.S. military pounded Fallujah with air strikes and artillery for two months before Operation Phantom Fury officially began, on November 8, 2004. Thirteen thousand troops took part in the assault—six times the troop strength deployed in the first battle of Fallujah. The Americans' first move was to capture and occupy Fallujah General Hospital,[73] cutting off the city's access to medical care on the eve of bloody urban fighting that marine commanders likened to the Battle of Hue during the Vietnam War.[74] Bombs and artillery shells destroyed many of the insurgents' fortified positions, and America's total air superiority gave them a huge tactical advantage over insurgents, who could not effectively coordinate their defense of the city.[75]

Faced with the overwhelming military strength of the American assault, insurgents laced the streets with homemade bombs and barricaded themselves in their homes. Fierce house-to-house fighting lasted a full week and left fifty-four marines killed and over four hundred wounded.[76] Moqtada al-Sadr denounced the attacks on Fallujah, but unlike in April, the rest of the country did not rally to support the city's resistance.[77] Fallujah could not hold out for long on its own against the focused intensity of the American attack. Hundreds of insurgents managed to slip out of the city, leaving behind the few who chose to die as martyrs. After weeks of mop-up operations,

Phantom Fury finally ground to a halt on December 23. Fallujah lay in ruins, but it was now firmly in American hands. An estimated eight hundred civilians had been killed,[78] but U.S. forces had failed to capture Zarqawi or any of its other most wanted insurgents.[79]

The two battles of Fallujah provide bookends for the nationalist insurgency in Iraq. In April, a united insurgency sparked uprisings across the country that forced the Americans to withdraw from Fallujah. By November, Sunni-Shiite solidarity had been broken down, and no one rushed to the city's defense.

THE WOLF BRIGADE

Wissam glances over his shoulder, nervous in the sudden silence. He clutches a sheaf of papers and pulls a keffiyeh up over his face. "I can't begin to describe the terror." The pages are filled with photographs of his neighbors' corpses, horribly disfigured by torture. He says they were all kidnapped by Shiite death squads operating inside the Iraqi police.

"The Sunnis were fighting the Americans, and the only way to shift these attacks was to change it into a fight between the Sunni and the Wolf Brigade—who were trained and armed by the United States. . . . The Americans were the fuel of the sectarian violence in Iraq."

Phantom Fury cleared Fallujah, but it did nothing to dampen the Sunni insurgency, and attacks on U.S. troops rose unabated across western Iraq. Iraq's Sunnis were virtually unanimous in their support for the resistance, and fighters were harbored and protected in Sunni towns and neighborhoods across the country.[80] The United States prepared a counterinsurgency force to disrupt their support networks and undermine their civilian base of support.

James Steele, who had organized El Salvador's brutal counterinsurgency forces during that country's civil war, and Steven Casteel, who worked with paramilitaries in Colombia, had been brought in to help found an elite force of two thousand Iraqi police commandos—the Wolf Brigade.[81] The Americans originally formed the Wolf

Brigade out of a group of former Ba'athist intelligence officers,[82] but once the Shiite political parties came to power, they were quickly replaced by Badr Brigade members, and Abdul Walid was put in charge. To the Americans, they were an effective counterinsurgency force, but to Iraq's Sunnis, they were a Shiite death squad.

Under Walid's leadership, the Wolf Brigade attacked the civilian base of support for the Sunni insurgency.[83] Residents of Baghdad's Sunni neighborhoods complained of widespread abuses—police raids in which every male resident between the ages of fifteen and fifty was rounded up without being charged with a crime; extrajudicial killings, with horribly disfigured corpses dumped in garbage heaps; police checkpoints, where entire families disappeared.[84] Those who survived imprisonment by the Wolf Brigade told stories of torture with power drills, beatings, and electrocution. And then there was the Wolf Brigade's television show, *Terror in the Grip of Justice*, which twice a day broadcast the humiliating and obviously coerced confessions of Sunni insurgents but never interrogated Shiites.[85] Sunni neighborhoods across Iraq began to fear the Shiite Wolf Brigade more than the U.S. Army.

Sectarian violence in Baghdad escalated steadily throughout 2005. Shiite militias, operating within the Iraqi police and military, sowed fear in the city's Sunni neighborhoods. Sunni extremists responded with car bombs and suicide attacks against Shiite civilians, claiming hundreds of innocent lives. The anger inside Baghdad's sprawling Shiite slums was barely held in check by the Sadrist leadership. Moqtada al Sadr condemned the Wolf Brigade's attacks and continued to call for a unified national resistance,[86] but he was quickly losing control of his own militia. The Mehdi Army functioned more like an armed social movement than an organized army. Its fifty thousand young, dedicated, but poorly disciplined fighters were just waiting for a spark to set them off.[87] And once the fire started, their leadership would be powerless to stop it.

TODAY IS BETTER THAN TOMORROW

That spark came on February 22, 2006, when a bomb ripped apart the golden dome of the thousand-year-old Al-Askari Shrine—one of the holiest Shiite sites in Iraq.[88] The United States immediately blamed Al Qaeda in Iraq for the attack. The American occupation's ruling Shiite coalition called for three days of "national mourning," and thousands of angry men and boys poured into the streets. Ayatollah Ali Sistani, the Shiite cleric followed by SCIRI and Dawa, released an ominous statement: "If [the Iraqi government's] security institutions are unable to provide the necessary security, the faithful are able to do that by the will and blessings of God." [89]

Trucks rolled through Baghdad calling residents out to protest, and thousands gathered in front of the Sadrists' main office in Baghdad. A cleric shouted Moqtada al Sadr's party line to the angry crowd through a megaphone. He said the Al-Askari bombing was not an attack by Iraq's Sunnis, it was an attack by the American occupier and their Zionists allies who wanted to start a civil war.[90] Moqtada al Sadr called for the Association of Muslim Scholars and other Sunni groups to join the Sadrists in a coalition to prevent sectarian attacks, and he ordered the Mehdi Army to defend Sunni mosques.[91] His calls and his orders were ignored.

Thousands of armed Shiites—many of them Mehdi Army members—rolled out of Sadr City on flatbed trucks and descended on Baghdad's Sunni neighborhoods. They burned scores of Sunni mosques, killed imams, ran families out of their homes, and seized control of entire neighborhoods. The Association of Muslim Scholars, who had once welcomed humanitarian aid caravans from Sadr City into Fallujah, claimed that 168 Sunni mosques were attacked in the first two days of violence.[92] The U.S. occupation would never again be threatened by insurgency. The insurgents had turned their guns on one another.

As 2006 opened, the U.S. occupation had weathered its most serious military challenge, but it looked nothing like the New Iraq that Bremer and American neoconservatives had once dreamed of. In 2003, the United States imported secular Iraqi leaders from

Washington and London and set out to build a pro-Western, neoliberal democracy. By 2006, power had been put in the hands of the most sectarian Shiite parties—SCIRI and Dawa—who were more closely allied to Iran than to the United States. U.S. policy makers had once planned to build a new Iraqi army from scratch—a force linked from the ground up to the American military that created it. Under the new strategy, the military and police were handed over to sectarian Shiite militias.

In a perverse military logic, it could be argued that the Salvador Option was a success. The insurgency had turned its weapons on itself and the United States would never again face the threat of a unified national uprising. Thousands of American troops would be killed in the coming years, and the Americans would kill thousands of Iraqis. But those deaths would make up a small fraction of the hundreds of thousands of Iraqis who would be killed by their own countrymen.

These years have taught us calculations that should never be made," said Abu Zeinab. "Dictatorship is better than occupation, but anything, anything is better than civil war. . . . Today is better than tomorrow.

6

IRAQ, PART II—
FEBRUARY 2006–DECEMBER 2012:
NEW ALLIES, OLD TACTICS

David Enders

After the invasion of Iraq in 2003, a nationalist Iraqi resistance, with nominally Shiite and Sunni wings, briefly coordinated to battle the U.S. military. As the occupation progressed, Iraq's civil war eventually subsumed most of these groups, and the country descended into rounds of violence whose beginning is often marked by the bombing of the Askariya Shrine in Samarra, a Shiite pilgrimage site in a largely Sunni city. The mosque, with its gleaming golden dome, was almost completely destroyed, and the image has become iconic for Iraqi Shia as a symbol of what they had endured and overcome.

The bombing of the Askariya Shrine and the sectarian militia violence that followed forced the United States to again revamp its counterinsurgency strategies and assumptions. As the political forces shifted in Iraq, the two main guerrilla groups fighting the United States began attacking each other more frequently than they did American soldiers, creating a rift the U.S. military would increasingly exploit. The continued marginalization of Sunnis, especially Sunni tribes that had once held positions of privilege under Saddam Hussein, also contributed to this development. Iraqis themselves don't agree on the use of the term "civil war" for this period of worsening political and sectarian hostilities. Depending on their perspective, they generally refer to it as "the troubles," or *harb taifia*, which means "sectarian war."

The Askariya Shrine was likely bombed by Sunni extremists

intent on fomenting sectarian warfare, although by February 2006 there was little need for further provocation. Since 2003, Sunni guerrillas had increasingly attacked Shiites and collaborators with the U.S. military and Iraqi governments in Baghdad, and across central Iraq more broadly. Some formerly mixed villages around Baghdad had already been emptied of their Shiite populations, and refugee camps were forming on the edges of the capital's already overcrowded Shiite slums. The ranks of Shiite militiamen grew in response as Shiite guerrillas continued to fight U.S. forces and effectively took over most of Baghdad in 2006. The United States allowed Shiite guerrillas to operate in the capital with near impunity until late 2007, helping to send the largest part of the Sunni guerrilla movement into the arms of the U.S. military.

The guerrillas who became known as "the insurgency" were composed of networks of Sunni religious extremists, Iraqi nationalists (largely Sunni military veterans), and Ba'athist fighters, more than 90 percent Iraqi, that made up the groups fighting the U.S. military and Iraqi government at the time. By no means monolithic, the Sunni insurgency included groups like Ansar al Sunna, Al Qaeda in Iraq, and the Islamic State of Iraq, each of which held sway in particular areas.[1] In northern cities like Mosul and Kirkuk, support for guerrillas was partially linked to fears of ethnic cleansing and marginalization of Arabs by Kurdish forces.

It was against this backdrop that the "troop surge," arguably the most publicized U.S. strategy for limiting violence in Iraq during the entire war, began. Though American lawmakers and policy wonks have given the additional "surge" of thirty thousand combat troops credit for stopping sectarian violence, the truth is much more local, and lies with what has popularly become known as al Sahwa, or the "The Awakening" movement. It was less a coup of counterinsurgency strategy than a reassessment of facts on the ground by the Sunni tribes who had either openly or tacitly supported the resistance, as many of the United States' former enemies became its allies. The cooperation of Sunnis who had previously fought the U.S. military and Iraqi government allowed the United States to assist the Iraqi army in quelling rebellious Shiite factions in Baghdad and the south. To understand the events that have taken place from 2006 until now, it is useful to begin in western Iraq, and move east, to Baghdad.

AL SAHWA: THE AWAKENING

Al Sahwa began inauspiciously in Al Qaim, a town along the Syrian border in Anbar Province that had been controlled outright at times by Sunni guerrillas and had been subjected to repeated U.S. incursions. One round of fighting in 2004, which involved U.S. snipers, left more than fifty civilians dead, according to local hospital staff who documented the casualties. The city was divided into quarters and surrounded by U.S. checkpoints, in an operation that would become a blueprint for dealing with Anbar. By 2006, much of Fallujah and Ramadi, the two largest cities in Anbar, lay in rubble, and their names were synonymous with resistance to the occupation and Al Qaeda in Iraq.

In late 2006, Faisal al-Goud, the head of the al-Goud tribe, approached U.S. soldiers in Anbar province with a request for assistance in fighting Al Qaeda in Iraq. He and his tribe had come to the conclusion that support, tacit or otherwise, for al Qaeda was no longer worth it and would only result in continued devastation for Anbar. More practically, al-Goud's tribe, with members on either side of the Syrian/Iraqi border, had controlled lucrative smuggling routes for decades. Previously, al Qaeda had been content to work with them to smuggle weapons and fighters. Now the terrorist organization was trying to take over the smuggling trade exclusively. To safeguard its major source of income, the al-Goud tribe raised a militia, and after they proved their commitment to fight, the United States began providing material support for what would soon become widely known as al Sahwa, or "The Awakening."

The exploitation of sectarianism was not unprecedented in the country's history. The Ottomans and the British had similarly raised tribal levies in Iraq, where factional fighting often needed little foreign encouragement. The Awakening movement also drew on earlier mercenary schemes employed by the Americans. As early as

2004, individual units of the U.S. military were striking deals with tribes in their areas. Shiites living north of Baghdad accused one such project, intended to guard an oil pipeline near Taji, of providing a local Sunni tribe with weapons and trucks, which were used not just to guard the pipeline but to drive Shiites out of the area. While al-Goud's motivations were primarily economic, the al Sahwa movement received popular support in Anbar due to an increasing dissatisfaction with the insurgency, which from 2004 to 2007 more or less controlled Ramadi, the province's capital of approximately three hundred thousand. The Awakening movement spread from Al Qaim southeast through the Euphrates River towns, eventually reaching Baghdad. Approximately one hundred thousand Iraqi fighters were on the U.S. payroll from 2007 to 2009.

Across Anbar Province, tribal leaders who had been marginalized by Saddam Hussein's government, as well as those who had received his patronage, saw a chance to ascend to new levels of power. Sheikh Ahmed Sattar Abu Risha, who became the face of the Awakening movement in 2007—superseding the al-Goud who was assassinated in Baghdad that same year—was largely regarded by other tribal leaders in Ramadi as a bit player but an astonishingly smooth talker. An outlaw under Saddam Hussein, Abu Risha made his living robbing convoys on the highway between Baghdad and Amman before he made common cause with the military. Abu Risha's "construction company" was soon flush with "reconstruction" contracts from the United States. Though he too was assassinated in September 2007, shortly after a photo op with President Bush, Abu Risha remained the icon of the Awakening movement, which resulted in significant improvements in security across Anbar.

As the Awakening spread to the few remaining Sunni enclaves in Baghdad, it became known by monikers ranging from "Sons of Iraq" to "Concerned Local Citizens," depending on the neighborhood and the group. In and around the capital, the movement was more driven by unemployment and fears of the Shiite-led Iraqi government than by the threat of an Islamic-leaning insurgency taking over cities and villages. Sunnis had nearly been driven out of Baghdad in the sectarian cleansing that took place from 2004 to 2007, another reason for the dissipation of violence—there was almost no one left for the Shiite militias to drive out. With nowhere else to turn, Sunnis and former Ba'athists embraced the United States as their only hope. Nowhere was this dynamic more clear than in Adhamiya, in northern Baghdad.

The residents of the predominantly Sunni neighborhood of Adhamiya, formerly home to many of Saddam Hussein's officers, were more likely to be secular nationalists than Islamists. Adhamiya had been a center of resistance activity from the beginning of the occupation. When I tried to visit in 2007, it proved impossible: the neighborhood was entirely controlled by Sunni militiamen hostile to the U.S. military and the Iraqi government.

By 2008, things were different, and the al Sahwa were in control, essentially reconstituting many of the former government's security forces in Adhamiya. Farouq al-Obaidy, the commander of one of the al Sahwa groups there, was cagey about what his position had been in the old government, but he stood proudly on the roof of his office and told a story that has become famous in Baghdad. "On April 9th, Saddam appeared here," he said, pointing to the Aimmah Bridge, which links Adhamiya to Khadamiya, a largely Shiite neighborhood on the other side of the river. "You see that spot, near those trees? He appeared by those trees. Then he crossed to Khadamiya. The last city that fell during the occupation was Adhamiya. And it didn't fall; it was occupied." [2]

Like most Iraqis, al-Obaidy viewed military resistance to the occupation as legitimate. His men had set up their own checkpoint leading to the bridge—about thirty-five feet in front of the one manned by the Iraqi army. The relationship between the army and al Sahwa was wrought with friction. As al Sahwa became increasingly marginalized, the army arrested many of its leaders, often on charges of collaborating with insurgents before and during the Awakening movement. It was no secret that many of the men who had driven hundreds of thousands of Shiites from their homes were now on the American payroll.

Al-Obaidy readily admitted there were many former guerrillas in his group, some of whom spouted anti-American sentiments while their boss spoke. His group rejected the "Awakening" moniker; in Adhamiya, he said: "We are the White Revolutionaries. We do not call ourselves The Awakening. We were never asleep. Iraq's current ruling parties were formed in Iran, let's be honest! They went to Iran when they were very young. They came back old. They don't have compassion for this country or their people. And their loyalty is to Iran. This is the truth that needs to get out. We want a leader to be an Iraqi from this land. We don't want a 'leader' to be a chess pawn, placed and removed by others."

Driving through Baghdad, especially in 2007 and 2008, required the negotiation of various walls and checkpoints, policed by any—or all—of three forces: a local militia, the Iraqi police, and the Iraqi army, all of them united by their distrust of the others. In Sleikh, a neighborhood across the highway from Adhamiya, Sunni and Shiite militias and government security forces battled for control. The Awakening members in Baghdad, desperate for jobs, even if they weren't as good as government ones, stepped in to fill the vacuum in 2007, attempting to ensure that Sunnis would not lose any more ground.

"Each guard here from the 'Sons of Iraq' gets paid $300 a month," said Abu Feras, the commander of a U.S.-allied Sunni militia in Sleikh. Soldiers in the Iraqi army, he complained, "get $700 a month," though he contended that "the Sons of Iraq are doing more than the Iraqi army to secure the area." Like many in the area, Abu Feras complained that Iraqi special forces—trained by the United States and allied with militias loyal to Shiite political parties—carried out raids and conducted arrests in Adhamiya beginning in 2004 in an attempt to crack down on the Sunni resistance. By 2005, the Jeish Al Mehdi, the Shiite militia nominally loyal to Shiite cleric Muqtada al Sadr, was also active in the neighborhood, fighting with Sunni militias it claimed were targeting Shiite civilians and providing protection for Sleikh's Shiites.

In Adhamiya and Sleikh, the Sahwa came to function as a job rehabilitation program for former members of Saddam's military and security forces who were purged in the U.S.-supported de-Ba'athification following the invasion. Abu Feras served for eleven years as a member of Saddam's secret police. The U.S. military unit he was working with had only been in Iraq for three months when it became aligned with Abu Feras. When the Awakening movement began, U.S. soldiers were blithe about the idea of joining forces with former enemies and supporting possible war criminals. "You have to start somewhere," one U.S. soldier said when asked how he felt about the new arrangement. A U.S. Army lieutenant who said he spoke daily with Abu Feras made only vague reference to the "vetting" process that had taken place before he arrived. If he had any concern about Adhamiya's history of resistance to the occupation, the lieutenant took pains to avoid speaking about it. The occupation had been full of contradictions and false promises up to that point. What was one more?

The Sahwa succeeded in securing the release of more than a thousand prisoners, and the Americans were in many cases happy to help build the reputation of their new allies. American soldiers openly called it the "make a sheikh" program, a name both mocking and naive, depending on the American soldier using the phrase. Sahwa commanders were sometimes consulted on prisoner releases, since the Americans had no desire to release enemies of the men with whom they were now allied.

In Fallujah, once the most potent symbols of resistance against the occupation, Sheikh Afan al Issawi committed his tribe to the Sahwa in early 2007. His meeting room was decorated with pictures of himself shaking hands with American and Iraqi politicians, including President Bush and Prime Minister Nouri-al Maliki. In 2008, Afan hadn't yet hung his picture of Barack Obama, and professed little interest in how Obama's election might affect U.S. policy in Iraq.

"The policy is the same," he sighed. "He is an American."

As a major Sahwa commander in Fallujah, Afan worked directly with the marines as they prepared to turn control of Fallujah over to the Iraqi government. The character of a meeting between Afan and a U.S. Marine Corps captain in July 2007 was telling. At one point, the captain began describing the rift between al Sahwa and the Iraqi Islamic Party as if Afan were a child. He spoke of "commitment" to Iraq and not taking sides. When Afan pressed the captain—in nearly accentless English—for support and concessions, such as keeping one of Afan's enemies in prison, the marine talked past him, moving back to broad generalizations. At one point in the meeting, the captain and Afan left the room to deal with the issue of money. Shortly after the closed-door part of the meeting, I saw Afan paying his men with vacuum-packed stacks of hundred-dollar bills. His two-year-old son Sadoon wandered around the office, happily waving one of the bills.

After the meeting, Afan drove me around Fallujah. The city still bore the scars of the heavy U.S. bombardments in 2004 and remained hostile toward the Iraqi government, which made promises to compensate residents whose homes and property had been destroyed but backed off when Ibrahim Jaffari, the leader of the Dawa Party, part of an alliance of religious Shiite groups, took control of the government the next year. To rebuild Fallujah, the U.S.-appointed prime minister, Ayad Allawi, delivered more aid and reconstruction funds than any of his successors, though it was still insufficient. Unemployment in Fallujah remained well over 30 percent, as it did in most of Iraq. Hospital and other services existed but were far from what was needed for a city its size. The martyr's cemetery, which occupies a former soccer stadium, was still conducting burials. The dead were now the victims of fighting between the Sahwa and the anti-government guerrillas instead of the victims of the Americans. As local elections neared in 2009, there were also tit-for-tat killings between the Sahwa and other more established Sunni political forces, such as the Iraqi Islamic Party. Even Afan admits he came to work with the United States grudgingly and still refers to those killed by the occupation as martyrs.

Sheikh Afan was so accommodating and frank during our tour of Fallujah that I asked him a favor I doubted he could fulfill: Could he help me interview someone affiliated with al Qaeda? Afan thought about it and replied: "Anyone from al Qaeda was killed or fled." I pressed a little further, and then he turned to one of his aides and said, in Arabic, "Call that son of a bitch." Half an hour later, one of Afan's cousins, Sheikh Ritha'a Jassim Hamed Abu Ahmed, arrived. By his own admission, Ritha'a planned bombings and attacks with al Qaeda until 2006, when his relatives discovered his involvement and gave him a choice: work with us or be killed. Ritha'a spent a year as a kind of double agent, spying on al Qaeda on behalf of the United States and the Awakening, but it was clear he hadn't fully redeemed himself: when lunch was served, he was explicitly not invited to the table, a serious snub.

"When the Americans first arrived, they met with sheikhs and said that they are a peaceful people, and that this country shouldn't be ruined, and that they don't have an agenda or anything," Ritha'a said. "The sheikhs agreed and told them, 'You have come to remove the leader of a country and leave after that.' But they never left. When the Americans didn't leave, the jihad began. We became an occupied country."

Though he said he now supported the Awakening, Sheikh Ritha'a still put the highest priority on bringing the occupation to a swift conclusion. "America will vanish with the help of God," he said. "History repeats itself. Muslims unite to defend their homeland and honor. America will not remain. These dogs will be kicked out, and the big dog who came with them as well. I kick out those who are crueler than the Americans. I kick out those who sold their honor and homeland," he said, referring to the Shiite parties that dominate the Iraqi government. "Then if the Americans don't leave, I will be the first one to blow myself up."

Leaders like Afan attempted to turn their new power into political clout, but they have fared poorly overall, trapped between a Shiite majority that now controls the government and more conservative Sunnis who reject any dealings with the government. He blames the occupation.

"They didn't protect Iraq from Iran. They didn't build good democracy in Iraq. They promised many things and they didn't do them. When they entered Iraq, I thought they would come to build Iraq and make it like Germany or France. Now after I see all the things that happened, I believe that they didn't come to help but to destroy Iraq," Afan said in October 2011, the same month he was promoted to parliament after one member of his party became a minister and another was killed in a bombing.

"Al Qaeda still exists in Iraq because they didn't do a good job with the Sahwa people and they don't trust the government anymore. They say, "Why do we fight? It's because the government lied to us. They said they would give us jobs, and they didn't.'"

"I don't have a big hope that Iraq will be safe. I think we have a big challenge to make Iraq safe," Afan said, adding that he will move his children to another country when they are old enough to go to school. "What I see now, the situation I see now, the picture under my eyes, there is no hope that Iraq will be safe soon. I think we need lots of years to be safe enough."

By the end of 2011, virtually all U.S. troops had left Iraq. But the gains of the Awakening reflect the continued factionalization of the country and will likely be short-lived. In October 2011, Sunni sheiks accused Iraqi army units answering directly to the prime minister's office of continuing the cycle of displacement that had begun under Saddam Hussein, only in reverse: they say Maliki's government had been driving Sunni families out of the town of Abu Ghraib in recent months in an effort to permanently change the area's demographics. The Iraqi government was also simultaneously continuing its campaign to purge Sunnis from government jobs.

THE SADRIST INSURGENCY AND THE OTHER SIDE OF COIN

Al Sahwa, of course, is only part of the story. Throughout the occupation, the United States was involved in two distinct counterinsurgencies, often at the same time. By 2007, the Mehdi militia had taken over a number of neighborhoods in Baghdad, cleansing Sunnis across the capital. After heavy fighting during March and April 2008, the U.S. military erected a wall along the southern edge of Sadr City, part of a spree of wall building across Baghdad.

Baghdad began as a walled city—and perhaps it will always be. For a brief period after the invasion, it looked like the walls were coming down. I remember watching Iraqis removing the bricks

of Saddam's feared Abu Ghraib prison to construct housing and
sensing the potent symbolism of that gesture. But the trend of tear-
ing down walls was soon reversed. Within a year, Saddam's palace
complex in central Baghdad—what would later become the Green
Zone—went from a compound guarded by a handful of soldiers
who had sandbagged small machine-gun emplacements to miles
of walls and wire and clogged traffic, causing confusion and transforming areas into "no-go" zones for average Iraqis. The American
presence, per se, was not a problem for most people, but American
attempts to extend power and to control ground were. Guests were
welcome. Occupiers were not.

The walls in Baghdad are no different from those the Israeli government has constructed to surround the West Bank. Constructed
of Jersey barriers, or T-Lok barriers (interlocking pieces that are
lifted into position with a crane and stand anywhere from four to
eighteen feet high), the walls first appeared like oversized concrete
LEGOs around U.S. installations in 2003 to stop car bombers. The
fortifications grew larger and more complex as the city became more
dangerous. Then they began to appear in other parts of Baghdad,
blocking roads and choking an urban core already beset by traffic
problems. On some streets, the walls have been painted with mu-
rals; in others they are covered with advertisements.

Sadr City had been a locus of violence against the occupation
since 2004. The walls were a de facto U.S. military endorsement of
Baghdad's new order, and Sadr City was the last neighborhood to
succumb. There, the wall demarcating the U.S. area of operations
was painted a "calming" blue, and the area was dotted with circular
concrete watchtowers at major intersections.

After the fight over the construction of the wall, which turned
most of the buildings on both sides of the corridor to rubble and
left nearly one thousand fighters and civilians dead, the Iraqi government and the Sadrieen, the political wing of Sadr's movement
that holds seats in parliament, negotiated a settlement whereby only
Iraqi soldiers could patrol north of the wall. Some militia leaders and
political figures were exempted from arrest, and time was granted to

militia leaders to flee and for weapons to be hidden before the Iraqi army entered Sadr City.

Abu Zeinab is a journalist who lives and works in Sadr City. In 2008, he refused to be photographed or appear on camera, fearing reprisals from the Iraqi government and military.

"During the days of Saddam there was oppression, suffering, and misery—and they still exist," he said, sitting in an open-air café in the middle of one of the district's markets. "If we get one minister or one member of parliament, it doesn't mean that our political situation has changed for the neighborhood. The poor are still very poor—and even worse than before."

It was midday, and the café in which we sat was largely empty, save for a few young men smoking water pipes and watching a European soccer match on satellite TV. The couches were threadbare and saggy.

"From the beginning, when the city was founded, it was called Thawra (Revolution) City. And it truly was a revolution against poverty—a revolution against despotism. Whether it was the domination during Saddam days or the domination of the occupier today, our response is the same—everyone refuses the occupation."

"The rich Shia live in Karrada," Abu Zeinab said, referring to a neighborhood in central Baghdad where many government figures have taken up residence, some in houses that formerly belonged to Hussein's deputies. "We are the underclass here in the east. Of course, their goal is to curb our freedom, to control our movement, to diminish our humanity in the neighborhood and instill fear in us again. They aim to keep us haunted with fear—to dominate us and force us into submission. To turn this all into a prison."

South of the wall, where the U.S. military continued its operations, soldiers proudly guided journalists through markets where merchants could once again operate without paying taxes levied by the militia.

"The wall and all the operations that accompanied the wall were all in an effort to cordon off Sadr City and sort of isolate it. This was their home base," said Captain Andrew Slack of the First Armored

Division. "Their capabilities are severely, severely degraded," he explained. "They have talking power—threats, graffiti—but they don't
have the means to contest coalition forces right now."

When the occupation began, I was right out of college, often
younger than the U.S. soldiers I was interviewing. By 2008, that
dynamic had changed, and as I walked around their sector, it occurred to me that some of Slack's men hadn't been old enough to
drive when U.S. tanks first entered Sadr City. Worse, as I watched
the troops fruitlessly search for suspects at homes they had visited
two and three times before, I realized that many of them didn't even
know why they were here. Their knowledge of Iraqi society was
minimal, and they often relied on *my* limited Arabic to communicate. I was happy to do what I could, especially for bored troops pulling a cordon, reduced to smiling weakly at the Iraqis passing by or
communicating in single words ("Stop," "Yes," "No"). Through his
translator, the platoon leader badgered residents about the whereabouts of their sons and took pictures of faces to be uploaded to biometric databases. No one seemed to know where their sons were,
and Slack's soldiers were incredulous.

I often found it hard to listen to U.S. troops speak of the situation in Iraq, but Slack was soft-spoken and likeable. He saw heavy
combat while serving in Anbar province in 2005 and 2006 and displayed an understanding and willingness to engage the dualities,
complexities, and contradictions of the military's years of occupation. This was a subject many officers and soldiers avoided, insisting they had only been serving in a particular area a short amount of
time and were unable to discuss the conduct of the previous units.
I do not doubt that some of their refusals were sincere and that the
soldiers had little sense of even recent history, but it painted a picture of a military with a fragmented and disconnected view of a fight
that is seen in very different terms by Iraqis. Iraqis tend to mark
time not by events like Saddam Hussein's capture or the turnover
of power from the U.S. occupation authorities to a handpicked government, but by the rounds of sectarian cleansing, destruction of
cities, and uprisings, or worse, when a family member was blown

up, assassinated, kidnapped, or incarcerated. Many cannot forget the chaos and looting that followed the invasion.

"The Mehdi Army was kind of able to step into that vacuum," Slack said, "and they became the government that provided fuel, basic needs, and services, all the essentials that people needed. People depended on them to get . . . sugar, flour, water, electricity, and fuel—everything they needed to survive."

Slack stopped and pointed to a small poster of Sadr on the wall of a market across the street. "People know that it's not tolerated by coalition forces or the Iraqi Army to display propaganda that shows guys with weapons. . . . You still will see propaganda like what you see on the wall right there," he said. "Things like that are all over the city," Slack said, "although it's hard to take in and comprehend that JAM [the U.S. military's acronym for Jeish al-Mehdi] is also a political party—it's one of the most popular in Iraq."

Before long, especially within Sadr City, people began to draw comparisons to the British occupation that followed World War I. British tactics of the early twentieth century called for building a circle of blockhouses around a defiant village or neighborhood and essentially starving the residents. Aylmer Haldane, the British general who commanded forces in Iraq against insurgents during and after an uprising in 1920 and 1921, wrote frequently of his requests to the Ministry of Defense for more troops. In the meantime, he secured what ground he could by ringing garrisons with fortified blockhouses and wire and relying on air power and tactics like cutting off the water supply to the rebellious city of Karbala—a practice pioneered during World War I in nearby Najaf. The tactic of building walls is not much different; both are "force multipliers," a term used by the U.S. military that could be read, in the starkest sense, as a sign of an insufficient number of boots on the ground.

The 1920 rebellion forced the British to secure their own local proxies, just as the Sadrist rebellion against the ham-fisted political management of the Coalition Provisional Authority forced a hasty reassessment of the inclusion of Iraqi politicians in the management of their country. The British also employed Arab and Kurdish proxy forces, a tactic the United States finally arrived at in 2006 and 2007 as it looked for ways to use sectarian fighting to its advantage. The Shiites of Sadr City still remember the British exploitation of sectarian divides, empowering the minority Sunni tribes that would set the political tone of modern Iraq and oppress all who opposed them. This was the era the United States had promised to end when it overthrew Saddam.

In 2005, Sheik Ghaith al Tamimi lived with his wife and two young sons in a tiny two-room apartment with no running water above a garage in Sadr City. Young and charismatic, Ghaith was the son of a doctor and a journalist, but he had taken a different path, participating in the resistance against Saddam Hussein and going to jail twice in the 1990s for his efforts. After the invasion, he was free to organize and did so.

I first encountered Ghaith on the street in front of the Ministry of Oil, where members of the Jeish al-Mehdi were holding a demonstration to protest the shortage of cooking and heating oils, as well as gasoline. Sadr had agreed to a cease-fire, albeit a shaky one, in September of the previous year. Ghaith said that at one point he had been forced to stand in front of an American tank to prevent some of the young men in his neighborhood from attacking it.

As the demonstrators, many holding empty oil lamps, prayed in the street in front of the ministry, a trio of Humvees pulled up on the other side of the median strip. Ghaith urged his angry but unarmed followers to refrain from violence. Had he given the word, those hundreds of men would have readily set upon the soldiers.

Ghaith's rise within the Sadrieen was not unique. The previous spring and summer had seen the first two Sadrist intifadas against the U.S. military culminate in Jeish al-Mehdi's takeover of the Imam Ali Shrine in Najaf. Ghaith had been in Najaf and nearby Kufa during the fighting and inside the shrine during the siege. When I asked him what his role had been, he smiled and pointed an imaginary rifle, making little popping noises. Those killed were mourned as martyrs, their faces added to the signs dotting the median strips in Sadr City that already displayed the faces of men martyred by Saddam during the Shiite uprising in 1991, immediately after the first Gulf War. Ghaith and the other young men that led the fighting in Najaf became heroes.

After a deal was brokered, the militia melted away in Najaf but remained in control of Sadr City. The United States, finally forced to take Sadr seriously, dropped a warrant it had issued for his arrest and redoubled overtures for him to join the political process. For me, the defining moment of that summer came when I happened to meet a U.S. tank platoon that had been responsible for the destruction of Sadr's main political office in Sadr City in May 2004. The platoon bragged about reducing the office to rubble after fierce fighting. I didn't tell the soldiers what I saw the day after their victory in Sadr City: men and boys from the neighborhood gathering together and rebuilding the office, larger and better fortified than before.

By the time I met Ghaith, the nature of Shiite resistance was shifting. The previous intifadas had been popular uprisings, difficult to control. As the civil war intensified and people were being displaced by the thousands, the Mehdi Army began carrying out its own retaliatory attacks and cleansing. It was growing and becoming better organized. Though rival factions inside the militia sometimes clashed violently, it was clear that anyone who opposed the Sadrieen from the outside would bear the brunt.

Very few members of the Supreme Islamic Iraqi Council (SIIC), the wealthy ruling Shiite party in the government that initially allied itself with the Americans before becoming increasingly marginalized by the Sadrieen, complained about the sectarian cleansing in Baghdad. Although they were not excited to share power with the lower-class Sadrieen, they certainly didn't mind letting the militia take on mutual enemies. The Mehdi militia's offensive was an important dynamic in driving many of Baghdad's Sunnis into cooperating with the U.S. military. Arguably, it made the Jeish al-Mehdi the most powerful force in the Iraqi political landscape in 2004. But in 2005, how far the militia would spread across the city was only just being realized. As Sunni guerrillas inflicted casualties on Shiite civilians in ever greater numbers, refugee camps of Shiites cleansed from mixed areas of Baghdad became recruitment centers for the militia, which formed first to protect neighborhoods and then began to carry out retaliatory attacks. Cooperation between Sunni guerrillas and the Jeish al-Mehdi that had existed in 2004 during dual uprisings against the U.S. military fully disintegrated as Shiite fighters accused the Sunni resistance of supporting attacks on civilians and harboring perpetrators.

The Shiite underclass complained that Sunni members of the government were allied with the militias responsible for sectarian cleansing. But as the violence mounted, Sadr approved the killing of Ba'athists and Takfiris—radical Sunnis who believe Shiites are heretics—and those categories were being loosely interpreted by many of the militia's commanders. The general feeling that all Sunnis were being targeted led some neighborhoods to form larger, more open militias of their own for protection. As the violence grew, distinctions that formerly had little or no meaning in Iraqi society became sharper. People who professed not to care about sectarian identity found themselves forced to choose sides. Sunni-Shiite marriages, once common, ended, and some couples found themselves under pressure to divorce.

Sunni rebels attempted to create a ring of territory in mixed villages and cities around Baghdad from which to operate, driving out Shiites and claiming they were collaborators with the U.S. military. But in Iraq, with twenty million Arabs, where the ratio is a lop-sided two-to-one in favor of Shia, the retaliation was bound to be devastating.

Shiite militias took the bombing of the Askariya Shrine as an excuse to act on long-standing grievances. Ghaith took over a mosque less than a block from the apartment he had rented on Palestine Street. The mosque had been taken from a Shiite cleric in 1980, during one of Saddam Hussein's purges of politically active Shiite Islamists. Ghaith had court papers from a judge in Baghdad who had ruled in favor of the mosque's former tenants, but the decision was never enforced by the Iraqi police. Given the opportunity, Ghaith had taken matters into his own hands. And while the Askariya bombing was provocation, plans for many of the attacks against the mosques had been made far in advance.

I didn't see Ghaith again until a few months later, when I visited him at the mosque. The building was surrounded by heavily armed guards, including uniformed policemen, and the streets leading to the mosque had been blocked off. It looked more like a forward operating base than a house of worship. Ghaith was on the front line, and the city was "falling" again, this time to the Sadrieen.

"On the bus, people talk about the American soldiers losing the war," he said. "Someone else must fight the terrorists."

This time, he was holding a real Kalashnikov rifle as he spoke.

Ghaith was arrested by the U.S. military in February 2007.

"Those who support the Sadrieen are young and they support using weapons," Jenan al-Obaidi, an SIIC member of parliament, told me. "Of course, there are older and more educated people in the Sadr movement who believe in using weapons. But they saw what happened when they tried to fight." Al-Obaidi and other SIIC members denied that the government was using the military for political purposes and seemed to have forgotten her own party's longstanding militia, the Badr Brigade, which had been integrated into the Iraqi security apparatus. "We are prosecuting the outlaws even if they are in the mosques," she said.

I visited Ghaith's family twice while he was in prison. His young son suffered a shrapnel injury to his head when the mosque was attacked by gunmen later in 2007. The grass in the courtyard had turned brown, and the entrance to the mosque was padlocked. Ghaith was not in Sadr City to see the militia defeated in 2008.

North of the Sadr City wall, the area was being patrolled by Iraqi soldiers from the 11th Division, the only division said to be operating "autonomously"—that is, without direct U.S. support. For many worshipers, the presence of the army at Friday prayers, the same place the militia first rallied in 2003, conjured memories of the previous government. They were well aware that the Iraqi military had shut down many of the Sadrists' mosques and arrested hundreds in parts of southern Iraq, and they were increasingly suspicious that similar efforts were afoot here.

One Friday in the summer of 2008, before prayers, worshipers used chains and trucks to pull down two of the twelve-foot-tall T-Lok barriers, which broke apart as they hit the ground, exposing rebar skeletons. The Iraqi Army had parked a Humvee next to the gap. Representatives from the Sadr office had to link arms to hold back young men at prayers from confronting the army.

The anger stemmed from the establishment of a small Iraqi Army firebase constructed in the neighborhood, across the street from the Sadrieen headquarters. The party's representatives called the base a violation of the cease-fire agreement. On the outside wall of the base, someone had plastered a poster of Sadr. The word "NO" was printed in red letters in front of the black-cloaked, black-turbaned leader, who lifted his finger, as if making a point. He looked serious. The young men shared his expression.

With the help of the American military, the Iraqi government had been arresting Sadr supporters across the south and stopping public Friday prayers from taking place.

"They banned prayers in Amara and Diwaniya and now they want to ban them here?" another preacher asked, speaking from a lectern in front of a ten-foot-tall picture of Sadr's father. "If they are here to kill us, then we welcome martyrdom. . . . Is democracy over? Is freedom finished? Have their empty slogans expired? The elections are about to take place, and this is all to prevent the Sadrieen from participating. They want to dismantle and shut down the Friday prayers so that we cannot take part." After prayers, men demonstrated, shouting epithets at the Iraqi military, waving Iraqi flags, and reciting poetry.

Later, when I arrived at the firebase, some of the men in the Iraqi military unit recognized me from Friday prayers and chided me for going, emphasizing the danger. After helping the Iraqi soldiers connect a digital projector to a laptop (both donated by the Americans), I sat through a PowerPoint briefing in preparation for a cordon-and-search operation that would begin before daylight. On the Iraqi officer's desk sat a miniature T-Lok wall, a model of the blast barriers that have gone up all over the city. The trinket was boldly covered with the patches of the U.S. unit that presented it to the commander, as well as the words "OIF 2008," Operation Iraqi Freedom, a tacit endorsement of the larger strategy: segregation for peace.

I followed the troops out into the streets as they searched houses, detaining a dozen men and collecting nearly fifty light weapons, mostly AK-47s and a handful of World War II–vintage automatic rifles.

"A lot of gangsters and militias controlled the neighborhood and the poor people," Colonel Nadum Khadim told me. "The law was imposed. The army came in. . . . If you ask me if the Mehdi Army will come back—I don't think so."

Saleh al-Obaidi, the Sadrieen's official spokesman, wore a light gray dishdasha rather than his cleric's robes. Many of the group's officials were moving undercover now. I had arranged to meet al-Obaidi at the Sadr office in Khadhmiya, but when I arrived at the checkpoint to enter the neighborhood, the Iraqi police insisted that there was no longer a Sadr office there. A few minutes later, al-Obaidi called and gave us directions for an alternative location. For all the cloak-and-dagger, al-Obaidi was surprisingly frank in describing the continued necessity of the Sadr movement.

"In 2007, the U.S. sent more troops to Iraq," he said. "We were in need of a popular style of opposition. Now the situation has developed. The Americans have started to think of reduction of their troops. They have started to think of longtime bases in Iraq, big bases in Iraq, and to pull out of Iraqi cities. They have started to change their thinking, and we have to change our thinking. We have made the decision to freeze Jeish al-Mehdi, but still, as long as there are occupying troops, we have to keep some people working for opposition." He was not angry, just matter-of-fact. "We hope that negotiations between the Iraqi government and the American government will reach a timetable [for American withdrawal] and we will not be in need of these groups. We are not anti-American, we are not anti-British, but at the same time, we want the liberation of our country."

Al-Obaidi accused the SIIC of using the cover of law to disenfranchise the Sadrieen ahead of January's provincial elections. SIIC was widely accused of fraud in the 2005 parliamentary elections, though the Sadrieen still won the most seats in the largely impotent Iraqi parliament and control of some governorates that would later be wrested away by force. The Sadrist parliamentary bloc staged a

number of walkouts, primarily over the Iraqi government's refusal
to demand a timetable for a complete U.S. withdrawal. The Sadrieen
have seen their cabinet ministers purged from their posts, accused
of misusing government funds and weapons. Meanwhile, the SIIC
and virtually every other Iraqi party stood accused of the same: simultaneously operating military and political wings. The SIIC had
been successful, however, in legitimizing its militia's presence by
"integrating" it into the Iraqi military, special police forces, and death
squad units, all with the training and backing of the United States.

Nonetheless, by the end of 2006, Prime Minister Nouri al-
Maliki had begun demanding that the U.S. military agree to
a complete withdrawal and a date for it—the first time since the
occupation began that a nominal Iraqi head of state had done so.
Whether he was sincere or simply trying to placate Sadr's base is
debatable, but it was a sign of the political winds in Iraq, where most
people have seen a drop in their standard of living since the U.S.
invasion and most of the more than four million that have been displaced from their homes to other areas of the country or neighbor-
ing countries are unlikely to return anytime soon.

Al-Obaidi also addressed with surprising candor the issue of the
Sadrieen's links to Iran, an issue he had always been cagey about
prior to 2008.

"We have the right to cooperate with anyone who can help us
here and there, including the Iranians. But we are not the followers
of the Iranian decision," he said. "Our agenda is working against the
occupation."

Though Sadr City remained under Mehdi surveillance, in January 2009, the Sadrieen was emptier than I had ever seen it. From
2003 to 2008, it had been a place where people came to offer support or seek assistance. To sit in its lobby and observe the foot traffic
was to understand how Sadr City operated. But over several visits in
January 2009, I encountered only one other visitor—a woman from
the neighborhood who came in complaining that her new neighbors
were prostitutes. She pleaded with the men in the office to do something about it.

"Go ask the army," the men in the office told her. "We're civilians now."

In most of Baghdad's other neighborhoods, it was clear the militia was not missed, and that if walling in Sadr City was what had to be done, then so be it.

People were drinking again in public for the first time since 2003. At a newly opened nightclub only ten minutes' drive from Sadr City, the owner smiled broadly.

"No more Jeish al-Mehdi," he said. When I asked if all this was really attributable to the containment wall, one of my friends chimed in, smiling as well and breaking into a derisive laugh.

"It is like a zoo."

On the other side of the wall, however, the shop owners of Sadr City were not so happy.

"Your business dies because of these stones," one shop owner said. He was standing on the eastern edge of the Sadr City, near where another wall had been built, running almost the entire length of the district.

"The Americans . . . the Americans . . . This is *their* plan, not Iraqis. They directed the Iraqi government to do this—to hurt Sadr City and especially the Sadr movement. The neighborhood is already suffocating. And they put these stones to suffocate it more?"

As he spoke, an old woman squeezed through an opening in the barrier just large enough for a single person. After her came a man carrying a canister of cooking gas who tossed his purchase over the wall to a helpful bystander before squeezing through the crack and continuing on his way.

"Is *this* Iraq?" the shop owner asked.

As the United States reduced its forces and became less involved in day-to-day combat operations, the political winds began to shift once again. Sadr returned from exile in Iran in January 2011. His political party had done well in Iraq's second national parliamentary elections, in 2010, and in the wrangling among parties for the position of prime minister, Sadr once again found himself in the position of kingmaker. As he did in 2005, he decided to support al-Maliki, despite al-Maliki's having sicced the U.S. military on the Sadrists two years before. Recent history seems ready to repeat itself, though this time without the U.S. military, which helped to set it in motion. Sadr was emboldened enough to threaten renewed attacks by fighters loyal to him if U.S. soldiers attempted to remain in Iraq past the withdrawal deadline set for the end of 2011. As the United States relinquished its Iraqi prisoners ahead of the withdrawal deadline, many of the Sadr loyalists who had been held since 2008, including Ghaith, were simply released. And perhaps most telling, the wall cutting Sadr City off from the rest of Baghdad came down in summer 2011.

At Friday prayers in late 2011, the Iraqi soldiers on the cordon were at ease. No longer were they there to protect the worshippers from the rest of Baghdad but simply to protect the worshippers. At the time of this writing, Sadr City continues to be the target of bombings that are presumably the work of Sunni extremists still intent on fomenting sectarian violence in Iraq. After one bombing in October 2011, a statement from Sadr's political office urged the young men of Sadr City not to take revenge against Sunnis, but it hardly seemed necessary. The Sadrieen, for now, had won. Their office in Sadr City, reduced to rubble by U.S. tanks in 2004, was now bigger than ever.

7

AFGHANISTAN, PART I— "YOU HAVE TO NOT MIND KILLING INNOCENTS": AMERICAN COIN OPERATIONS IN AFGHANISTAN AND THE VIOLENCE OF EMPIRE

Jeremy Kuzmarov

"COIN is a form of warfare and thus involves violence. Don't be fooled by the fact that Petraeus found some useful idiots to make it sound more palatable and humanitarian."
—COIN theorist and military official [1]

Billy Waugh is a seasoned CIA paramilitary specialist from Bastrop, Texas, with a long career in the business of espionage and killing. A decorated veteran of the Korean and Indochina wars who led mercenary forces in the secret war in Laos and clandestine missions in Libya alongside the disgraced CIA operative Edwin Wilson, he has been in dozens of countries since 1989. After 9/11, the seventy-two-year-old was asked to lead a CIA-paramilitary unit in Afghanistan's Southern Logar province whose goal was to send to Washington Osama bin Laden's body in a box. Threatening any media that came within three kilometers, Waugh and his men set up networks of intelligence "assets" and trained local Afghans, many of whom said they joined for the money and to even the score with clan rivals. Among them were Zahim Khan and Pacha Khan Zadran, Northern Alliance warlords who called in a U.S. air strike on a delegation of Pashtun tribal elders on their way to congratulate the newly elected President Hamid Karzai in Kabul.

A precursor to mercenaries affiliated with Blackwater (later Xe Services, now Academi) and DynCorp (formerly California Eastern

Airways), Waugh's unit had authorization to assassinate enemy combatants and to call in air strikes using smart bombs and hell-fire missiles controlled by remote-control joystick. He told a reporter that the way to win the war is to "let them kill each other. Send up a satellite and take pictures. Keep the Special Operations teams in the hills, fifty miles out of the towns. Then go in at night and do your work. Kill them. Kill like we did in Germany. Flatten the place. You have to not mind killing innocents. Even the women and children." [2]

Waugh's candid comments epitomize the violence and terror underlying U.S. counterinsurgency (COIN) strategy in Afghanistan, which has been concealed from the public with the complicity of the mainstream media and prowar intellectuals. Furthermore, Waugh's career is significant because he embodies the continuity in American policy from wars such as Vietnam where similarly repulsive tactics were employed. [3]

Defined by the anthropologists Roberto Gonzalez, Hugh Guster-son, and David Price as efforts to "eliminate an uprising against a government," the term "counterinsurgency" was formally adopted by the Kennedy administration in the early 1960s and has been a feature of American military strategy since the late-nineteenth-century Indian wars and the colonization of the Philippines. Throughout the decades, extensive atrocities have resulted from the use of high-tech weapons and espousal of what the historian Richard Drinnon characterized as a "savage war" doctrine in which the supposed "uncivilized" nature of the enemy was used to justify parallel or greater barbarity by American troops and their proxies. [4] One can see echoes of this doctrine today in the proclamation by military officers that life, to Afghans, is "cheap."

During the Cold War, in the attempt to counter wars of national liberation, military intellectuals sought to emulate the tactics of the revolutionary commanders Mao Zedong, Che Guevara, and Vo Nguyen Giap, who effectively mobilized peasant armies to defeat better-armed forces. Drawing on the writings of European colonial strategists such as Britain's Sir Robert Thompson, they devised strategies to undercut guerrilla movements by isolating villagers through forced relocation into strategic hamlets (which often entailed spraying their fields with chemical defoliants), developing skilled police and intelligence agencies, and adopting such civic action programs as building schools and setting up medical clinics in the attempt to win "hearts and minds." They also sanctioned night raids, police sweeps, and targeted assassination, along with scorched-earth campaigns designed to intimidate or punish the population for supporting the insurgents.[5]

In theory, counterinsurgency experts aimed to minimize "collateral damage" by cultivating effective intelligence networks and building proxy forces to pinpoint the enemy. In reality, however, levels of violence are impossible to manage in a war zone. In Vietnam, Laos, and Cambodia during the 1960s and 1970s, like Afghanistan today, the fact of foreign occupation ensured that U.S.-backed forces lacked the support necessary to successfully track their adversary, who, motivated by a nationalist and revolutionary cause, was able to sink deep roots in the population. Foreign aid enhanced corruption, while air attacks yielding "methodical devastation," as one observer put it, drove villagers into the resistance.[6]

In 1967, the journalist I.F. "Izzy" Stone perceptively observed that "in reading the military literature on guerrilla warfare now so fashionable at the Pentagon, one feels that these writers are like men watching a dance from outside through heavy plate glass windows. They see the motions but can't hear the music. They put the mechanical gestures down on paper with pedantic fidelity. But what rarely comes through to them are the injured racial feelings, the misery, the rankling slights . . . the desperation. So they do not really understand what leads men to abandon wife, children, home, career, friends to take to the bush and live gun in hand like a hunted animal; to challenge overwhelming military odds rather than acquiesce any longer in humiliation, injustice or poverty."[7] These comments still resonate, even though the character of the movements the United States is fighting today are radically different.

An important model for American COIN strategy in Afghanistan is the Vietnam Phoenix program, whose goal was to eliminate the "Viet Cong" infrastructure (VCI) through the use of sophisticated computer technology, intelligence-gathering techniques, and improved coordination among military and civilian intelligence agencies.[8] In a secret blueprint for Phoenix, Frank Armbruster of the Hudson Institute referred favorably to a RAND Corporation study by Chong Sik-Lee on Japanese tactics during World War II and the anti-Huk campaign in the Philippines, and stressed the importance of identity cards, police roundups, and interrogation in pinpointing enemy cadres. Effective counterinsurgents were best recruited from the native population, because they knew the terrain. Once identified, hard-core VC (South Vietnamese guerrillas; the National Liberation Front) would be isolated and never allowed to return to their communities or executed outright. The rest of those detained could be won over through political indoctrination built around a counter-ideology.[9]

Calculated to promote terrorist methods, Armbruster's essay reflects how COIN specialists conceived of Phoenix—like its Afghan counterparts—as a clinically managed operation capable of dismantling the VCI. In practice, however, Phoenix was anything but precise in its application of violence, contrary to the claims of right-wing mythologists. Internal reports point to the corruption of Provincial Reconstruction Units (PRUs—trained as "hunter-killer teams) who used their positions for revenge and extortion, threatening to kill people and count them as VC if they did not pay them huge sums. The South Vietnamese government (GVN) under Nguyen Van Thieu, who ousted Nguyen Cao Ky in a power struggle centered in part on control of the $88 million heroin industry, used PRUs to eliminate rivals. Numerous "atrocities" were committed by "VC avenger units" prone to rape, pillage, and body mutilation.[10]

Robert Komer, director of pacification, lamented the large number of "phantom kills" and "flagrant" cases of report padding, most egregiously in the province of Long An, where Evan Parker Jr., a CIA operative, noted that "the numbers just don't add up." Dead bodies were being identified as VC, rightly or wrongly, in the attempt to at least approach an unrealistic quota. The catalog of agents listed as killed included an inordinate number of "nurses," a convenient way to account for women killed in raids on suspected VC hideouts.[11]

On the whole, an estimated twenty thousand to eighty thousand

people were killed under Phoenix and thousands more were subjected to torture, with the CIA promoting interrogation techniques
designed to emphasize the prisoner's dependence on his captor. In
one case, a detainee was kept in an air-conditioned room for four
years to exploit his fear of the cold and was later ordered to be thrown
into the South China Sea from a height of ten thousand feet.[12] Many
others died in overcrowded prisons run by the Office of Public Safety
(OPS) at the United States Agency for International Development
(USAID), which lacked sanitation and were sometimes flooded
with raw sewage. After touring prisons in the Mekong Delta, the
adviser John Paul Vann noted, "I got the distinct impression that
any detainees not previously VC or VC sympathizers would almost
assuredly become so after their period of incarceration."[13]

Flash forward forty years, and American COIN operations are
yielding similarly deadly and counterproductive consequences,
contributing to a resurgence of the Taliban. After the withdrawal of
Mullah Omar into Pakistan following the September 2001 invasion,
the U.S.-NATO coalition worked to stabilize the power of Hamid
Karzai, a former deputy foreign minister whose father was assassinated by Taliban agents. Born to a distinguished Pashtun family
of the Popalzai clan in Kandahar, Karzai ran an NGO in Pakistan
during the 1980s assisting the anti-Soviet mujahideen, earning
the nickname the "Gucci guerrilla" for spending most of his time
networking in the lobby of the Islamabad Holiday Inn. Meena Sid-
diqui, a human rights attorney in Kabul, noted: "When someone
has not arisen from the people they cannot work on behalf of the
people. Karzai had a good past, a good life, and ate well but he cannot do good for his people because he did not come from the people."
Like many other colonial creations, his regime has been beset by
corruption, epitomized by his brother, Ahmed Wali, who used drug
proceeds to fund state terror operations and relied on fundamentalist warlords implicated in serious human rights crimes during the
1990s civil war.[14]

Analogous to its British and Russian predecessors, the U.S.-
NATO occupation has uprooted communities, altered local power
structures, and aggravated tensions among the Tajik, Uzbek,

Hazara, and Pashtun, boding ill for future peace prospects. A key reason the war has gone on for so long is that American war planners see Afghanistan not only as a base of terrorist operations but a country of strategic importance in accessing Central Asian oil and gas resources in the new "great game" of imperial competition with China and Russia.[15] Afghanistan's connection to 9/11, meanwhile, is ambiguous. A New York University study released in 2011 points to long-standing friction between the Taliban and al Qaeda, which, according to the former commanding general Stanley A. McChrystal, have fewer than one hundred fighters stationed in Afghanistan.[16] The U.S. military consequently has spent an inordinate amount of time enmeshed in local disputes, fighting farmers driven into opposition by their hatred of the government. The journalist Anand Gopal described the insurgent movement as a "mélange of nationalists and Islamists, shadowy kohl-eyed mullahs and head-bobbing religious students as well as erudite university students, poor illiterate farmers and veteran anti-Soviet commanders" unified in their aversion to foreign occupation.[17]

New York Times columnist Nicholas Kristof, a member of what Edward S. Herman characterized as the "cruise missile left," predicted in September 2001 that "our invasion of Afghanistan may end up saving one million lives over the next decade," and that "troops can advance humanitarian goals just as much as doctors or aid workers." The reality has been completely opposite. After the ouster of the Taliban, Northern Alliance militias backed by the United States killed thousands of civilians alongside U.S.-NATO forces, with thousands more dying from suicide bombs directed against "occupational collaborators."[18] A UN official complained about the use of "cowboy-like excessive force" by Special Forces in "snatch and grab" raids and their "blowing doors open with grenades rather than knocking." Atrocities at checkpoints have also been routine, with some units playing macabre games where soldiers were rewarded for high kill-totals and took photos that included mutilated body parts.[19]

During the fall 2010 offensive in Kandahar, a district governor acknowledged large-scale demolition of homes by U.S.-NATO troops in violation of the Geneva Accords. Displaced Afghans saw subsequent offers of compensation as akin to "kicking dirt in our eyes."[20] The victims of errant bombing strikes have undoubtedly felt the same way. The *Times of India* reported on a typical incident in November 2001, where "a U.S. bomb flattened a flimsy mud-brick home in Kabul, blowing apart seven children as they ate breakfast with their father. The blast shattered a neighbor's house killing another two children. . . . [T]he houses were in a residential area called Qalaye Khatir near a hill where the hard-line Taliban militia had supposedly placed an anti-aircraft gun." Despite government claims of surgical precision, several villages were subsequently wiped out by U.S. warplanes, and at least four wedding parties were destroyed, including one in Nangarhar Province in which the bride and forty-six others were killed, prompting even Hamid Karzai to plead for greater restraint.[21]

Some of the deadliest bombings have been carried out in the remote Pakistani border region by computerized drone machines that have killed ten civilians for every "militant," according to the Brookings Institution. A precedent was established during the secret war in Laos, which, according to the peace activist Fred Branfman, saw the development of a "new type of warfare . . . fought not by men but machines and which could erase distant and unseen societies clandestinely, unknown to and even unsuspected by the world outside." In May 2009, a strike on the village of Bala Boluk in Afghanistan's Western Farah Province resulted in the deaths of approximately one hundred twenty people, including fifty-three girls under the age of eighteen whose bodies were torn to shreds by the blast.[22] The mainstream media did even not bother to cover the story. Pervez Hoodbhoy, a Pakistani physicist and political activist, noted that the usual outcome of drone attacks was "flattened houses, dead and maimed children and a growing local population that seeks revenge against Pakistan and the U.S."[23]

Much of the intelligence has come from American-trained commando units built up as part of a strategy of "tribal engagement" in which Special Forces immerse themselves in local cultures in order to forge alliances with village chiefs. Civic-action programs, including food drops, building rural schools, and vaccinations, have been adopted for the same purpose by Provincial Reconstruction Teams (PRTs), though these have been undercut, like their predecessors in Vietnam, by communication difficulties and the displacements fueled by the war. The PRTs, in effect, serve as a "military tool to achieve military ends," in the words of one army veteran, and as a means of manipulating poor and starving civilians by dispensing aid in exchange for information.[24] NGOs have aroused added hostility by being staffed with "scores of overpaid young people who flaunted their high salaries and motor vehicles," according to Frederick Starr, a specialist on Central Asia. "Their well funded activities highlighted the poverty and ineffectiveness of the civil administration and discredited its local representatives in the eyes of the populace."[25]

As a central facet of COIN, the United States has invested billions of dollars trying to create professional army and police forces whose main function is to "kill and capture terrorists." Quoting favorably from British colonialist T.E. Lawrence, Lt. Col. John Nagl wrote in his influential manual *Learning How to Eat Soup with a Knife: CI Lessons from Malaya and Vietnam*: "Local forces have inherent advantages over outsiders in a COIN campaign. They can more easily gain intelligence. They don't need to hire translators to run patrols and understand local behavioral patterns and the local terrain."[26]

While purporting to offer lessons from history, Nagl and other COIN gurus fail to mention that internal security forces built up by the United States have historically been poorly motivated, undisciplined, and often ruthless, owing largely to the cynical reasons people have joined. Financed almost entirely by the United States, the South Vietnamese army and police forces had among the highest desertion rates in history and committed myriad atrocities extending into Cambodia. Their Korean counterparts executed thousands of prisoners, as American soldiers wondered why "North Koreans fight like tigers and South Koreans run like sheep." The CIA's clandestine Hmong army in Laos was known for cutting off ears and burning villages while USAID-trained secret police were implicated in torture and death-squad activity throughout Latin America.[27] Gabriel Kolko explained in *Anatomy of a War: Vietnam, the United*

States, and the Modern Historical Experience that "the functions, actions and values of officers and soldiers are the inevitable conse-quence of the kinds of society they are seeking to create or defend," which, in the cases cited above, were corrupt, quasi-colonial cre-ations of the United States.[28]

History is repeating itself in Afghanistan, where the journalist Ann Jones notes, "Taliban fighters seem so bold and effective, while the Afghan National Police [ANP] are dismally corrupt and the Af-ghan National Army [ANA] a washout." Built out of Northern Alli-ance militias, the ANA was headed by General Muhammed Fahim, a successor to the Tajik warlord Ahmad Shah Massoud, who had been accused of overseeing the massacre of Shiite Hazara and other rivals during the 1990s battle for Kabul. Starting combat operations in 2003, the drug-tainted organization was overrepresented by Ta-jiks at the officer level and staffed with Soviet army veterans known for suppressing their own population. Reports indicate that it was underequipped and engaged more with rival clan militias than the Taliban or al Qaeda. A Pentagon study in June 2008 determined that well over half the units were "only partially or unable to conduct their primary mission."[29]

Commanders were known for taking sex slaves, raping girls, stealing food and land, and robbing homes. (A witness told Hu-man Rights Watch: "[T]hey gamble, bet money and when they lose, go and enter the houses to steal.") They threatened and kidnapped journalists, held people for ransom in "private prisons," and re-cruited child soldiers. They even beat or arrested musicians at wed-dings, destroying their instruments, and in one case assaulted a UN staffer. Matthew Hoh, a State Department envoy who resigned in protest of the war, stated that ANA officers were often stationed in territories distant from their homes, which made them seem like an occupying force. The ANA's brutality was epitomized in an incident in June 2004 in which soldiers beheaded four Taliban prisoners in what Human Rights Watch characterized as a war crime.[30]

In 2010, Jones observed recruits going through basic warrior training to get the promised Kalashnikov and pay, and then going home and enlisting under another name. In a country where 40 percent of the men are unemployed, she states, "joining the ANA for ten weeks is the best game in town." During a visit to one of the training camps, she overheard American trainers referring to their protégés in the "same racist terms once applied to African slaves, lazy, irresponsible, stupid and child-like." The Taliban "fight for something they believe—that is that their country should be freed from foreign occupation, our Afghans try to get by."[31]

In Naghlam Province, true to Jones's observations, ANA soldiers were found stealing equipment and cowering in ditches rather than fighting. Michael Bell, who headed a team of Hungarian trainers, stated: "They don't have the basics so they lay down. I ran around for an hour trying to get them to shoot [which they did not]." Many were suspected of being paid off by the Taliban, prompting the removal of their cell phones before battle to make sure they didn't tip off the enemy. This policy exemplifies a lack of trust between U.S.-NATO forces and their proxies, which is characteristic of colonial interventions. With time, the ANA began killing their own advisers, prompting the U.S. Army, in January 2012, to warn of "a rapidly growing systematic homicide threat on a magnitude of which may be unprecedented in the history of modern warfare."[32]

The ANP have proven to be as disloyal and corrupt as the ANA. After nearly nine years and over $7 billion spent on training and salaries, *Newsweek* reported in a March 19, 2010, cover story, "The Gang That Couldn't Shoot Straight," that officers could barely shoot a rifle or hit a target fifty meters away and sold or provided ammunition to insurgents. Mohammed Moqim, an eight-year veteran of the force, is quoted as stating that "we are still at zero. [Recruits] don't listen, are undisciplined and will never be real policemen."[33] Peter Galbraith, a former UN envoy, stated on *60 Minutes* that the ANP was unsalvageable as an institution. A taxi driver told Seth G. Jones, a RAND Corporation analyst, "Forget about the Taliban, it is the police we worry about."[34]

Embodying a U.S. imperial style grounded in the quest for serviceable information but not deep knowledge of the subject society, policy makers and think-tank intellectuals have long emphasized the importance of a professional police in stabilizing the post-Taliban order. Released to great fanfare by the University of Chicago Press in 2007, with a foreword by Nagl and Sarah Sewall, a lecturer in public policy at Harvard's John F. Kennedy School of Government, the army counterinsurgency manual relates that local "police are often the best force for countering small insurgent bands supported by the local population [as a result of their frequent contact with the population]. In COIN operations, special police strike units may move to different AOs [areas of operation] while patrol police remain in the local area on a daily basis and build a detailed intelligence picture of the insurgent strength, organization and support."[35] This prescription is contingent, however, on the legitimacy of the incumbent government and the ideological motivation of state security forces, as well as the competence of civilian advisers, which has been lacking in Afghanistan. Furthermore, it ignores the danger of an evolving police state, a central legacy of many previous interventions dating to the Progressive Era. (In the Philippines, for example, the United States built up a police constabulary, which pioneered coercive psychological warfare techniques that contributed to significant human rights violations and stifled democratic development for decades).[36]

Particularly stark was the fact that COIN aficionados overlooked the failure of police training programs in Afghanistan during the Cold War. In the 1950s, the State Department provided over three hundred thousand dollars in modern equipment to the police. Their aim was to gain leverage among the security forces and suppress demonstrations against King Muhammed Zahir Shah and Prime Minister Mohammed Daoud led by procommunist elements and "religious fanatics" from Kandahar (whom the CIA ironically recruited twenty years later to fight the Soviets).[37]

In the fall of 1957, the State Department sent Albert Riedel, a polygraph specialist with the Berkeley, California, Police Department, to Kabul under the top-secret 1290-d program, whose mission was to develop local police and security forces to "provide internal security in countries vulnerable to communist subversion."[38] Riedel's experience was not pleasant. He could barely communicate with officers who did not know English, and he had difficulty finding a qualified interpreter. While accepting American supplies, including tear gas, walkie-talkies, handcuffs, and repressive instruments such as leg irons, the Afghan police barely acknowledged Riedel's presence and refused to take any advice on how to manage the police force. Riedel noted to his superiors that he was not even allowed to tag along with cops on their patrols and was made to feel like an "old colored gentleman he once interrogated back in Oregon" who was "left to sit idly, completely, but however politely ignored." He added that the "Prime Minister never wanted a police adviser. Yes, he would take any free donations of equipment, but they would use it the way they wanted." In his view, the government did not want to be exposed to any new ideas, and the king "could not tolerate any change."[39]

Besides the insight into existing racial mores, Riedel's comments exemplify the difficulty of trying to impose a Western-style security apparatus in a country where strong nationalist sensibilities prevail and foreigners are viewed with suspicion owing to historical circumstance. They also highlight the dangers inherent in police programs providing weaponry to the security forces of authoritarian leaders who invariably appropriate them for their own ends, in a pattern that is being repeated.

After the ouster of the Taliban, Germany took the lead in police training, receiving criticism from NATO commanders for mismanagement and poorly integrating the programs into COIN. The State Department subsequently gave DynCorp International of Falls Church, Virginia, which trained internal security forces in Kosovo (where employees were linked to the child sex trade and illegal arms sales), a $1.1 billion contract.[40] New precincts were constructed—shoddily, in a number of cases, due to cost-cutting measures by private contractors, forcing police at times to interrogate people in their private residences. Riedel's heirs traveled around the country seeking to upgrade record-keeping, communications, and riot control capabilities. Training centers were established with short, two- to eight-week courses in handcuffing, weapons maintenance, constitutional procedure, and guerrilla warfare. British and Canadian soldiers provided lectures in crime scene investigation, evidence collection, and dismantling IEDs (improvised explosive devices).

Most of the recruits were illiterate. They sat on hard benches in classrooms that baked in the summer and froze in the winter listening to English-speaking instructors and poorly trained translators who were unfamiliar with police terminology. Journalist Ann Jones noted that the exercises looked like military maneuvers.[41]

Coming primarily from low-paid police forces in Texas, South Carolina, Georgia, and Florida, DynCorp employees made six-figure salaries, fifty times more than their Afghan counterparts. Operating under limited legal oversight, they alienated Afghans through such practices as "driving through the streets fast and furious without regard for the locals," as one contractor put it, public drunkenness, whoring, torture, and shooting civilians. One of DynCorp's slogans was: "I do this job for the opportunity to kill the enemies of my country and also to get that boat I always wanted. . . . [W]hen engaged I will lay waste to everything around me." A number of staff previously served under repressive regimes, including apartheid South Africa, Alberto Fujimori's Peru, and Augusto Pinochet's Chile. Others, like Waugh, long operated in the dark shadows of American foreign policy.[42]

With such men in charge, the ANP emerged at the center of the repression gripping Afghanistan, routinely shaking down civilians, shooting demonstrators, terrorizing people in raids, and intimidating voters during fraudulent elections. In Babaji north of Laskgar Gah, police bent on taking revenge against clan rivals abducted and raped preteen girls and boys. In 2006, Jamil Jumbish, the Kabul chief of police, was implicated in murder, torture, and bribery, and his replacement, Amanullah Guzar, of extortion, land grabbing, and kidnapping three UN workers.[43] The above abuses fit a historical pattern and are partly a product of the social polarizations and corruption bred by the U.S.-NATO intervention and mobilization of police for military and political ends.

WikiLeaks's "Afghan War Logs" confirm wide-scale police brutality and its cover-up. In one incident, the chief of police in Balkh Province raped a sixteen-year-old girl and ordered his bodyguard to fire on a civilian who tried to report the incident. When the bodyguard refused, he was shot to death.[44] Some police cultivated poppy within compound walls and even robbed banks. When a Kabul man reported that he found a policeman's identity card in his shop after it was burglarized, the commander warned him not to tell anybody or his life would be at risk.[45]

The lack of an effective judicial or legal system and the Bush administration's support for torture hastened the ANP's lawlessness. The Red Cross reported massive prison overcrowding, "harsh" conditions, a lack of clarity about the legal basis for detention, and inmates being subjected to "cruel" treatment in violation of the Geneva Conventions, including hanging from the ceiling and sexual abuse of women and juveniles incarcerated for escaping bad marriages. Sensory deprivation and other forms of psychological torture were common, leading prisoners to go insane. Many were held without charges for years in facilities lacking rudimentary toilets. An undisclosed number died in custody, including hundreds transported by the army's chief of staff, Rashid Dostum, in unventilated containers where they suffocated to death or were shot.[46]

The scale of abuse paralleled Iraq, where DynCorp was given a $750 million contract in 2004 to professionalize the police and other security forces implicated in torture and death-squad activity. Robert Cole, a police officer from East Palo Alto, California, and an employee of DynCorp, explains that racist attitudes were engrained in a mini–boot camp training session, where he was "brainwashed, reprogrammed and desensitized" and "morphed" into a "trained professional killer." Taught that Arabs only understood force, he was instructed to shoot first and think later and to command police to do the same. "If you see a suspicious Iraqi civilian, pull your weapon and gun him down," he was told, "you don't fire one . . . or two shots. . . . You riddle his sorry ass with bullets until you're sure he's dead as a doorknob."[47] This is an inversion of democratic police methods and Western counterinsurgency doctrine, which in theory advocates a moderation of force in order to avoid antagonizing the population and creating martyrs.[48] No wonder the scope of violence has been so high.

As with the Iraqi police, Americans established an identity card system and biometric archive of Afghan fingerprints and head shots that were electronically scanned by satellite to Washington. According to the historian Vikash Nadav, these efforts exemplified the deep mistrust of the population inherent in COIN operations and an imperial drive for control reminiscent of the British in India.[49] As in Vietnam decades earlier, the sophistication of new policing technology did not translate into greater efficiency in identifying guerrilla forces, owing to a variety of factors, including the weakness of the Karzai government and excessive firepower by U.S.-NATO troops and their proxies, which drove Afghans into the resistance.

Showing where their loyalties rested, in May 2006, when a U.S. tank smashed into a traffic jam in Kabul, police threw off their uniforms and joined protestors in looting buildings, vehicles, and police posts, denouncing the occupation.[50] According to a 2009 report by General Stanley A. McChrystal, a onetime Special Forces assassin, prisons have served as a key recruiting base and "sanctuary [for Islamic militants] to conduct lethal operations" against government and coalition forces, including the bombing in 2008 of the Kabul Serena Hotel, which was allegedly planned, without interference, from prison. At the Pul-e Charkhi facility, eighteen prison officers, one of them a colonel, were arrested for taking bribes from Taliban commanders. In the Sarposa Prison in Kandahar, guards were stoned on drugs when close to five hundred inmates escaped in April 2011.[51]

While there is limited evidence of Taliban involvement (despite hysterical claims by CNN and other media), the United States has supported leading narcotics traffickers such as Haji Juma Khan, commander of the Hezb-i-Islami party, and his son, General Abdul Khalil Andarabi, head of the Northeast Highway Police, causing production to escalate to over eight thousand tons per annum.[52] According to WikiLeaks documents, Hamid Karzai pardoned five border police officers caught with 124 kg (273 pounds) of heroin and intervened in a drug case involving the son of a wealthy supporter. Karzai's close friend Sher Muhammed Akhundzada, governor of Helmand Province, was found with more than nine tons of opium in his office by the DEA in 2005 (he subsequently took up a seat in the Senate). Izzatullah Wasifi, whom Karzai appointed anticorruption chief in 2007, spent almost four years in a Nevada prison for selling heroin to an undercover cop. Meanwhile, Vice President Ahmed Zia Massood was caught by the DEA entering Dubai with $52 million in cash. A CIA officer commented that during the period of the U.S.-NATO occupation, "Virtually every significant Afghan figure has had brushes with the drug trade. If you are looking for Mother Theresa [sic], she doesn't live in Afghanistan."[53]

Cheryl Bernard, a RAND analyst and the wife of Zalmay Khalilzad (who was, consecutively, U.S. ambassador to Iraq, U.S. ambassador to Afghanistan, and U.S. ambassador to the United Nations) explained one of the key reasons for the lack of good governance: "[To defeat the Soviets] we threw the worst crazies against them that we could find and there was a lot of collateral damage. . . . Then we allowed them to get rid of, just kill all the moderate leaders. The reason we don't have moderate leaders in Afghanistan today is because we let the nuts kill them all. They killed all the leftists, the moderates, the middle-of-the-roaders. They were just eliminated, during the 1980s and afterwards." The United States continues to tolerate high levels of corruption out of perceived geopolitical expediency and by claiming that it is ingrained within the political culture of Afghanistan. In reality, however, it is a product of historical contingencies, the breakdown of social mores caused by the war, and the need among officials who are lacking popular legitimacy to obtain money for counterinsurgency.[54]

Similar factors were at play during the 1960s, when Vietnam and Laos were at the center of the world drug trade, which benefited from American backing of corrupt officials who controlled the traffic, with the CIA overseeing the production and sale of opium by Hmong guerrillas in order to finance the secret war against the Pathet Lao.[55] History is thus coming full circle in Afghanistan, which produces 93 percent of the world's heroin and has been characterized by even Fox News as a "narco-state."[56] The drug trade first exploded in the 1980s with the destruction of rural agriculture by the Soviet invasion and the CIA's support for heroin traffickers such as Gulbuddin Hekmatyar of the Hesb-i-Islami.[57] Drug money has since corrupted all facets of society and made it nearly impossible to carry out development projects. As in South Vietnam under U.S. occupation, the main airport has become a transshipment point for heroin, and positions for police chief are auctioned off due to their enormous graft value. The cost for a job as chief of police on the border is rumored to be upward of one hundred fifty thousand dollars. Brig. Gen. Abdul Razik, a brutal DynCorp-trained warlord who bragged about not taking prisoners alive, pulled in $5 million a month as chief of the counternarcotics police in Kandahar (he later became police chief).[58]

Special Envoy Richard Holbrooke characterized the $800 million counternarcotics campaign run by DynCorp as "the most wasteful [government program]" he had seen in forty years. Targeting predominantly competitors of U.S.-backed warlords, police counternarcotic teams armed with hoes, sticks, and weed whackers eradicated a paltry 2,373 acres of poppy in raids that killed and wounded dozens of Afghans and were met with stones, snipers, roadside bombs, and angry mobs. Fearful of being forced to sell their children to pay off opium debts, many farmers contracted militiamen equipped with state-of-the-art satellite phones, semiautomatic weapons, and Toyota pickup trucks to protect their fields. Aerial defoliation destroyed watermelons and wheat crops, an outcome that was unsurprising, given that DynCorp was facing a class-action suit by Ecuadorian peasants for spraying herbicides in Colombia that drifted across the border, resulting in the poisoning of food crops, contamination of drinking water, and the death of several children. In 2007, William Wood, the U.S. ambassador to Colombia nicknamed "Chemical Bill" for his advocacy of herbicides, was transferred to Afghanistan, showing a continued commitment to repressive eradication.[59]

Also in 2007, the U.S. military took over police training from DynCorp and tried to clean up corruption by raising salaries, providing electronic pay, and dismissing abusive chiefs (or so it claimed). Little changed apart from further militarization. Journalist Nir Rosen overheard a U.S. sergeant telling his men: "Throw some fuckin' grenades, we're not there to arrest people, just fuckin' kill people."[60] Because of the ANP's inability to provide security, village elders and provincial governors increasingly looked either to the Taliban or to independent militias led by mujahideen fighters and ethnic warlords, many of whom had abhorrent human rights records. Attempting to replicate Iraq's "Sunni awakening," the military backed some of these militias while stepping up training of auxiliary paramilitary units, including those dedicated to protecting industrial facilities and pipelines. It has also bolstered financing of the CIA-trained National Security Directorate (NSD), staffed by many former KGB "assets," who cultivate informants nationwide and carry out Phoenix-style assassinations in a program frequently exploited by agents pursuing personal feuds.[61]

In 2004, as the war expanded into Pakistan, the Bush administration began providing tens of millions of dollars in technical aid, training, and equipment to the Pakistani police through the Department of Justice's International Criminal Investigative Training Assistance Program (ICITAP) and the Drug Enforcement Administration (DEA). Coinciding with the provision of $15 billion in military aid, which General Pervez Musharraf diverted to bolster the Taliban's insurgent network and prepare for war with India, American advisers introduced a computerized security system to monitor movement across the border and created counternarcotics units and a police air wing equipped with three caravan spotter planes and eight Huey helicopters to aid in counterinsurgency operations.[62] According to Amnesty International, U.S.-trained forces have been implicated in "large-scale disappearances" primarily of "activists pushing for greater regional and ethnic rights . . . in Baluchistan and Sindh," with the government using the "rhetoric of fighting terrorism to attack its internal critics." Meanwhile, the Pakistani Inter-Services Intelligence (ISI) has long been infiltrated by the Taliban, ensuring that the United States is, in essence, financing its own assassins.[63]

The Obama administration's troop surge in 2010 generally deepened the humanitarian crisis in a region of the world already ravaged by decades of conflict. Amid escalating violence, unemployment in Afghanistan hovers around 60 percent, and child mortality is among the worst in the world. Many go hungry in refugee camps, with malnutrition rates estimated at around 70 percent. The empowerment of fundamentalist warlords has ensured that between 60 and 80 percent of marriages remain forced, with girls deprived of education and traded and sold like commodities. Prostitution is also at a record high due to wide-scale displacement, with one woman commenting: "During the Taliban era, if a woman went to market and showed an inch of flesh she would have been flogged—now she's raped." [64]

Malalai Joya, a courageous critic, wrote in *A Woman Among Warlords*: "Afghanistan has long been used as a deadly playground in the 'Great Game' between superpowers, from the British Empire to the Soviet empire, and now the Americans and their allies. They have tried to rule Afghanistan by dividing it. They have given money and power to thugs and fundamentalists and warlords who have driven our people into terrible misery. . . . [This] endless U.S.-led 'war on terror' . . . is in fact a war against the Afghan people. The Afghan people are not terrorists; we are the victims of terrorism." [65]

Joya's words resonate with this study of COIN operations. From Billy Waugh's escapades in 2001 to the disastrous efforts at police and military training, American intervention has contributed immeasurably to the climate of misery to which she is alluding, while failing to win "hearts and minds." The unleashing of violent social forces and ethnic hatred will be difficult to contain over the long term. Afghanistan is only the latest country to be the victim of American COIN strategies, which have changed little over the past half century and draw directly on colonial precedents. Joya writes that the only positive outcome of the U.S.-NATO intervention has been the development of a political consciousness among many Afghans. One can only hope the same will hold true in America, where the population has been lulled into acquiescence by the sanitized rhetoric of politicians, COIN theorists, and the mainstream media, which belies the grisly reality on the ground.

8

AFGHANISTAN, PART II— COUNTERINSURGENCY IN AFGHANISTAN: MYTH OR REALITY?

Jean MacKenzie

Author's note: April 2012
The first draft of this manuscript was completed in August 2011.
Since then, the situation in Afghanistan has, if anything, wors-
ened. What might have been a controversial conclusion in 2011—
that counterinsurgency, or COIN, had failed in Afghanistan—is
now all but accepted wisdom.

Incidents of Afghan soldiers firing on their international
mentors multiplied in the final months of 2011. By April 2012,
ten "green on blue" attacks had resulted in the deaths of nineteen
foreign servicemen, and analysts began referring to the problem
as "systemic."

The burning of copies of the Koran on an American base
near Kabul in February 2012 produced violent protests across the
country in which at least two dozen people died. Photographs and
video of U.S. soldiers desecrating the corpses of Taliban also dam-
aged the image of the American military with the Afghan popu-
lation, making the battle for hearts and minds all but impossible.

As the date for withdrawal nears, the U.S. military is trying
its best to create an illusion of victory in a war that has seen very
limited progress over the past decade. But an examination of the
facts from this period will reveal that COIN, to the extent that
it was ever really practiced in Afghanistan, contributed little to
resolving what has become a disastrous war.

INTRODUCTION

It is April 27, 2011. I am sitting in my office in Kabul, with a young Afghan journalist working at the next desk. The shocking news comes across the wires that an Afghan Air Force pilot has just shot and killed nine people—eight U.S. military officers and a contractor—at Kabul International Airport.

The Afghan journalist—let's call him Aziz—is urban, well educated, and has benefited greatly from the presence of the international forces and the small army of aid workers that followed in their wake. He makes a hefty salary, has traveled abroad extensively, and is in line for a prestigious scholarship in the West. He is not in the least aggressive and seems well disposed toward me and other foreigners with whom he has come into contact.

When he heard the report of the rogue pilot, he let out a victory whoop and pumped the air with his fist.

"Good for him!" he cried. I knew then that something had gone terribly wrong with the battle for hearts and minds in Afghanistan.

MISSED OPPORTUNITIES AND THE RISE OF THE TALIBAN

It is not too soon to say that the U.S.-NATO intervention in Afghanistan has failed, doomed by a series of miscalculations, incompetence, hubris, and a persistent failure to understand the country.

That is the bad news. The "good" news, at least judging by the recent dearth of media reports on the decade-long war, is that nobody will know much about it when the country enters the final and disastrous phase of this ill-considered conflict.

Much as in Iraq, the U.S. government will spin a narrative of victory, while media attention, now focused on Libya, Somalia, Yemen, or numerous other, more recent stories, will not be on hand to correct the overly rosy assessments coming out of Washington.

It did not have to be this way. In 2001, when the United States invaded Afghanistan in retaliation for the horror of 9/11, the Afghan people were staunchly opposed to the brutal, repressive Taliban government and the misery and isolation it had brought to their lives.

At that time, despite the long history of attempts by great powers to conquer their country, contributing to a general mistrust of foreigners, Afghans were prepared to accord the foreign troops a honeymoon period—a chance to prove that they had something better to offer than the unpopular regime they had toppled.

This should not have been a difficult task. Given the Taliban's penchant for snuffing out any form of pleasure, from kite flying to chess playing; for restricting girls' education and women's employment; for beating men whose beards were too short or whose hair was too long, it should have been possible to win the hearts and minds of the exhausted, frustrated Afghan people.

"I remember the exhilaration of those first few days," said A., a young Afghan who lives in a neighborhood in northwestern Kabul. "We would go up to the roof every night to watch the air strikes. It was exciting. We wanted this dark regime to go."

The death and destruction of the invasion did not unduly disturb the populace. They had seen much worse. "The Americans were pretty careful," said W., a medical student in Kabul at the time of the invasion. "They did not kill many civilians, and people were very happy that they had come."

But the euphoria was short-lived. The International Conference on Afghanistan in Bonn in December 2001 went a long way toward short-circuiting Afghan hopes for a brighter future. The gathering was supposed to assemble the players in the future democratic state of Afghanistan and, along with the international community, develop a road map for helping to bring the country to stability. But according to Lakdar Brahimi, the United Nations Special Representative at the time and one of the chief architects of post-Taliban Afghanistan, the seeds of future disaster were sown in Bonn: "The most important . . . mistake was the fact that we did not reach out to those who were not represented in Bonn, at the Bonn conference, and in particular to the Taliban," Brahimi said at an interview with the Century Foundation in April 2010. "The Taliban had been routed, they had been beaten, but not defeated—they didn't recognize or accept their defeat. Where did they go?"[1]

It is now quite obvious where they went: to lick their wounds and nurse their grievances, to regroup and plan their revenge. The other major miscalculation of Bonn was inviting the "warlords" back into the fray. As even a cursory reading of Afghan history would have revealed, the "political factions" that tore Afghanistan apart during the civil-war years of the 1990s were largely responsible for the emergence of the Taliban in the first place. The warlords who had united in the fight against the Soviet invaders soon split apart once the common threat was gone. They were grouped, not by ideology or conviction, but by ethnic and regional interest; in most cases they amounted to little more than heavily armed thugs. Anger and revulsion at the predations of armed gangs loyal to one or another warlord who robbed, kidnapped, raped, even killed with impunity, spurred the population to embrace a regime that promised a cleaner, quieter, more secure life.

But after Bonn, there they were, back in the public eye: Ismail Khan, Abdul Rashid Dostum, Abdul Rassoul Sayyaf, Haji Mohammad Mohaqeq—men whose names and faces were just as appalling to many as those of Mullah Omar or the other outcast, Gulbuddin Hekmatyar. For Afghans, it was the worst of both worlds: the warlords were back in power, and, deprived of any possible constructive role in a new government run by their historical enemies, the Taliban became even more of a danger to the population.

As Alex Strick van Linschoten and Felix Kuehn have pointed out, "A combination of factors caused the leadership to begin an insurgency. Internal factions, in particular a younger generation, opposed a political process. Arguably more important, however, was the lack of real options. The counterterrorism policies of the United States at that time threatened the security of Taliban who might have been willing to join the process, and Afghan officials with whom the Taliban communicated said they could not protect them from detention by the United States."[2]

The Taliban are largely drawn from the Pashtun ethnic group, the largest in Afghanistan, and their exclusion set off a wave of ethnic resentment. Although Bonn installed a Pashtun—the little-known

Hamid Karzai—as the head of the interim government, and virtually enthroned another Pashtun—Zalmay Khalilzad—as the U.S. Special Envoy for Afghanistan, average Pashtuns still felt marginalized. The exclusion of the major Pashtun groups (the Taliban and Gulbuddin Hekmatyar's Hezb-i-Islami) from power, as well as the execution of military operations almost exclusively in Pashtun areas, made the rank and file feel that they were targets rather than partners.

In those early days, the watchword was "counterterrorism"—finding, detaining, and in some cases killing those seen as an integral part of the Taliban. As the cells in the U.S. military prison in Guantánamo Bay, Cuba, filled with Pashtun men suspected of links to Taliban and al Qaeda, many of whom would later be set free with no charges against them, things in Afghanistan were slowly changing.

With the populace still more or less on their side, the United States and its allies set about transforming Afghanistan from a perennial problem state into a "fledgling democracy." A constitution was produced in 2003–4; presidential elections were held in October 2004. A parliament emerged from a rather messy campaign in 2005, and many international observers thought that a corner had been turned. Afghanistan's democratic institutions were now tenuously in place; the rest was supposed to be fine-tuning.

The first four years of the international presence in Afghanistan do not play a significant role in the history of counterinsurgency. There was, according to the military wisdom of the time, no insurgency to speak of, just a few isolated pockets of resistance that needed mopping up. The international community, made up of the military forces, the diplomatic institutions, and the small army of nongovernmental institutions who implemented various programs, was intent on "nation building," while ignoring the fact that many of the prerequisites for that task were simply not in place.

Upward of 70 percent of the population in Afghanistan was illiterate. The Afghan government, riddled with incompetence and corruption, could not even begin to supply basic needs, and the international community did not have the knowledge or the commitment to remake Afghanistan. The country entered a period of dangerous disillusionment. This gave the groups that opposed the NATO intervention the opening they needed. By the winter of 2005–6, any hopes for a dramatic transformation were gone, and the insurgency was mobilizing throughout the country.

But it took a while for the countries that constituted NATO's Internal Security Assistance Force (ISAF) to realize this fact. As David Kilcullen, a COIN expert, writes, "Back in the spring of 2006, the war was also changing. Indeed, it was heating up dramatically. The winter of 2005–6 saw . . . a spreading and intensifying Taliban insurgency in Afghanistan." But efforts to map out a plan to deal with the growing problem, argues Kilcullen, were "hampered by a . . . reluctance on the part of some troop-contributing nations to grasp that the conflict had evolved from a reconstruction mission into a full-blown counterinsurgency."[3] The delay on the part of the international community to recognize what was happening may have contributed to the quagmire we find ourselves in today.

A DECADE OF COIN

Ten years after the initial intervention, Afghanistan was an unalloyed disaster. The insurgency had gained ground steadily since 2005; the "fragile but reversible" gains ubiquitously touted by General David Petraeus had proven to be illusory, as attacks, explosions, casualties, and other disasters continued to mount. Individual communities experienced a temporary lull in violence when huge influxes of heavily armed marines arrived on their doorsteps, but the Taliban who were "cleared" from the area reemerged once the boots moved to other ground.

"The truth of it is, they never left," said one journalist who has covered Helmand Province over the course of several counterinsurgency campaigns there in five years. "They blend into the population, become farmers and shopkeepers, and then dig up their guns from their backyards once the military's focus has shifted." The constant presence of the insurgency among the people undermines many of the principles of classic counterinsurgency, in which the goal is to separate the insurgents from the population. Afghans are well aware that the military, however strong their patrols, however many air strikes they are prepared to call in, cannot protect them from their next-door neighbor.

"How do they expect people not to cooperate with the Taliban?" demanded the journalist. "The people *are* the Taliban. Are people supposed to stop talking to their uncles, fathers, brothers, friends? We have never understood the extent to which the Taliban are part of the general population." Indeed, the concept is a difficult one to grasp; the Taliban were seen by much of the international community—both military and civilian—as an imposed regime, bitterly resented. While this is undoubtedly true in the northern parts of the country, in the south and east, where Pashtuns dominate, the Taliban were and remain much more representative of local cultural norms. This seems to be a central problem in the formulation of a counterinsurgency strategy for Afghanistan. As long as the Taliban are seen as an outside or occupying force, rather than an integral part of the population to be won over, any plans put in place are unlikely to work.

The difficulties begin with the very name used for the insurgency. The term "Taliban" has been used indiscriminately to identify those who are fighting the international coalition and the Afghan government it supports. However, almost no one who has spent time in the real Afghanistan—as opposed to the artificial construct visited by most diplomats and high-ranking officers—can pinpoint who the insurgents are; there are many disparate groups fighting for very different reasons. In the north, for example, the insurgency began in earnest only when a local Tajik leader in Balkh Province began targeting Pashtun elders; the population resisted, and another locus of "insurgency" was born. In Helmand Province, the center of the opium poppy industry, the insurgency began in earnest when a strong but highly corrupt governor was removed at British insistence. The governor had kept competing drug lords at bay by superior force; in his absence, the local mafias began to battle each other and the foreign forces, mostly British, who were trying to conduct a counternarcotics campaign.[4]

One military historian who is studying the problem refuses to call Afghanistan's fighters an "insurgency" at all. "What we have here is a multi-focal civil war," he said, speaking on condition of anonymity. "There are various groups settling internal scores, and using ISAF as they wish to accomplish their goals." The international forces remain committed to a description of a unified enemy, although they do recognize some stratification among them. The concept of "First Tier" versus "Third Tier" Taliban was introduced by the military under the tutelage of General Stanley McChrystal, the ISAF commander, and eagerly embraced by diplomats hoping to jump-start peace talks. However, other experts argue that such terminology is merely a tool to allow military strategists to hold out hope for "reintegration" of the less ideologically committed, while providing a justification for the policy of stamping out the "irreconcilables."

In general, the military and diplomatic arms of the international community have been intent on demonizing the insurgents. The "Taliban" have become the bogeyman, the inhuman force that must be destroyed. The term "Taliban" has also been used interchangeably with "terrorist" in many U.S. military reports. There is very little inclination to understand or address the actual grievances of the Taliban or the attraction they still hold for many in Afghanistan. These days, with the rise of kidnapping for profit and other forms of criminality, a corrupt government that seems to recognize no law, and the comeback of armed groups loyal to thuggish "warlords," there is a reluctant nostalgia among many in Afghanistan for the days when no one dared to step out of line for fear of swift and violent punishment.

But the international military, in particular, paints the Taliban as monsters. Indeed, General David Petraeus, commander of NATO forces in Afghanistan from 2010 to 2011, set off a major fracas in February 2011 when he suggested that injuries suffered by children in Kunar Province, in an ISAF operation, were actually inflicted by Taliban parents on their own offspring to up the casualty count.

The Afghan president was reported to have found this deeply offensive, and even the multi-ethnic parliament protested Petraeus's statement.⁵ Other media reports implied that the Taliban burn their own children to gain access to international military bases; under the guise of asking for medical care, they are actually spying for the insurgents.⁶

These claims are part of what the U.S. military calls "STRATCOM," or strategic communications, which, according to the late Richard Holbrooke, U.S. Special Envoy for Afghanistan and Pakistan, is another term for "propaganda." They ultimately undermine any chance of political settlement. Once you have painted the other side as inhuman fiends, it becomes difficult to suggest a civilized sit-down.⁷ The propaganda, which is aimed largely at the home front, serves only to alienate the local population, whose hearts and minds the international forces claim they are so intent on capturing. Meanwhile, "psyops," psychological operations directed at the indigenous population, consists largely of inept attempts to influence local opinion through the ISAF newspaper—which is seen more often wrapped around kebabs than in front of anyone's eyes—and the "radio in a box" broadcasting efforts that are dismissed by the local population as Western-backed propaganda. No amount of STRATCOM can counter the reality on the ground.

The rising tide of civilian casualties, a deeply corrupt government, rampant unemployment, and growing insecurity have combined to radicalize an angry and disaffected population. The ISAF troops are increasingly seen as invaders and occupiers. Soon, the term "Taliban" may have to be applied to the Afghan population as a whole.

CLASSIC COUNTERINSURGENCY?

For the bible of counterinsurgency in Afghanistan, one need look no further than the U.S. Army Field Manual, FM 3-24. Produced in 2006 by a team under the tutelage of General David Petraeus, it purports to "merge traditional approaches to COIN with the realities of a new national arena shaped by technological advances, globalization, and the spread of extremist ideologies—some of them claiming the authority of a religious faith."[8] FM 3-24 lays out the chapter and verse of COIN: including definitions of insurgency and counterinsurgency, using intelligence in the field, designing counterinsurgency campaigns, and leadership and ethics.

But as Frank Ledwidge, author of *Losing Small Wars: British Military Failure in Iraq and Afghanistan* (2011), points out, it is COIN itself that has attained the status of a quasi-religious faith:

> Whilst its believers would state that it is rather in the nature of an applied science perhaps a more appropriate analogy might be a somewhat cultish religion. One "does" COIN in much the same way as one practices Catholicism. Doctrine must be followed, and fiercely defended if attacked. When believers are shown evidence that COIN is all too often only so much snake oil, the response is that COIN is not being "done." . . . The idea that COIN itself is a bankrupt idea that had run its course by the 1960s is simply not acceptable. Yet it is becoming rather clear that this is in fact the case.[9]

Ledwidge's sweeping denunciation of COIN will raise hackles, but it does help provide an explanation for why things have gone so disastrously wrong in Afghanistan. The application of outmoded but revered concepts helped those in charge to avoid confronting the actual situation they were facing.

If Ledwidge is right, then the proponents of counterinsurgency in Afghanistan will need all of their faith to keep believing in the face of the perpetually gloomy picture that has been emerging over the past few years. A study sponsored by the RAND Corporation in 2011 gave counterinsurgency in Afghanistan a very low chance of success. The study parameters asked eleven experts for a "worst-case" scenario emerging from a set of "Good and Bad COIN Factors and Practices," in which "good" refers to conditions and actions that have proven successful and "bad" refers to those that have led to failure.

After a complex mathematical process of toting up the negatives and positives, Afghanistan was rated +3.5—too low to be optimistic, but not a complete failure: "This score is lower than [Croatia] the lowest-scoring COIN win in the past 30 years [which was +5], but it is higher than [Nicaragua] the highest-scoring loss [which was 0]. This highlighted that certain factors are absent whose presence would likely increase the prospects for success."[10]

Even this sober and supposedly objective assessment is too rosy. For example, the experts gave COIN a full point for "earnest IO (Information Operations), PSYOP/strategic communications effort." But "earnest" does not necessarily mean "effective." The experts also gave a point for "intelligence adequate to support kill/capture or engagements on COIN force's terms." But as countless examples have shown, intelligence has all too often been fatally flawed in Afghanistan, leading to botched raids, with the wrong people killed or captured.[11] The study lacks internal consistency as well: while gaining points for avoiding "excessive collateral damage" and "disproportionate use of force," which would supposedly indicate that the international military was not wreaking havoc with the civilian population, COIN gets a rap on the knuckles for contributing "to substantial new grievances claimed by the insurgents."

Whatever metrics the panel used, it does not seem that they have spent much time talking to the supposed focus of COIN in Afghanistan: the Afghan people themselves. The relentless propaganda machine of the U.S. military does its best to paint a picture of a friendly, helpful force with the best interests of the Afghan people at heart. But a few hospitals being opened, wells dug, or a school for midwives dedicated cannot erase multiple scenes of mayhem: hundreds killed in Shindand, a tragedy in Herat Province well documented by the United Nations, the Afghan government, and journalists, but never fully acknowledged by the military; fifty people killed at a wedding in Jalalabad, including the bride; hundreds killed at a bazaar in Helmand Province in a failed attempt to kill a noted Taliban leader who was not even in the area at the time.

This is war, and collateral damage is inevitable. But the anger and frustration at these mistakes are also inevitable and will undercut most attempts to win over the population. After almost every civilian casualty inflicted by foreign forces, the U.S. military attempts to lay the blame on the Taliban for "endangering non-combatants by hiding behind women and children." This explanation is not convincing to many Afghans. While numerous studies have shown that the bulk of civilian casualties are caused by the insurgents, the bulk of the anger is still directed at the international troops.

THEORY VERSUS REALITY

In his 2009 book *The Accidental Guerrilla*, David Kilcullen puts forth a fairly unconventional theory of the Afghan insurgency. The Taliban, or however we choose to name the variety of groups who are fighting the international forces in Afghanistan, are not primarily motivated by ideology, he argued. Instead, they are fighting us because we are there. We have, in effect, brought the war to them, making them "accidental" fighters. Though his thesis implied that the only permanent way to end the fight would be to withdraw, Kilcullen nonetheless argued that there was hope for COIN by convincing the local population that they are better off with the international forces protecting them than they are when left alone with the insurgents.

In *Counterinsurgency* (2010), Kilcullen appears to turn back the clock in his thinking, returning to the fold of classic theorists in the field. This retrograde sequel spins an elaborate scheme of theory and practice that Kilcullen hopes will serve as a complement to the 2006 Counterinsurgency Field Manual, which, he explains, is "less about how a given military force actually behaves than how it wants to behave." [12] In a conscious homage to "Twenty-Seven Articles" (1917), T.E. Lawrence's ruminations on dealing with rebel forces during the Arab Revolt against the Ottoman Turks,[13] Kilcullen then outlines his "Twenty-Eight Articles," whose application should bring victory in counterinsurgency.

Kilcullen begins with a definition of counterinsurgency that puts the population squarely at the center: "What is counterinsurgency?" he asks. "This is a competition with the insurgent for the right and the ability to win the hearts, minds and acquiescence of the population."[14] Kilcullen is a persuasive writer and a cogent thinker. But while his "Twenty-Eight Articles" may provide an elegant theory, they are hopelessly divorced from Afghan reality.

Kilcullen rightly draws attention to the power of popular perception: "In this battlefield," he writes, "popular perceptions and rumor are more influential than the facts and more powerful than a hundred tanks."[15] But if that is the case, then much more effort must be directed at determining what popular perceptions actually are.

When I first went to Helmand Province, in 2006, just as the insurgency was heating up, it took me about a month of intense conversations with locals to ascertain that the British, whose troops were running operations in the area, were universally distrusted and despised. This had less to do with the rather dismal performance of the British troops than with historical resentments. During the second of their three ill-fated forays into Afghanistan, the British suffered a painful defeat at the hands of Afghans in Maiwand, an area between Helmand and Kandahar. Maiwand may not figure prominently in the British war pantheon alongside Waterloo or Trafalgar, but every child in Helmand can recite the stirring words of a national epic about the Battle of Maiwand (1880), where the valiant female warrior, Malalai, rode into the fray, using her headscarf as a standard, and exhorting all the men of Afghanistan to lay down their lives or forever bow their heads in disgrace: "Young love! If you do not fall in the battle of Maiwand, by God, someone is saving you as a symbol of shame!"

With this as the historical backdrop, the choice of sending the British to Helmand could hardly have been more ill-fated. Even though Helmand was a hotbed of narcotics trafficking and brutality, it was still relatively peaceful before the British came. Within months of the British takeover, it was in the grip of a full-blown insurgency. The British committed a series of missteps: the forced removal of a thuggish but effective governor, who had kept the local strongmen in check through a complex web of threats and enticement; a counternarcotics campaign that saw output double, while resentment against the foreigners increased exponentially; and the classic mistake of any counterinsurgency: promising too much and delivering too little.

But rather than simply deride the British for incompetence, the local population in Helmand saw the deteriorating situation as a function of British malfeasance. "The Ingrezi [a derogatory term for the British] are just trying to get revenge for the Battle of Maiwand," was the common mantra. When I tried to tell this to the political officers at the local military base, known euphemistically as the Provincial Reconstruction Team (PRT), they dismissed it out of hand. Only one, a political adviser, decided to check it out. He was more than surprised. "I had no idea how much they hated us," he said. "It turned my thinking on Helmand around 180 degrees."

With the British already behind in the "hearts and minds" campaign, there was little hope of obtaining accurate and objective intelligence from the local population. Instead, time after time, the ISAF or NATO troops became pawns in intertribal rivalries, with one group "informing" on another to get the well-equipped foreign soldiers to deal with their opponents.

This problem was not limited to Helmand. As Elizabeth Rubin brilliantly outlined in her reporting for the *New York Times* from Kunar Province, the NATO forces were at times responsible for creating an insurgency where none had previously existed, by playing the pawn in an all-Afghan chess match. In the Korengal Valley, which became one of the most violent theaters of the war in 2007–10, the Americans teamed up early on with a group of wealthy timber lords who led them to believe that a local rival, Haji Matin, was allied with the Taliban. At the time, this was not the case. An air strike on Haji Matin's compound killed many members of his family, but Haji Matin survived, joining with a local Arab leader to mount a campaign of revenge against the Americans.[16] Within months, the insurgency was in full swing. This scenario has been repeated over and over in Afghanistan, needlessly multiplying areas of resistance.

All successful counterinsurgencies, Kilcullen argues, "have

been willing and able to kill the enemy, often with great ruthlessness. But all have clearly distinguished that enemy from the population in which it hides, have applied violence as precisely and as carefully as possible, have acted scrupulously within the law, and have emphasized measures to protect and win over the population."[17] Distinguishing the enemy from the surrounding noncombatant population is key, Kilcullen emphasizes, but in a country like Afghanistan it is almost impossible.

As the tragic death of the BBC reporter Ahmed Omed Khpulwak in July 2011 demonstrated, in a crisis situation, any Afghan can be perceived as a threat. Khpulwak was in the governor's compound in Tirin Kot, the capital of Uruzgan, when it came under Taliban attack. He hid in a bathroom but was shot and killed by Mohammad Mohaqeq, a NATO soldier, in the aftermath. NATO maintains that the soldier was justified in shooting, thinking that Khpulwak was about to fire a weapon or detonate an explosive vest. But the reporter was unarmed and, his relatives insist, clearly showing his journalist's ID. There are many more examples of how the failure to distinguish between the insurgents and the population as a whole has affected the counterinsurgency in Afghanistan.

As the Afghanistan Analysts Network (AAN) so clearly demonstrated in its May 2011 report on targeted assassinations, intelligence is all too often misguided. Worse still, the military coalition typically refuses to admit wrongdoing, even when it is presented with proof that it has killed the wrong person. According to the AAN, an attack on an election convoy in September 2010 killed ten people and injured seven. ISAF claimed that it had killed the Taliban's deputy shadow governor of Takhar, who was also a senior member of the Islamic Movement of Uzbekistan. ISAF claimed success. But according to the report, as well as the testimony of many who were involved in the research, the man they insisted they were targeting and had killed was nowhere near the convoy. Instead, the dead were all parliamentary election workers out on the campaign trail.[18] This mistake, still unacknowledged by ISAF, contributed to the renewed legacy of anger and bitterness toward the presence of foreign military forces in Afghanistan.

Another of Kilcullen's tenets that supposedly gives the advantage to the counterinsurgents is the fact that insurgents must rely on local populations for support. This gives the counterinsurgency a simple way to limit the insurgents' effectiveness: "We can asphyxiate the network by cutting the insurgents off from the people," he asserts. "We can drive the insurgents away from the population, and then introduce local security forces, protective measures, governance reforms, and economic and political development, all designed to break the connection between the insurgents and the population."[19]

But how is this possible when the population and the insurgents are so closely intertwined, both geographically and by ties of family and friendship? "Of course I know Taliban," laughed a young reporter in Helmand Province. "I have friends, I have relatives. My uncle rides with the Taliban at night. During the day he is a shopkeeper." Many of Kilcullen's formulas for victory bear little relation to this reality. In addition to the near impossibility of separating the insurgency from the population, the Afghan security forces that are supposed to come in to protect the population are in some cases worse than the insurgents. A journalist who has covered Afghanistan from 2004 to 2010, particularly in the volatile south, had this to say: "I have been to dozens of Shura Councils after clearing operations. At every single one, the local elders come up to the international forces, gesture to the local police, and say, 'Please do not leave us alone with these guys.'"

Good governance has also proved elusive. As Karl Eikenberry, the ambassador at the time, outlined in a "secret" cable to Washington in November 2009 that was widely leaked to the press, the major impediment to victory in Afghanistan was the absence of conditions on the ground that would make COIN possible. Eikenberry argued against President Barack Obama's troop surge, explaining that it was too much money and effort for too little return. President Karzai, he wrote, "is not an adequate strategic partner," and the Afghan security forces will not be able to shoulder a fair share of the burden in the near future. Civil society, he argued, is also lacking, and internationals deployed for development assistance are largely unable to do their jobs, due to inadequate security. Most important, argued Eikenberry, "More troops won't end the insurgency as long as Pakistan sanctuaries remain." [20]

The White House ignored Eikenberry's critique of the new COIN strategy. The leaking of his cable, with its damning characterization of the Afghan president, crippled the ambassador's relationship with Karzai and cast a pall over the remainder of his tenure. Eikenberry left Afghanistan in July 2011, but much of his assessment has proved correct.

"LEGITIMACY IS THE GOAL"

If, as the Counterinsurgency Manual clearly states, "The primary objective of any COIN operation is to foster development of effective governance by a legitimate government," [21] then the counterinsurgency effort in Afghanistan must be deemed a failure. The Afghan government arguably had less legitimacy than it did more than a decade earlier, when the interim administration was installed by the international conference in Bonn. Afghans are disgusted by the corruption and incompetence of their leaders and have made this clear in survey after survey. [22]

Grievances within the government also increased in this period. Ministers speaking privately had harsh words for their president. Even First Vice President Marshal Mohammad Qasim Fahim, speaking on September 9, 2011, at a ceremony marking the tenth anniversary of the death of the legendary commander Ahmad Shah Massoud, called for a "national leader" to bring the country out of crisis. Those present saw this as a direct slap in the face to the president, Hamid Karzai, who should, in fact, be filling that role.

Over the past decade, corruption has reached unprecedented heights, epitomized by the Kabul Bank scandal that leached nearly $1 billion from the Afghan economy into the pockets of the politically well connected. Two deeply flawed elections—the one that returned Karzai to office in 2009, and the chaos of the parliamentary poll in 2010—have undermined what little faith the population still had in democracy as a concept.

The economic and development aid that is supposed to convince the local population that they are better off with the international forces has become something of a bitter joke. Numerous reports, including one in August 2011 by the Commission on Wartime Contracting, indicate that much of the aid money has been mismanaged or wasted, or has ended up in the hands of the Taliban.[23] Money has fueled government corruption, encouraged a short-term grant mentality, and fostered almost no sustainable growth.

Kilcullen is, of course, correct in saying that no counterinsurgency can work without a detailed knowledge of the country, without a deep and accurate assessment of the mission, and without precise intelligence that provides insight into "enemy" operations. But almost none of this was done before the invasion of Afghanistan, and very little since.

A COUNTERINSURGENCY IN SEARCH OF A MISSION

A central problem that has plagued the war in Afghanistan from the beginning has been a failure to define what the actual mission was, what success would look like, and how the international intervention could be brought successfully to an end. This made it all but impossible to measure progress.

In the first days after the horrific attacks of 9/11, America and the world stood among the ruins of their old world order. For the United States, the sense of superpower invulnerability had been shattered, perhaps irrevocably. Something had to be done; someone had to be punished. The United States demanded retribution, and few in the world were prepared to deny the country its revenge.

On October 7, 2001, less than a month after 9/11, the United States launched Operation Enduring Freedom, in the beginning a small effort to dislodge al Qaeda from the country. A few hundred Special Forces and a few dozen air strikes were initially successful: al Qaeda was effectively chased out of Afghanistan within a few weeks, although the central prize, Osama bin Laden, slipped through a flimsy U.S. cordon, presumably to Pakistan.

But American ire was not yet satisfied: Operation Enduring

Freedom evolved into the Global War on Terror, with a concentrated focus on Afghanistan and, later, on Iraq. GWOT, as it was known, never really made sense for Afghanistan. In *An Enemy We Created: The Myth of the Taliban/al Qaeda Merger in Afghanistan, 1970–2010*, Alex Strick van Linschoten and Felix Kuehn (popularly known as Strick and Kuehn) insist that the Taliban had no foreknowledge of, or complicity in, the 9/11 attacks. Their role was in providing sanctuary for Osama bin Laden, a man who had largely funded the war against the Soviets in the 1990s. They owed him a debt of gratitude, and he was further protected by the Pashtun laws of hospitality.[24]

Still, they might have been willing to give him up, provided that the international community had been willing to work with the Taliban regime to make this possible. Mullah Wakil Ahmed Mutta-wakil, then the Taliban's Foreign Minister, an educated and urbane man, is quite open about the challenges. "We had no way to talk to the Americans," he said. "They had never recognized the Taliban regime. We were looking for solutions—perhaps a third country—but we were given an ultimatum to hand over Osama." According to Muttawakil, the Taliban would have been more than willing to furnish guarantees that al Qaeda would not be allowed back into Afghanistan. "We want them here even less than you do," he said during an interview at his home in Kabul in March 2009.

But the Bush administration was in no mood for compromise. It needed a reason to strike, and Afghanistan's delay in handing over bin Laden provided one. Operation Enduring Freedom had begun. Most experts agree that al Qaeda had been effectively pushed out of Afghanistan by November 2001. Estimates from intelligence of-ficials, including Leon Panetta, at that time the Director of Central Intelligence, have placed the number of operatives left in the coun-try at no more than one hundred.[25]

Yet, close to a decade later, Kilcullen argued that we were battling a global Jihadist insurgency, philosophy-driven and implacably hos-tile to the West. "[T]he 'War on Terrorism' is a defensive war against a worldwide Islamist jihad," he writes in *Counterinsurgency*.[26] Those who know Afghanistan well are equally adamant that this is not the case. The insurgency here is driven by local grievances, they say. There is no real top-down command structure, and no one is quite sure how powerful Mullah Omar and his Quetta Shura really are.

In fact, several experts argued that peace talks could not really progress because the Taliban are afraid to show their weakness. "If we negotiated a cease-fire with the Quetta Shura, would they be able to enforce it?" asked one military historian who specializes in Afghanistan. He asked that his name not be used since he is not authorized to speak on the record. "I am afraid they could not do it."

If the Taliban were really not in control of the disparate fighting groups, then very little about the U.S. strategy made sense. There was, however, a determination to forge on to "victory." On September 9, 2011, speaking at a Massoud anniversary ceremony, Ryan Crocker, the U.S. Ambassador to Afghanistan, called for "more pain" to force the Taliban to the negotiating table.[27] So the war continued, with a vaguely understood mission against a poorly defined enemy, and absolutely no idea of what an acceptable end state might be.

NIGHT RAIDS: PART OF A
POPULATION-CENTRIC APPROACH?

Instead of developing a strategy to deal with the actual situation on the ground, the international community, with the United States at its head, made a bad situation even worse by pursuing a tactic of counterterrorism, with its night raids and body-count metrics, and calling it counterinsurgency.

"They are waging counterinsurgency only with a gun; it cannot be expected to work," said an official in the Afghan Foreign Ministry in November 2011. Night raids, part of the kill/capture program in which Special Operations forces parachute into a village, knock down doors, search homes, and detain or sometimes kill the inhabitants, became a main bone of contention between the Afghan government and the international coalition. "The president has called for a stop to night raids," continued the Foreign Ministry official.

"They must end. Afghanistan will never negotiate away its sovereignty." Indeed, Karzai had been thundering against night raids for years; in May 2011 he vaguely threatened the foreign troops with revenge attacks if the raids and air strikes continued: "If [NATO] does not stop air strikes on Afghan homes, their presence in Afghanistan will be considered that of an occupying force," he said at a news conference on May 31. "History has shown how Afghans deal with occupiers."[28]

But Karzai's impotent tirades did little to stop the violence. Instead, night raids were hailed as an essential tool in the fight against the insurgency. This perhaps encapsulates the problem: in the drive to stamp out the enemy, NATO employed a tactic that, more than any other single issue, turned the population against them.

Gareth Porter, an investigative journalist for Inter Press Service (IPS), published a report in June 2011, demonstrating the dangers of this approach. Using the military's own data, Porter showed that in a ninety-day period in 2010, more than 80 percent of those detained in such raids were later released because they were found to have been innocent civilians.[29] The military did not bother to investigate the affiliations of the people they actually killed. Most COIN experts agreed that night raids are counterproductive, although some, like Lieutenant Colonel John Nagl (Ret.), who advises the Pentagon, praised their efficacy and precision. In 2011, he told PBS's *Frontline*:

> We're getting so good at various electronic means of identifying, tracking, locating members of the insurgency that we're able to employ this extraordinary machine, an almost industrial-scale counterterrorism killing machine that has been able to pick out and take off the battlefield not just the top level al Qaeda–level insurgents, but also increasingly is being used to target mid-level insurgents.

Frontline's report showed that night raids had actually misidentified and wrongly targeted several supposed miscreants, a fact that neither Nagl nor his boss, General David Petraeus, was willing to acknowledge.[30] Even Kilcullen argued that such tactics are self-defeating:

> Enemy focused strategy, which seeks to attack the guerrilla forces directly, risks dissipating effort. . . . Counterinsurgents who adopt this approach risk chasing their tails and so exhausting themselves, while doing enormous damage to the noncombatant civilian population, alienating the people and thus further strengthening their support for the insurgency. This, indeed, is precisely the trap we fell into . . . in Afghanistan.[31]

Still, the raids continued.

WHAT DOES COIN MEAN TO THE TROOPS?

COIN, of course, cannot work if the troops who are supposed to be carrying it out are not convinced that it will work. Foreign soldiers are not apt to be successful at persuading the population that they are there to protect them when, in fact, the troops see the local population as the enemy. One example is the behavior of U.S. forces on the road, which, Kilcullen points out, is a good indicator of their attitude toward the local population.[32]

I have seen firsthand how the U.S. military interacts with Afghans on the road, and it was a sobering experience. In early 2005, soon after my arrival in Afghanistan, I was on my way to Jalalabad in a Toyota TownAce van with a group of Afghans. I was the only foreigner and the only female. In those halcyon days, there was no insurgency to speak of. The worst part of a road trip was the lack of restrooms.

On the way out of Kabul we were stuck behind an American convoy. Our driver was the calmest of men. He did not seek to pass the convoy. He did not get too close to the heavily armored vehicles. So one wonders what motivated the soldier who was riding shotgun to wave his M16 at us, making a threatening gesture with his arm, and mouthing "Fuck you" at our car. I was furious. In anger, I stood up through the sunroof, took off my headscarf to expose my blond hair, and made an equally rude gesture right back at the soldier. He had the grace to look embarrassed. No one at that time wanted fellow Americans to see them mistreating the population.

I escaped unharmed. But incidents of road rage often end badly for the Afghan side. It is called, euphemistically, "escalation of force" and involves a car or other vehicle that does not or cannot heed signs to stop. In many cases, the car turns out to have civilians in it—a husband speeding to take his wife to the hospital in time to give birth; a family on the way home from a picnic; a group of young men out for a joy ride. Or it could be a passenger bus full of civilians, as happened in Kandahar in April 2010. U.S. forces strafed the bus, killing five and injuring as many as eighteen. They insisted that the bus had failed to heed hand signals to stop.

The incident ignited protests and inflamed already fierce anti-American sentiment in the area, but the military was unapologetic. One prominent military blogger, Rajiv Srinivasan, was brutally blunt:

> Why does its matter that it was a bus full of civilians? . . . *If I felt even the slightest suspicion that this vehicle was a VBIED* [Vehicle Borne Improvised Explosive Device], *an intoxicated driver, or even a bus with no brakes, I would have firmly ordered my men, "You fire if you feel unsafe."* [Emphasis added.] . . . Lights, lasers, or nothing, if those soldiers felt threatened, they had every right to engage.

This flies in the face of the "population-centric" strategy that was supposedly then in place. But Srinivasan is not a fan of the policy:

> Maybe us platoon leaders need to assume some more risk with our own soldiers' lives in order to win this war on terror. . . . But the minute a soldier feels his life is at risk, his inclination is to turn to the leaders he trusts. *If those leaders*

turn to him and explain that his "life is being risked for Afghan civilians" . . . well . . . what would you do? Personally, I would stop trusting my leaders."[33] (Emphasis added.)

If American soldiers are not willing to put their lives at risk for Afghan civilians, then the whole "protecting the population" aspect of COIN becomes nothing more than feel-good rhetoric.

BODY-COUNT METRICS

Almost everyone in the U.S. policy establishment, from Hillary Clinton, the former secretary of state, on down, emphasized that we cannot "kill our way to victory" in Afghanistan. Yet that seems to be the main tactic in the so-called counterinsurgency. Body counts are not supposed to be the metric; in fact, in a country like Afghanistan they are egregiously deceptive.

When General McChrystal took command of ISAF in June 2009, he stopped the practice of issuing Taliban body counts. In a speech that October, at London's prestigious International Institute for Strategic Studies, he explained why: "At the end of the day we don't win by destroying the Taliban," he said. "We don't win by body count. We don't win by the number of successful military raids or attacks. We win when the people decide we win."[34] Kilcullen also pointed out that body counts are virtually worthless as a measure of progress: "At the start of a conventional engagement, if we are facing one hundred of the enemy and we kill twenty, we can assume that eighty are left. In counterinsurgency, this logic does not hold: the 20 killed may have 40 relatives who are now in a blood feud with and are obligated to take revenge on the security forces who killed the 20, so the new number of the enemy is not 80 but 120."[35]

Nevertheless, body counts are one of the main indicators of progress touted by the military. The International Joint Command (IJC), which handles press releases for NATO and ISAF, publishes numbers of Taliban killed and captured daily and constantly drags out numbers of killed and detained as a measure of progress. Mullah Abdul Salaam Zaeef, the Taliban's former ambassador to Pakistan, recalls a tragicomic incident during his interrogation in Guantánamo: "They kept telling me 'there are only thirty-five hundred of you guys, and when we kill you all, you are finished,'" he said in an interview in his Kabul home. "But by my count, the foreigners have killed some twenty thousand Taliban over the past eight years, and the Taliban are now stronger than ever."[36]

Another important but misleading metric constantly cited by the military is "area cleared." In fact, "clearing operations" are known inside the military community as "mowing the lawn"—do it once, and you have to come back in a few months to do it again. Others have likened clearing operations to squeezing a water balloon: dislodge the insurgents from one area, and they concentrate elsewhere. This is exactly what happened in Helmand. As parts of the province became more secure with the addition of tens of thousands of U.S. marines, previously safe areas of the country became increasingly unstable.

THE FUTURE OF COIN IN AFGHANISTAN

In 2011, an Afghan security specialist who had spent several years in Afghanistan concluded that COIN was no longer relevant there. "We have lost," he said, speaking on condition of anonymity. "COIN no longer matters. What matters is how we withdraw. Afghans are getting ready for the next civil war. The government is hopelessly dysfunctional, and Afghans are fed up. . . . It does not matter whether we leave in three years or twenty—this internal war will take off once we are gone."

After a decade, thousands of lives and more than $3 trillion had gone into the effort to stabilize Afghanistan. Doctrines were adopted and abandoned; strategies were designed and revised. COIN was to provide the silver bullet; instead, it seemed only to prolong and deepen the agony. Perhaps, as many experts advise, the fault lies with an incorrect application of COIN. Perhaps we gave too little, too late. Or perhaps, as Frank Ledwidge tells us, COIN itself is no more than smoke and mirrors, a rhetorical Band-Aid placed on a gaping wound.

Could the Afghanistan debacle lead to an overall degradation of COIN as a theory? It may be too soon to make such a sweeping statement. But it is not too soon to state, categorically, that in this war, COIN has failed.

NOTES

Introduction *by Hannah Gurman*

1. For examples of this or related invocations, see "The Age of Counterinsurgency," *World Politics Review*, March 31, 2009, www.worldpolitics review.com/features/11/the-age-of-counterinsurgency; David Ucko, *The New Counterinsurgency Era: Transforming the U.S. Military for Modern Wars* (Washington, DC: Georgetown University Press, 2009).

2. For a report of the conference, go to: usacac.army.mil/cac2/coin/ repository/coin_symposium_may_2010/final_products/COIN_Sympo sium_2010_Final_Report.pdf.

3. U.S. Army/Marine Corps, "Counterinsurgency," FM 3-24, December 2006, www.fas.org/irp/doddir/army/fm3-24.pdf; *The U.S. Army/ Marine Corps Counterinsurgency Field Manual* (Chicago: University of Chicago Press, 2007).

4. Hannah Gurman, "The Iraq Withdrawal: An Orwellian Success," *Salon*, August 15, 2010, www.salon.com/news/feature/2010/08/15/iraq_with drawal_success.

5. Thomas Ricks, "The COINdinistas," *Foreign Policy*, December 2009, www.foreignpolicy.com/articles/2009/11/30/the_coindinistas.

6. "ISAF Commander's Counterinsurgency Guidance," International Security Assistance Force, North Atlantic Treaty Organization, August 26, 2009, www.conflictmonitors.org/countries/afghanistan/daily-briefing /archives/briefing-details/!k/afghanistan-conflict-monitor/2009/08/28/ isaf-commanders-counterinsurgency-guidance.

7. I learned of the conference through the website of the U.S. Army Counterinsurgency Center, which I had been perusing as part of my research related to a course I teach at NYU on the Vietnam War. The website, which was a source for both the U.S. military establishment and the American public, is itself a reflection of counterinsurgency's emphasis on marketing.

8. In April 2010, Afghan officials reported that the Taliban in Marjah had "recovered momentum." Six months later, residents of the town reported that the area was "more insecure than ever," and the Associated Press called it a "full-blown insurgency." Many real Taliban simply relocated from rural

Kandahar to Kandahar City, where the levels of violence actually increased in the wake of the campaign and the deputy governor was assassinated in February 2011. Others left for their seasonal safe havens across the border in Pakistan. Richard A. Oppel Jr., "Violence Helps Taliban Undo Afghan Gains," *New York Times*, April 3, 2010; Todd Pitman, "Marjah Insurgency Full-Blown," Associated Press, October 8, 2010; Gareth Porter, "Ninety Percent of Petraeus's Captured 'Taliban' Were Civilians," Inter Press Service, June 12, 2011, www.ipsnews.net/news.asp?idnews=56038.

9. "ARM Annual Report Civilian Casualties of War: January–December 2010," Afghanistan Rights Monitor, February 2011.

10. "Upcoming Kandahar Offensive Stirs Fear in Residents," *CNN Online*, May 24, 2010, afghanistan.blogs.cnn.com/2010/05/24/upcoming-kandahar-offensive-stirs-fears-in-residents; Afghanistan Human Rights Commission, "63 Civilians Killed in Afghanistan in the Last Two Weeks," press release, February 23, 2010, www.aihrc.org.af/English/Eng_pages/Press_releases_eng/2010/Pre_23_Feb_2010.pdf; Gareth Porter, "The Non-Existent City the Military Said We Conquered in Afghanistan," *AlterNet*, March 9, 2010, www.alternet.org/story/145971/marjah%3A_the_non-existent_city_the_military_said_we_conquered_in_afghanistan?page=1; Matthew Hoh, "On Anniversary of Marjah Push, Escalation Strategy Still Failing," *Daily Kos*, February 13, 2011, www.dailykos.com/story/2011/02/13/943893/-On-Anniversary-of-Marjah-Push,-Escalation-Strategy-Still-Failing.

11. Joshua Foust, "The Unforgivable Horror of Village Razing," *Registan.net*, January 13, 2011, www.registan.net/index.php/2011/01/13/the-unforgivable-horror-of-village-razing/.

12. Abubakar Siddique and Mohammad Sadiq Rishtinai, "Picking Up the Pieces Following Kandahar Offensive," Radio Free Europe, February 4, 2011, www.rferl.org/content/picking_up_the_pieces_following_kandahar_offensive/2298031.html; Will Keola Thomas, "Is This What Population-Centric Counterinsurgency Looks Like?" *Afghanistan Study Group*, March 10, 2011, www.afghanistanstudygroup.org/2011/03/10/is-this-what-population-centric-counterinsurgency-looks-like.

13. Rajiv Chandrasekaran, "U.S. Sending Tanks to Hit Harder at Taliban," *Washington Post*, November 19, 2010.

14. "Despite Gains, Night Raids Split U.S. and Karzai," *New York Times*, November 15, 2010; "NATO Gunships Kill 9 Afghan Children; 3rd Reported Attack on Afghan Civilians in 2 Weeks," *Democracy Now!*, www.democracynow.org/2011/3/3/us_apologizes_to_afghan_people_for.

15. "Kill/Capture," *Frontline*, PBS, May 10, 2011.

16. Gareth Porter, "New Light Shed on US's Night Raids," *Asia Times*

Online, September 17, 2010, atimes.com/atimes/South_Asia/LI17Df03 .html.

17. "Separating the Taliban from Al-Qaeda: The Core of Success in Afghanistan," NYU Center on International Cooperation, February 1, 2011.

18. Missy Ryan, "Afghans Turn from West Despite Military Gains: Study," Reuters, May 16, 2011; Tom A. Peter, "In Deadly Kandahar, Skepticism Over Gains Cited in Afghan War Review," *Christian Science Monitor*, December 16, 2010.

19. Peter, "In Deadly Kandahar"; "Separating the Taliban from Al-Qaeda"; Joshua Partlow and Habib Zahori, "Afghan Officials Allege that 65 Civilians Were Killed in U.S. Military Operation," *Washington Post*, February 20, 2011; Ernesto Londoño, "Petraeus Apologized for NATO Strike That Reportedly Killed Nine Afghan Children," *Washington Post*, March 3, 2011.

20. Ray Rivera, "Karzai Gives 'Last' Warning to NATO on Airstrikes," *New York Times*, May 31, 2011.

21. Noah Schachtman, "No Let Up for Afghan Air War, Despite Karzai's Threat," *Wired*, June 8, 2011, www.wired.com/dangerroom/2011/06/ no-let-up-for-afghan-air-war-despite-karzais-threat.

22. According to a UN report released in August 2012, 83 civilians were killed by air strikes between January and June 2012, eighteen of them during an attack on insurgents in Logar Province in June. The UN reported that insurgent-caused civilian casualties decreased in this period for the first time in five years, down by 22 percent from the previous year, although the head of the UN Assistance Mission in Afghanistan called this trend "hollow," noting that casualties were increasing again in the early summer months. "UN: Overall Afghan Civilian Deaths Fall, But Targeted Killings Surge," Associated Press, August 8, 2012.

23. "What Is the Secretive U.S. 'Kill/Capture' Campaign?" *Frontline*, PBS, June 17, 2011, pbs.org/wgbh/pages/frontline/afghanistan-pakistan/ kill-capture/what-is-the-secretive-us-killca/#ixzz1ShEHdX5J.

24. Julian Borger, "Afghanistan War Tactics are Profoundly Wrong, Says Former Ambassador," *The Guardian*, May 25, 2011; Mansoor, quoted in Spencer Ackerman, "This Is the End of Counterinsurgency in Afghanistan," *Wired*, June 28, 2011.

25. "Hard Choices: Responsible Defense Spending in an Age of Austerity," Center for a New American Security, October 2011; Spencer Ackerman, "Obama's Favorite Think Tank: Cut the Army, Forget Counterinsurgency," *Wired*, October 4, 2011, www.wired.com/dangerroom/2011/10/cnas-army -cuts/; Thomas Ruttig, "Destruction Is Rebuilding, or: Fare Thee Well, Population-Centric COIN," Afghanistan Analysts Network, March 18, 2011, aan-afghanistan.com/index.asp?id=1560; Thomas Ruttig, "A Back

Somersault in the US Strategy: Lower Aims, Higher Risks," Afghanistan Analysts Network, October 16, 2010, aan-afghanistan.com/index.asp?id=1231.

26. David Howell Petraeus, "The American Military and the Lessons of Vietnam" (PhD diss., Princeton University, 1987), via Proquest.

27. In addition to the 2006 field manual, the canon of counterinsurgency history included new and recent popular books on the history of counterinsurgency, such as John Nagl's *Learning to Eat Soup with a Knife: Counterinsurgency Lessons from Malaya and Vietnam* (New York: Praeger, 2002) and David Kilcullen's *The Accidental Guerrilla: Fighting Small Wars in the Midst of a Big One* (New York: Oxford University Press, 2009). Old "classics" of counterinsurgency were also revived, including, for example, the colonial French military officer David Galula's *Counterinsurgency Warfare: Theory and Practice*, first printed in 1961 and reprinted in 2006.

28. "Remarks on Signing the Afghanistan Day Proclamation," March 10, 1982, American Presidency Project, presidency.ucsb.edu/ws/index.php?pid =42248&st=&st1=#axzz1a6qJxKa1.

29. U.S. Army/Marine Corps, "Counterinsurgency," 5-20.

30. Lieutenant Colonel James Gant made a brief splash within the circles of military intelligentsia through his advocacy of tribal engagement. He published *One Tribe at a Time* as an e-book in October 2009, garnering a high-level audience and praise from General Petraeus. However, attempts to implement tribal engagement in Afghanistan have revealed a complex web of long-standing local rivalries that are often exacerbated by foreign intervention. See Hannah Gurman, "Tribal Engagement and the Heavy History of Counterinsurgency Light," *Small Wars Journal*, June 6, 2010, smallwars journal.com/blog/journal/docs-temp/452-gurman.pdf.

31. Nagl's *Learning to Eat Soup with a Knife* is the most prominent example of references to Malaya in COIN. The Algerian War entered the official COIN discourse in 2003, when experts on guerrilla warfare in the Defense Department hosted a screening of Gillo Pontecorvo's 1965 film *Battle of Algiers*.

32. Mohamed Amin and Malcolm Caldwell, eds., *Malaya: The Making of a Neocolony* (London: Spokesman Books, 1977); Jomo Kwame Sundaram, *A Question of Class: Capital, the State, and Uneven Development in Malaya*, (New York: Oxford University Press, 1986); David Prochaska, *Making Algeria French: Colonialism in Bône, 1870–1920* (New York: Cambridge University Press, 1990); Ngô Vĩnh Long, *Before the Revolution: The Vietnamese Peasants Under the French* (New York: Columbia University Press, 1991).

33. Lippmann, quoted in Ronald Steel, *Walter Lippmann and the American Century* (Boston: Little, Brown, 1980), 237.

34. Kilcullen, *Accidental Guerrilla*.

35. "Terror Watch List Counter: A Million Plus," ACLU, www.aclu.org/technology-and-liberty/terror-watch-list-counter-million-plus; Center for Human Rights and Global Justice, *Targeted and Entrapped: Manufacturing the "Homegrown Threat" in the United States* (New York: NYU School of Law, 2011); "CIA Helping NYPD Spy on Muslim Communities," Associated Press, August 24, 2011.

36. Paul Lewis, "Surveillance Cameras Spring Up in Muslim Areas—The Targets? Terrorists," *The Guardian*, June 4, 2010; "German Minister Slammed Over Proposed Security Partnership with Muslims," *Der Spiegel*, March 30, 2011; "Preventing Violent Extremism: Winning Hearts and Minds," Department for Communities and Local Governments: London, April 2007; "Muslims in Europe: Promoting Integration and Countering Extremism," CRS Report for Congress, Washington, DC, September 7, 2011.

1. Malaya *by Karl Hack*

1. Fong Chong Pik, *Fong Chong Pik: The Memoirs of a Malayan Communist Revolutionary* (Petaling Jaya: SIRD, 2008), 9.

2. For "loyalists" in Kenya, see Daniel Branch, *Defeating Mau Mau, Creating Kenya: Counterinsurgency, Civil War, and Decolonization* (Cambridge: Cambridge University Press, 2009).

3. See Peter Rimmer and Lisa Allen, eds., *The Underside of Malayan History: Pullers, Prostitutes, Plantation Workers* (Singapore: Singapore University Press, 1990); and J.F Warren's works, including *Ah Ku and Karayuki-san: Prostitution in Singapore, 1870–1940* (Singapore: National University of Singapore Press, 2003).

4. Karl Hack, "Iron Claws on Malaya: The Historiography of the Malayan Emergency," *Journal of Southeast Asian Studies* 30, no. 1 (1999): 99–125; and Karl Hack, "The Malayan Emergency as Counter-Insurgency Paradigm," *Journal of Strategic Studies* 32, no. 3 (2009): 383–414.

5. Richard Stubbs, *Hearts and Minds in Guerrilla Warfare: The Malayan Emergency 1948–1960* (Kuala Lumpur: Oxford University Press, 1989), 249–50.

6. Geoffrey Bourne, Director of Operations (DOO), Federation of Malaya, letter to General Templer, March 15, 1956, W0216/901, National Archives, London, UK.

7. The classic in this genre is Stubbs, *Hearts and Minds in Guerrilla Warfare*.

8. The classic account is C. Northcote Parkinson, *Templer in Malaya*

(Singapore: Donald Moore, 1954). See the discussion of this and the narrative as morality tale in Hack, "Iron Claws on Malaya," 99–100, especially footnote 5; and Karl Hack and Anthony Short, "Correspondence," *Journal of Southeast Asian Studies* 31, no. 2 (2000): 390–95.

9. Hack, "The Malayan Emergency," 249–50.

10. "Report of an Address to the Legislative Council, 18 November 1948," H.S. Lee Papers, Folio 55, Institute of Southeast Asian Studies, Singapore.

11. Huw Bennett, "A Very Salutary Effect: The Counter-Terror Strategy in the Early Malayan Emergency, June 1948 to December 1949," *Journal of Strategic Studies* 32, no. 3 (June 2009): 415–44; and Anthony Short, *In Pursuit of the Mountain Rats: The Communist Insurrection in Malaya* (Singapore: Cultured Lotus, 2000), 160–69.

12. Ian Ward and Norma Miraflor, *Slaughter and Deception at Batang Kali* (Singapore: Media Masters, 2008).

13. Short, *In Pursuit of the Mountain Rats*, 160–69.

14. By March 1953, 24,036 Chinese detainees and dependents had been deported, along with 1,893 Indians and Ceylonese. "Detention and Deportation in the Emergency," paper for the Legislative Council, March 9, 1953, Co1022/132, No. 24 of 1953, National Archives, London, UK.

15. William Williams, interview with Adrian Wood, in *Ruling Passions: Race, Sex and Empire*, BBC, tape recording, v68–9, British Empire and Commonwealth Museum Archives, Bristol, UK.

16. *Freedom News* no. 1, January 15, 1949, quoted in Kumar Ramakrishna, *Freedom News: The Untold Story of the Communist Underground* (Singapore: Rajaratnam School of International Studies, 2008), 27–30.

17. *Freedom News*, no. 26, June 15, 1952, quoted in ibid., 61–70.

18. Richard Stubbs, "Counter-Insurgency and the Economic Factor: The Impact of the Korean War Boom on the Malayan Emergency," Institute of Southeast Asian Studies (Singapore) Occasional Paper 19, 1974, 39–40, shows that real wages peaked in 1951. Stubbs takes 1947, not 1939, as 100, thus increasing the impression of how good wages were, producing index figures of 203 for the peak in 1951 and 159 in 1953, for example.

19. DOO Lt. Gen. R.H. Bowen, "Review of the Emergency in Malaya, June 1948 to August 1957," September 12, 1957, 4, 6, Air20/10377, National Archives, London, UK.

20. H.S. Lee 21.40 b, copy of Director of Operations Directive No. 17, October 12, 1951, "Protection of Concentrated Villages and Resettlement Areas," Institute of Southeast Asian Studies, Singapore.

21. The classic account is Parkinson, *Templer in Malaya*. See also Hack, "Iron Claws on Malaya," 99–100; and Hack and Short, "Correspondence," 390–95.

22. Malayan Communist Party, "October Resolutions," 1951, Co1022/187, National Archives, London, UK.

23. For coverage of communist strategy from Chin Peng's viewpoint, see C.C. Chin and Karl Hack, eds., *Dialogues with Chin Peng: New Light on the Malayan Communist Party* (Singapore: NUS Publishing, 2004), 19–20, 144–70.

24. Han Suyin, *My House Has Two Doors* (London: Granta, 1982), 79–80.

25. Ibid., 82.

26. "Press Release for 15th June 1951 on Food Control" under name of DOO, H.S. Lee Papers, File 7, Institute of Southeast Asian Studies, Singapore. For peak operations, see Karl Hack, "Corpses, Prisoners of War and Captured Documents: British and Communist Narratives of the Malayan Emergency," *Intelligence and National Security* 14, no. 4 (1999): 228–29; Hack, "The Malayan Emergency," 404; and Major General Lindsay, DOO Instruction Number 36, 24 June 1954, H.S. Lee Papers, File 7.44/1–19, Institute of Southeast Asian Studies, Singapore. This identified three main phases: (1) 1–2 months' preparation; (2) food and security control increases as operation begins; and (3) exploitation of increased information flow.

27. Hack, "The Malayan Emergency," 404; and Hack, "Corpses," 228–29. The figure of 67 percent (66.78 percent) is arrived at using the statistics for 1957. See DOO Lt. Gen. R.H. Bowen, "Review of the Emergency in Malaya, June 1948 to August 1957," September 12, 1957, Air20/10377, National Archives, London, UK.

28. Karl Hack, *Defence and Decolonisation in Southeast Asia: Britain, Malaya and Singapore, 1941–1968* (Richmond, UK: Curzon Press, 2001), 131–42.

29. "Progress Report on Home Guard for the Advisory Committee to the Federal War Committee," June 30, 1950, H.S. Lee Papers, File 21.70, Institute of Southeast Asian Studies, Singapore. See also Appendix D to "Agenda for the Federal War Committee Meeting of 15 Nov. 1951," H.S. Lee Papers, File 21.37a.

30. SWEC minutes on Broga and other New Villages, H.S. Lee Papers, File 79.10/2, Institute of Southeast Asian Studies, Singapore.

31. Though the MCP feared the effect enough to mock the exercise in a *Freedom News* report, see the April 15, 1954, edition, in *Freedom News*, 190–91.

32. *Straits Times*, July 11, 1952, 1, for Templer's 1952 visit. But see passim for new measures, July 1953, H.S. Lee papers, File 79.10/2, for "punishment for the uncooperative attitude of the Broga villagers."

33. *Straits Times*, June 27, 1952, 5.

34. For the police state accusation, see Victor Purcell, *Malaya, Communist or Free?* (London: Victor Gallancz, 1954). For a recent, balanced example of

the trend toward emphasizing the more abusive and coercive side of COIN, see David French, *The British Way in Counterinsurgency* (London: Oxford University Press, 2011).

35. "Memorandum Submitted to the Right Honourable O. Lyttleton by the MCA Delegation," headed by Dato Tan Cheng Lock for a meeting at King's House in Kuala Lumpur, December 2, 1951, H.S. Lee Papers, Folio 3.3/12–17, Institute of Southeast Asian Studies, Singapore.

36. Han Suyin, *And the Rain My Drink* (London: Cape, 1956), 44. Han Suyin is the pen name of Elizabeth Comber, originally Chow Kuanghu (or using today's Hanyu Pinyin form of transliteration, Zhou Guanghu). Note that these latter names are shown using the Chinese tradition of placing the family name first.

37. *Annual Report on the Malayan Union for 1947* (Kuala Lumpur: Government Printing Office, 1948), 1–3. Based on initial findings of the 1947 census, this gave a population of 4.9 million in 1957, including 2.1 million Malays, 1.88 million Chinese, 534,000 Indians, and 9,155 Europeans.

38. Han, *My House Has Two Doors*, 70.

39. *Annual Report on the Federation of Malaya* (Kuala Lumpur: Government Printing Office, 1949), 3; and Han, *My House Has Two Doors*, 70.

40. M.R. Stenson, *Repression and Revolt: The Origins of the 1948 Communist Insurrection in Malaya and Singapore* (Athens: Ohio University Center for International Studies, 1969), 9.

41. Karl Hack, "The Origins of the Asian Cold War: Malaya 1948," *Journal of Southeast Asian Studies* 40, no. 3 (2009): 471–96. For Chin Peng, see Chin and Hack, *Dialogues with Chin Peng*, 118–19.

42. Tim Harper, *The End of Empire and the Making of Malaya* (Cambridge: Cambridge University Press, 1999), 94–148.

43. *Annual Report on the Malayan Union for 1947*; "To Answer It with Struggle," translation of an editorial in the *Min Sheng Pau*, June 4, 1948, Co537/4246, National Archives, London, UK.

44. Rajeswary Ampalavanar, *The Indian Minority and Political Change in Malaya, 1945–1957* (Kuala Lumpur: Oxford University Press, 1981), 51; and Stenson, *Repression and Revolt*, 11.

45. Purcell, *Malaya: Communist or Free?*, 177–83.

46. Han, *My House Has Two Doors*, 78.

47. Harper, *End of Empire*, 135; and *Straits Times*, April 29 and 30, May 16 and 29, June 3 and 7, July 15, and August 24, 1947.

48. See *Straits Times*, June 9, 1948, 1; and the Malayan Security Service's *Political Intelligence Journal*, 11/1948, June 15, 1948, Mss. Indn. Ocn. S. 251/1948, Rhodes House, Oxford, UK.

49. "To Answer It with Struggle."

50. *Straits Times*, June 4, June 6, and June 29, 1948. For the critical detail on MCP intimidation, see also *Political Intelligence Journal*, no. 11 (June 15, 1948), Mss. Ind. Ocn. S. 251/1948, Rhodes House, Oxford, UK.

51. "Supplement 7 of the Malayan Security Service," July 15, 1948, Mss. Ind. Ocn. S. 251/1948, Rhodes House, Oxford, UK. Issued specifically for "Interrogation of Unnamed Perak MCP Area Representative," a political and "tough gun-man type" who had been arrested on June 23, 1948.

52. Ibid.

53. Ampalavanar, *Indian Minority*, 60–62, 178–80.

54. Chin Peng, *Alias Chin Peng: My Side of History* (Singapore: Media Masters, 2003), 9.

55. See Kevin Blackburn and Karl Hack, *War Memory and the Making of Modern Malaya and Singapore* (Singapore: NUS Press, 2012) for widespread Japanese anti-Chinese atrocities.

56. Tan Teng Phee, "Like a Concentration Camp, *lah*: Chinese Grassroots Experience of the Emergency and New Villages in British Colonial Malaya," *Chinese Diaspora Studies* 3 (2009): 225.

57. By January 1953, just 7.4 percent of insurgents killed since the Emergency began were non-Chinese, the majority of them Indians and Malays. See Purcell, *Malaya: Communist or Free?*, 146. By January 1, 1952, 2,778 "bandits" were killed, including 2,599 Chinese, 102 Malay, and 117 Indian and others.

58. Three of the most prominent "Malays" had Indonesian origins and claim influence from Malay anti-British revolts as well. See Abdullah C.D., *The Memoirs of Abdullah C.D. (Part One)* (Petaling Jaya: SIRD, 2009); Shamsiah Fakeh, *The Memoirs of Shamsiah Fakeh* (Petaling Jaya: SIRD, 2009); and Rashid Maidin, *The Memoirs of Rashid Maidin* (Petaling Jaya: SIRD, 2009).

59. *Annual Report on the Malayan Union for 1947*, 1–3. Based on initial findings of the 1947 census, this gave a population of 4.9 million in 1957, including 2.1 million Malays, 1.88 million Chinese, 0.534 million Indians, and 9,155 Europeans. By contrast, the 1931 census counted 47 percent Malays and Malaysians, 14 percent Indian, 37 percent Chinese, and 3 percent other. *Annual Report on the Malayan Union for 1946* (Kuala Lumpur: Government Printing Office, 1947), 1.

60. Purcell, *Malaya: Communist or Free?*, 221.

61. *Straits Times*, March 12, 1952, 4.

62. Agnes Khoo, *Life as the River Flows: Women in the Malayan Anti-Colonial Struggle* (Monmouth: Merlin Press, 2007), 186.

63. Chin and Hack, *Dialogues*, 9.

64. Han, *And the Rain My Drink*, 261 and title page.

65. Ibid., 260–61.

66. Khoo, *Life as the River Flows*, 186–87. Han's views are quoted above. Lucien Pye's classic work is *Guerrilla Communism in Malaya: Its Social and Political Meaning* (Princeton, NJ: Princeton University Press, 1956). One wonders if Han met Pye, since her novel writes witheringly of an "Australian" sent to study insurgents, and Pye did fieldwork in 1952–53, when she was in Johor.

67. "The AJUF of Malaya," Spencer Chapman Report, September 1, 1945, Garnoss-Williams Papers, vol. 3, 26–67, Imperial War Museum, London, UK.

68. Ibid., 46.

69. Ibid., 16–17.

70. Khoo, *Life as the River Flows*, 187.

71. Ibid.

72. DOO Lt. Gen. R.H. Bowen, "Review of the Emergency in Malaya, June 1948 to August 1957," September 12, 1957, Air20/10377, National Archives, London, UK. This gives detailed figures for insurgent eliminations as: killed, 6,398; captured, 1,245; SEP, 1,938, for a total of 9,581, plus wounded, 2,760. Total "CT" insurgent casualties: 12,341.

73. Tan Chin Siong, letter to Tan Cheng Lock, May 23, 1950, H.S. Lee Papers, Folio 24.30, Institute of Southeast Asian Studies, Singapore.

74. Tan Teng Phee, "The Case of Tras New Village and the Assassination of Henry Gurney During the Malayan Emergency," *BiblioAsia* 6, no. 4 (2011): 9–13.

75. Khoo, *Life as the River Flows*, 68–69. Chen lived in a wartime "red zone" and came from a family that supported the communists in and after the war. She joined the MNLA in 1954, at the age of seventeen.

76. Tan Teng Phee (Murdoch University) works on Chinese New Villagers, and Phoon Yuen Ming (NUS University Department of Chinese Studies) on gender and communists. Then there is older work: see Lim Hin Fui, "Poverty Among Chinese in Malaysia" (thesis, University of Malaya, 1990), on three Perak New Villages, and his *Poverty and Household Economic Strategies in Malaysian New Villages* (Petaling Jaya: University of Malaya Institute of Advanced Studies, 1994). Tan's works include "Like a Concentration Camp, *lah*."

77. Khoo, *Life as the River Flows*, 68–69.

78. *Report on the Food Searches at Semenyih in the Kajang District of the State of Selangor* (Kuala Lumpur: Government Press, 1956).

79. Khoo, *Life as the River Flows*, 69.

80. Liu Jun, *Deep in the Jungle*, trans. Chia Sze Soon (Singapore: Liu Jun Studio, 2010). Liu Dun is the pen name of Lai Yong Taw.

81. Khoo, *Life as the River Flows*, 71.

82. Cherries Seah and Christina Seah, "Unsung Heroes: Auxiliary Police at Simpang Tiga New Village, Perak," *The Guardian* 4 (August 2007): 13, based on an interview with Sdr Sheah Choi Yea. This entire edition of *The Guardian*, a Malaysian Chinese Association publication, is devoted to New Villages past and present and titled "Revisiting Our Roots: New Villages"; it is available at www.mca.org.my/Chinese/Guardian%20pdf/GUARDIAN%20 AUG.pdf.

83. Hack, "Iron Claws on Malaya," 122.

84. Ibid.; and Lim, *Poverty among Chinese in Malaysia*, 360.

85. Karl Hack, "Screwing Down the People: The Malayan Emergency, Ethnicity and Decolonisation," in *Imperial Policy and South East Asian Nationalism*, ed. Hans Antlov and Stein Tonnesson (Richmond, UK: Curzon, 1995), 98–109.

86. Fong Tian Yong, Ivy Tan, and Christina Seah, "Unsung Heroes: Home Guards of Bukit Tinggi New Village, Pahang," *The Guardian* 4 (August 2007): 12, based on an interview with Sdr Lu Yal You.

2. The Philippines *by Vina A. Lanzona*

1. Ann Jones, "Counterinsurgency Down for the Count in Afghanistan," *The Nation*, July 1, 2010, www.thenation.com/article/36948/counter insurgency-down-count-afghanistan.

2. Rikke Haugegaard, "Female Power: The Role of Afghan Women in Counterinsurgency," *Defence Viewpoints*, November 16, 2010, www .defenceviewpoints.co.uk/articles-and-analysis/female-power-the-role-of -afghan-women-in-counterinsurgency.

3. Ann Jones, "Counterinsurgency Down for the Count in Afghanistan."

4. For more on the U.S. counterinsurgency war in Vietnam, see Larry E. Cable, *Conflict of Myths: The Development of American Counterinsurgency Doctrine and the Vietnam War* (New York: New York University, 1986); John A. Nagl, *Learning to Eat Soup with a Knife: Counterinsurgency Lessons from Malaya and Vietnam* (London: Praeger, 2002); Donald W. Hamilton, *The Art of Insurgency: American Military Policy and the Failure of Strategy in Southeast Asia* (London: Praeger, 1998); Thomas L. Ahern Jr., *Vietnam Declassified: The CIA and Counterinsurgency* (Lexington: University Press of Kentucky, 2010).

5. See classic works on the Huk Rebelliion, including Benedict Kerkvliet, *The Huk Rebellion: A Study of Peasant Revolt in the Philippines* (Lanham: Rowman & Littlefield, 2002); Eduardo Lachica, *Huk: Philippine Agrarian Society in Revolt* (Manila: Solidaridad, 1971); Alfred Saulo, *Communism in the Philippines: An Introduction* (Manila: Ateneo de Manila University, 1969);

William Pomeroy, *The Forest* (1963; Quezon City: University of the Philippines Press, 2011); Luis Taruc, *He Who Rides a Tiger* (Santa Barbara, CA: Praeger, 1967); and more recently, Vina Lanzona, *Amazons of the Huk Rebellion* (Madison: University of Wisconsin, 2009).

6. Kerkvliet, *Huk Rebellion*, 92–94.

7. "Milestones in the History of the CCP," 1950, Secretariat, Politburo Exhibit no. O-180F, Special Collections, University of the Philippines, Dillman, Quezon City, Philippines.

8. Spencer Ackerman, "Women Prominent in Defense Movement," *Washington Independent*, July 8, 2008, washingtonindependent.com/673 /women-prominent-in-defense-movement. See also Erich Simmers, "Gender and Warmaking: The Women of Counterinsurgency," *Weaponized Culture*, July 11, 2008, weaponizedculture.wordpress.com/2008/07/11/women -of-coin.

9. Ackerman, "Women Prominent in Defense Movement."

10. See Alfred W. McCoy, *Closer Than Brothers* (New Haven, CT: Yale University Press, 2001).

11. The Huk campaign was used as a model for other counterinsurgency wars the United States and other nations like Britain waged in newly established nations in Southeast Asia after World War II. For treatments of these other COIN wars, see Michael McClintock, *Instruments of Statecraft: U.S. Guerrilla Warfare, Counterinsurgency, and Counterterrorism, 1940–1990* (New York: Pantheon Books, 1992); Ian F.W. Beckett, *Modern Insurgencies and Counterinsurgencies: Guerrillas and Their Opponents Since 1750* (London: Routledge, 2001); Nagl, *Learning to Eat Soup with a Knife;* Hamilton, *Art of Insurgency;* Gérard Chaliand, *Terrorism: From Popular Struggle to Media Spectacle* (London: Atlantic Highlands, 1987); Ian F.W. Beckett, ed., *The Roots of Counter-Insurgency: Armies and Guerrilla Warfare 1900–1945* (London: Blandford, 1988); Richard Stubbs, *Hearts and Minds in Guerrilla Warfare: The Malayan Emergency, 1948–1960* (New York : Oxford University Press, 1989).

12. Stephen T. Hosmer and S.O. Crane, R-412-ARPA, *Counterinsurgency: A Symposium, April 16–20, 1962* (Santa Monica, CA: RAND, 1963); and A.H. Peterson, G.C. Reinhart, and E.E. Conger, eds., RM-3652-PR, *Symposium on the Role of Airpower in Counterinsurgency and Unconventional Warfare: The Philippine Huk Campaign* (Chicago: RAND, 1963).

13. Colonel Napolean Valeriano, AFP, and Lieutenant Colonel Charles T.R. Bohannan, AUS, *Counter-Guerrilla Operations: The Philippine Experience* (New York: Praeger, 1962).

14. Colonel Laura C. Loftus, "Influencing the Forgotten Half of the

Population in Counterinsurgency Operations," USAWC Strategy Research Project, U.S. Army War College, 2008.

15. Ann Jones, "Woman to Woman in Afghanistan," *The Nation*, October 27, 2010, thenation.com/article/155623/woman-woman-afghanistan ?page=0,0.

16. Haugegaard, "Female Power."

17. Ibid.

18. Laleh Khalili, "Gendered Practices of Counterinsurgency," *Review of International Studies* 37 (2011): 1471–91.

19. Ibid., 1476.

20. My recent monograph, titled *Amazons of the Huk Rebellion: Gender, Sex and Revolution in the Philippines* (Madison: University of Wisconsin, 2009), is devoted entirely to the women who actively participated in the Huk movement.

21. For an in-depth treatment of the Huk Amazon, see ibid.

22. Jesus Lava, interview by author, Mandaluyong, Manila, November 1993. Unfortunately, there is no official record of the actual number of women directly involved in the Hukbalahap and HMB movements. But based on my interviews and conversations with former Huk men and women, the massive amount of coverage of "Amazon" captures in newspapers, and the considerable attention the Huk leadership paid to issues related to gender and family, I think 10 percent is the lowest possible estimate of the female composition of the Huk movement.

23. For more information on the success of U.S. counterinsurgency measures against the Huks, see Daniel B. Schirmer and Stephen Shalom, eds., *The Philippines Reader: A History of Colonialism, Neocolonialism, Dictatorship, and Resistance* (Cambridge, MA: South End Press, 1999), 105–23. For other works on counterinsurgency in the Philippines, see Alexander P. Aguirre and Ismael Z. Villareal, *Readings on Counterinsurgency* (Quezon City: Pan Service Masters Consultants, 1987); *The Insurgency Situation and Government Counter Measures* (Quezon City: Office of the Minister of National Defense, 1985), A.H. Peterson, G.C. Reinhard, and E.E. Conger, eds., *The Philippine Huk Campaign* (Santa Monica, CA: RAND, 1963); and Robert T. Yap-Diangco, *The Filipino Guerrilla Tradition* (Manila: MCS Enterprises, 1971).

24. See Lanzona, *Amazons of the Huk Rebellion*.

25. Valeriano, *Counter-Guerrilla Operations*, 15.

26. Ibid., 5.

27. Politburo documents reveal that there were no systematic plans to enlist women and train them as Huk soldiers.

28. Kerkvliet, *Huk Rebellion*, 94–95.

29. Benedict Kerkvliet writes that "in both size and organizational strength, the peasant rebellion grew between 1946 and late 1948." Kerkvliet, *Huk Rebellion*, 174. See also Victor Lieberman, *Why the Hukbalahap Movement Failed* (New Haven: Yale University Press, 1968). See also *Solidarity* 4 (October–December 1966): 22–30; and *New York Times Magazine*, March 14, 1965.

30. Araceli Mallari, interview by author, Caloocan City, Manila, October 1993.

31. Special Committee on Un-Filipino Activities, House of Representatives of the Republic of the Philippines, Report on "Communism in the Philippines."

32. "PI Awake to Menace, Magsaysay Tells Vets," *Manila Times*, September 18, 1952.

33. Civil Affairs Office, Department of National Defense, *Report on Communism and the Serviceman*.

34. "Magsaysay Fails to Nix Poll Aims," *Daily Mirror*, June 24, 1952; "Magsaysay Denies Aims in Politics," *Manila Times*, June 16, 1952.

35. Institute for Food and Development Policy, Walden Bello, *U.S. Sponsored Low-Intensity Conflict in the Philippines*, Food First Development Report No. 2 (San Francisco: 1987), 11–12.

36. Edward Lansdale was Magsaysay's frequent companion on trips around Central and Southern Luzon, as well as on official trips abroad. See "EQ, Others See Magsaysay Off, Lansdale Accompanies Secretary," *Manila Times*, June 8, 1952.

37. For biographies of Ramón Magsaysay, see Carlos P. Romulo and Marvin M. Gray, *The Magsaysay Story* (New York: J. Day Co., 1956); and the most recent, Manuel F. Martinez, *Magsaysay: The People's President* (McLean, VA: RMJ Development Corporation, 2005). Most works on Magsaysay are hagiographic presentations of what many believed to be the "most popular president" of the Philippines. They rarely criticized his close relationship with the U.S. government.

38. Kerkvliet, *Huk Rebellion*, 245.

39. Valeriano, *Counter-Guerrilla Operations*, 29.

40. Ibid., 29.

41. Ibid., 35.

42. Bello, *U.S. Sponsored Low-Intensity Conflict*, 12.

43. See "Secretary Awarded Medal," *Daily Mirror*, June 14, 1952; and the collection of speeches about Magsaysay in Jose T. Nueno, *The Knight of the Masses: Magsaysay, the Crusading President* (Tagaytay: 1957).

44. "Magsaysay's Bataan Day Speech," *Manila Times*, April 10, 1952.

45. "Bread but Not Bullets," *Manila Times*, February 21, 1952.

46. "What the Huks Think of Sex," *Philippines Free Press*, July 29, 1967.

47. Hosmer and Crane, *Counterinsurgency: A Symposium*, 63.

48. The depictions of Huk Amazons and their relationship with their children seemed to reflect the attitudes of Amazon women in Greek mythology, who had sex with men and disposed of their male children. See François Hartog, *The Mirror of Herodotus: The Representation of the Other in the Writing of History*, trans. Janet Lloyd (Berkeley: University of California Press, 1988), and Lanzona, *Amazons of the Huk Rebellion*.

49. José Veloso Abueva, *Raóon Magsaysay: A Political Biography* (Manila: Solidaridad, 1971).

50. Bello, *U.S. Sponsored Low-Intensity Conflict*, 21.

51. As recounted in Valeriano, *Counter-Guerrilla Operations*, 214.

52. See Jonathan Nashel, *Edward Lansdale's Cold War* (Amherst: University of Massachusetts Press, 2005).

53. Bello, *U.S. Sponsored Low-Intensity Conflict*, 22.

54. Valeriano, *Counter-Guerrilla Operation*, 50.

55. Hosmer and Crane, *Counterinsurgency: A Symposium*, 72.

56. The use of napalm was discussed by both Colonel Valeriano and Colonel Lansdale in Peterson, Reinhart, and Conger, *Symposium on the Role of Airpower in Counterinsurgency and Unconventional Warfare*, 36–37.

57. Bello, *U.S. Sponsored Low-Intensity Conflict*, 22.

3. Vietnam *by Hannah Gurman*

1. David Howell Petraeus, "The American Military and the Lessons of Vietnam" (PhD diss., Princeton University, 1987), via Proquest Dissertations Online.

2. U.S. Army/Marine Corps, "Counterinsurgency," FM 3-24, December 2006, fas.org/irp/doddir/army/fm3-24.pdf; *The U.S. Army/Marine Corps Counterinsurgency Field Manual* (Chicago: University of Chicago Press, 2007).

3. Brian Williams, interview with David Petraeus, First Draft of History Conference, Washington, DC, October 1, 2009, www.cbsnews.com/8301 -503544_162-5356921-503544.html. See also "Remarks by the President in Address to the Nation on the Way Forward in Afghanistan and Pakistan," speech, December 1, 2009.

4. See, for example, U.S. Army/Marine Corps, "Counterinsurgency," 2-12–2-13. For an earlier version of this argument, see Lewis Sorley, *A Better War: The Unexamined Victories and Final Tragedy of America's Last Years in Vietnam* (New York: Harcourt, Brace, 1999).

5. Quoted in Eric Bergerud, *The Dynamics of Defeat: The Vietnam War in Hau Nghia Province* (Boulder, CO: Westview Press, 1993), 59.

6. The most comprehensive English-language source for such material is the RAND compilation of interviews with NLF defectors: RAND Vietnam Interview Series (Santa Monica, CA: RAND Corporation, 1972). As David Hunt explains, despite the methodological issues, which include the fact that this research was sponsored and conducted by the U.S. government and focuses only on defectors, the material remains a valuable source of insight into the social revolution in Vietnam as understood by those who participated in it. David Hunt, *Vietnam's Southern Revolution: From Peasant Insurrection to Total War, 1959–1968* (Amherst: University of Massachusetts Press, 2009), 225–34.

7. Kurt Jacobsen, *Pacification and Its Discontents* (Chicago: Prickly Paradigm Press, 2009), 57. See also Ngô Viñh Long, *Before the Revolution: The Vietnamese Peasants Under the French* (New York: Columbia University Press, 1991).

8. James Walker Trullinger, *Village at War: An Account of Conflict in Vietnam* (Stanford, CA: Stanford University Press, 1994), 18, 19–22.

9. Thomas Ahern, *Vietnam Declassified: The CIA and Counterinsurgency* (Lexington: University Press of Kentucky, 2009), 118; Douglas Pike, quoted in Bergerud, *Dynamics of Defeat*, 57.

10. David Elliott, *The Vietnamese War: Revolution and Social Change in the Mekong Delta, 1930–1975* (New York: M.E. Sharpe, 2006), 96, 135; Hunt, *Vietnam's Southern Revolution*, 68–115; Trullinger, *Village at War*, 101.

11. Elliott, *Vietnamese War*, 156.

12. Howard Schonberger, "The Japan Lobby in American Diplomacy, 1947–1952," *Pacific Historical Review* 46, no. 3 (August 1977): 327–59; Noam Chomsky, "The Backroom Boys" (1973), in *For Reasons of State* (New York: The New Press, 2003), 31.

13. Chomsky, "Backroom Boys," 8, 54; Marilyn B. Young, *The Vietnam Wars, 1945–1990* (New York: Harper, 1991); Fredrick Logevall, *Choosing War: The Lost Chance for Peace and the Escalation of the War in Vietnam* (Berkeley: University of California Press, 1999), 388–93; Lloyd Gardner, *Pay Any Price: Lyndon Johnson and the Wars for Vietnam* (Chicago: Ivan R. Dee, 1995), 185.

14. Statistics for U.S. casualties can be found at the National Archives, "Statistical Information About Casualties of the Vietnam War." The exact number of Vietnamese deaths is less certain. According to the Agence France-Presse, which received an official report from the Vietnamese government in 1995, 1.3 million North and South Vietnamese soldiers died, and 1.8 million were wounded, with a total of 4 million civilian casualties. "Casualties—US vs NVA/VC," www.rjsmith.com/kia_tbl.html.

15. Roger Hilsman, *To Move a Nation: The Politics of Foreign Policy in the Administration of John F. Kennedy* (New York: Doubleday, 1967), 413. See also

David Milne, *America's Rasputin: Walt Rostow and the Vietnam War* (New York: Hill & Wang, 2008); Michael Latham, "Redirecting the Revolution? The USA and the Failure of Nation-Building in South Vietnam," *Third World Quarterly* 27, no. 1 (2006): 27–41.

16. Douglas S. Blaufarb, *The Counterinsurgency Era: U.S. Doctrine and Performance, 1950 to the Present* (New York: The Free Press, 1977), 55–56.

17. Walt Rostow, June 1961, quoted in ibid., 55–58.

18. Though the British campaign against the Malayan Communist Party and the U.S. effort to defeat the Huk Rebellion in the Philippines are frequently invoked as examples of "successful" counterinsurgency, these campaigns relied heavily on coercion and manipulation of the people by the state.

19. Elliott, *Vietnamese War*, 117.

20. Alfred W. McCoy, *The Politics of Heroin: CIA Complicity in the Global Drug Trade*, rev. ed. (1972; Chicago: Lawrence Hill, 2003), 200–207, 213, 259.

21. Elliott, *Vietnamese War*, 96, 227; Richard A. Hunt, *Pacification: The American Struggle for Vietnam's Hearts and Minds* (New York: Westview Press, 1995), 15.

22. Elliott, *Vietnamese War*, 101, 110; Ahern, *Vietnam Declassified*, 22–25.

23. Bergerud, *Dynamics of Defeat*, 20; Blaufarb, *Counterinsurgency Era*, 110–11.

24. SGM Herbert A. Friedman (Ret.), "PSYOP of the Strategic Hamlet in Vietnam," 25, www.psywarrior.com/VNHamletPSYOP.html.

25. Elliott, *Vietnamese War*, 104; Blaufarb, *Counterinsurgency Era*, 123; Bergerud, *Dynamics of Defeat*, 20; Hunt, *Pacification*, 20.

26. Lee Tong Foong, "The MPAJA and the Revolutionary Struggle, 1939–1945," and Michael Morgan, "The Rise and Fall of Malayan Trade Unionism," in *Malaya: The Making of a Neo-Colony*, ed. Mohamed Amin and Malcolm Caldwell (London: Spokesman Books, 1977); K.A. Hack, "The Malayan Emergency as Counter-insurgency Paradigm," and Paul Dixson, "'Hearts and Minds'? British Counter-Insurgency from Malaya to Iraq," both in *Journal of Strategic Studies*, June 2009. See also chapter 1 of this volume.

27. Blaufarb, *Counterinsurgency Era*, 114; Bergerud, *Dynamics of Defeat*, 51; Friedman, "PSYOP," 11; Marilyn B. Young, "Counterinsurgency Now and Forever," in *Iraq and the Lessons of Vietnam: Or, How Not to Learn from the Past*, ed. Lloyd C. Gardner and Marilyn B. Young (New York: The New Press, 2007), 217.

28. Leaflet 21501, quoted in Friedman, "PSYOP."

29. Blaufarb, *Counterinsurgency Era*, 20; Bergerud, *Dynamics of Defeat*, 36. Bergerud cites slightly different statistics—6,000 hamlets with 8 million people by the end of 1963.

30. Trullinger, *Village at War*, 73.

31. Friedman, "PSYOP," 18–19.

32. Hunt, *Pacification*, 23; Early Young, senior U.S. rep in Long An, quoted in Friedman, "PSYOP"; Bernard Fall, "Theory and Practice of Insurgency and COIN," *Naval War College Review*, April 1965.

33. Elliott, *Vietnamese War*, 166; Trullinger, *Village at War*, 97.

34. Elliott, *Vietnamese War*, 162.

35. Hunt, *Pacification*, 25; Elliott, *Vietnamese War*, 195–97, 208, 232.

36. Blaufarb, *Counterinsurgency Era*, 122; Elliott, *Vietnamese War*, 190, 220.

37. Lyndon B. Johnson, "Remarks at a Dinner Meeting of the Texas Electric Cooperatives, Inc.," May 4, 1965, in *Public Papers of the Presidents, 1965*, Book 1, www.presidency.ucsb.edu/ws/?pid=26942#axzz1WiiOYhlS; Gardner, *Pay Any Price*, 56, 191–92.

38. Bergerud, *Dynamics of Defeat*, 144; Friedman, "PSYOP," 4; Elliott, *Vietnamese War*, 199; Blaufarb, *Counterinsurgency Era*, 230; Hunt, *Vietnam's Southern Revolution*, 142.

39. Trullinger, *Village at War*, 119; Hunt, *Vietnam's Southern Revolution*, 162.

40. Jacobsen, *Pacification and Its Discontents*, 31; Chomsky, "Backroom Boys," 70; Derek Gregory, "Lines of Descent," author's draft, 8. Gregory quotes one air force officer on the bombing campaign in the north who told the *New York Times*: "This is different from air operations in South Vietnam. There is far more advanced planning here, far more experienced pilots and tight discipline."

41. Elliott, *Vietnamese War*, 221–48; Hunt, *Vietnam's Southern Revolution*, 156.

42. Gregory, "Lines of Descent," 13–15.

43. Truong Nhu Tang, *A Viet Cong Memoir: An Inside Account of the Vietnam War and Its Aftermath* (New York: Random House, 1986), 167–68; Hunt, *Vietnam's Southern Revolution*, 172, 125, 134.

44. Hunt, *Vietnam's Southern Revolution*, 120, 121, 123, 192.

45. Quoted in Chomsky, "Backroom Boys," 3.

46. Hunt, *Vietnam's Southern Revolution*, 141.

47. Wade Markel, "Draining the Swamp: The British Strategy of Population Control," *Parameters*, Spring 2006, 35–48.

48. Elliott, *Vietnamese War*, 338; David Hunt, "Dirty Wars: Counterinsurgency in Vietnam and Today," *Politics and Society* 38, no. 1 (March 2010): 39.

49. Quoted in Chomsky, "Backroom Boys," 84–85.

50. Douglas Valentine, *The Phoenix Program* (Lincoln, NE: Authors

Guild, 2000), 90; Hunt, *Pacification*, 40; RAND study, quoted in Chomsky, "Backroom Boys," 5.

51. Elliott, *Vietnamese War*, 263.

52. Ibid., 251–52; Young, "Counterinsurgency Now and Forever," 218.

53. Hunt, *Pacification*, 48–49; Bergerud, *Dynamics of Defeat*, 152–53.

54. Trullinger, *Village at War*, 151–58.

55. Chomsky, "Backroom Boys," 97.

56. Elliott, *Vietnamese War*, 323; Abrams, quoted in Hunt, *Pacification*, 193, 212.

57. U.S. Army/Marine Corps, "Counterinsurgency," 2-12–2-13. See also Lewis Sorley, *A Better War: The Unexamined Victories and Final Tragedy of America's Last Years in Vietnam* (New York: Harcourt, Brace, 1999).

58. Valentine, *Phoenix Program*, 43–56, 85, 170; Blaufarb, *Counterinsurgency Era*, 246–47; Jacobsen, *Pacification and Its Discontents*, 25–26; Chomsky, "Backroom Boys," 92.

59. Alfred W. McCoy, "Torture in the Crucible of Counterinsurgency," in Gardner and Young, *Iraq and the Lessons of Vietnam*, 238, 240–41; John Paul Vann, quoted in Hunt, *Pacification*, 239.

60. Hunt, *Pacification*, 247; McCoy, "Torture in the Crucible of Counterinsurgency," 241; Valentine, *Phoenix Program*, 259.

61. Hunt, *Pacification*, 189; Nick Turse, "A My Lai a Month," *The Nation*, November 13, 2008, www.thenation.com/article/my-lai-month?page=full.

62. Turse, in "A My Lai a Month," writes that the division claimed 10,899 VC killed and 748 weapons captured, with 267 U.S. casualties.

63. Turse, "A My Lai a Month"; Elliott, *Vietnamese War*, 336, 346; Hunt, *Pacification*, 189.

64. Turse, "A My Lai a Month"; Elliott, *Vietnamese War*, 337, 346.

65. Regarding the Department of Defense's acknowledgment, see William Haseltine, William R. Carter, and Ngô Vĩnh Long, "Human Suffering in Vietnam," *Science* 169, no. 3940 (July 3, 1970): 6; Elliott, *Vietnamese War*, 338.

66. Elliott, *Vietnamese War*, 338.

67. Hunt, *Pacification*, 204–6, 229, 230, 262; Hunt, *Vietnam's Southern Revolution*, 126; Bergerud, *Dynamics of Defeat*, 158; Elliott, *Vietnamese War*, 383.

68. Blaufarb, *Counterinsurgency Era*, 271; George C. Herring, *America's Longest War* (Boston: McGraw-Hill, 2002), 232; Bergerud, *Dynamics of Defeat*, 234; refugee adviser, quoted in Hunt, *Pacification*, 230.

69. Trullinger, *Village at War*, 193; Ahern, *Vietnam Declassified*, 375.

70. James Tyson, "Land Reform in Vietnam: A Progress Report," *Asian Affairs* 1, no. 1 (September–October 1973): 41; William Bredo, "Agrarian

Reform in Vietnam: Vietcong and Government of Vietnam Strategies in Conflict," *Asian Survey* 10, no. 8 (August 1970), 750; Bergerud, *Dynamics of Defeat*, 299; Elliott, *Vietnamese War*, 375; Jacobsen, *Pacification and Its Discontents*, 57.

71. Elliott, *Vietnamese War*, 372; Malvern Lumsden, "'Conventional War' and Human Ecology," *Ambio* 4, no. 5 (1975), 223–28; Michael Herr, *Dispatches* (1968; New York: Avon, 1978), 44.

72. Haseltine, Carter, and Long, "Human Suffering in Vietnam," 6.

73. Brian Williams, interview with David Petraeus, *NBC Nightly News*, October 1, 2009; Barack Obama, West Point speech, December 1, 2009.

4. El Salvador *by Joaquín M. Chávez*

1. See Leigh Binford, *The El Mozote Massacre* (Tucson: University of Arizona Press, 1996); and Mark Danner, *The Massacre at El Mozote: A Parable of the Cold War* (New York: Vintage Books, 1994).

2. See Juan José Dalton and Gerardo Arbaiza, "El Día que empezó el Proceso de Paz en El Mozote," *ContraPunto*, January 16, 2012.

3. See Gloria Morán, "Derecha 'encachimbada' por acto de Funes," *ContraPunto*, January 17, 2012.

4. The mandate of the Truth Commission for El Salvador reads: "The Commission shall have the task of investigating serious acts of violence that have occurred since 1980 and whose impact on society urgently demands that the public should know the truth." See United States Institute of Peace, www.usip.org/files/file/ElSalvador-Report.pdf (accessed October 3, 2012). Based on this mandate, the commission did not investigate the violence perpetrated by state agents against civilians prior to 1980, which arguably led to the radicalization of vast segments of the social movements and to the rapid expansion of the insurgency during the 1970s. In this sense, TCR offered a tautological explanation on the origins of political violence in El Salvador between 1980 and 1991.

5. Leigh Binford wrote about the convergence between the repressive mentality and trajectory of the Salvadoran elites and U.S. counterinsurgency in his study of the El Mozote Massacre. See Binford, *El Mozote Massacre*, 27–48. Greg Grandin also analyzed the confluence between U.S. counterinsurgency and the Guatemalan elites' genocidal policies in his study of the Panzós Massacre. See Greg Grandin, *The Last Colonial Massacre: Latin America in the Cold War* (Chicago: University of Chicago Press, 2004).

6. See Peter Maass, "The Salvadorization of Iraq?," *New York Times Magazine*, May 1, 2005.

7. Ignacio Martín-Baró studied the psychosocial impacts on Salvadoran society of the political repression carried out by the state forces in the 1970s

and 1980s. See Ignacio Martín-Baró, "The Psychological Value of Violent Political Repression," in *Writings for a Liberation Psychology* (Cambridge, MA: Harvard University Press, 1994), 150–64.

8. See José Roberto Cea, interview by the author, June 21, 2012. See also Jeffrey L. Gould and Aldo A. Lauria-Santiago, *To Rise in Darkness: Revolution, Repression, and Memory in El Salvador, 1920–1932* (Durham, NC: Duke University Press, 2008).

9. Ibid.

10. Ibid.

11. Ibid.

12. See Roque Dalton, *El Salvador Monografía* (San Salvador: UCA Editores, 2007), 115–16.

13. See Salvador Cayetano Carpio, *Secuestro y Capucha* (San José, Costa Rica: Editorial Universitaria Centroamericana (EDUCA), 1982).

14. Carpio claimed that José Urías Orantes and Daniel Menjívar, two police torturers, inflicted "the hood" on him. See Salvador Cayetano Carpio, "Secuestro y Capucha," in *Revista Universidad* (San Salvador: Editorial Universitaria, 1967), 111–16.

15. Ibid., 119.

16. Ibid., 102.

17. Ibid., 182, 195.

18. See Dalton, *El Salvador*, 116.

19. See José Roberto Cea, interview by the author, June 21, 2012.

20. See Fabio Castillo, "Episodios Desconocidos de la Historia Centroamericana," *CartasCentroamericanas*, July 1986, 5.

21. See Leslie Bethell and Ian Roxborough, "The Impact of the Cold War on Latin America," in *Origins of the Cold War: An International History*, 2nd ed., ed. Melvyn P. Leffler and David S. Painter (New York: Routledge, 2005), 299–316.

22. Scholars generally agree that the Lemus regime oscillated between a partial political opening and repression. Assessing Lemus's presidency, Tommie Sue Montgomery wrote: "The 1950s provided sufficient political latitude to permit the development of several center-to-left-leaning organizations. As demands for reform increased, however, the [Lemus] regime grew more defensive. Increased repression produced more opposition." See Tommie Sue Montgomery, *Revolution in El Salvador: From Civil Strife to Civil Peace* (Boulder, CO: Westview Press, 1995), 48–49. Paul D. Almeida posits that "collective military rule," which promoted economic modernization between 1948 and 1962, fluctuated between restricted political openings and repression. Emerging social movements and political parties such as Partido Revolucionario Abril y Mayo (PRAM) "benefited from the early years of Lemus'

reforms, which lifted the special state of emergency, allowed the return of exiles, and permitted the support of labor mobilizations and national conferences." Almeida also points out that social movements and left opposition forces overthrew Lemus in October 1960 and enjoyed "almost three months under a progressive civil-military Junta," which ended with the "conservative military" coup of January 1961. Security forces "massacred protesting civilians" during the coup, this incident prompted the Communist Party of El Salvador (PCS) to create "an underground guerrilla organization" the Frente Unido de Acción Revolucionaria (FUAR). See Paul D. Almeida, *Waves of Protest: Popular Struggle in El Salvador, 1925–2005* (Minneapolis: University of Minnesota Press, 2008), 61–63.

23. Members of PRAM included social democrats, "radicalized liberals," and communists. See Héctor Dada, interview by Joaquín Chávez, April 23, 2007. PRAM's name alluded to the civic-military movement that ousted the dictator Maximiliano Hernández Martínez between April and May 1944. The Frente Nacional de Orientación Cívica (FNOC) was a center-left coalition made up of political parties and social movements. FNOC was constituted by the PRAM, the Partido de Acción Renovadora (PAR), the Radical Democratic Party (PRD), the General Association of Salvadoran University Students (AGEUS), and the General Confederation of Salvadoran Workers (CGTS). See Víctor Valle, *Siembra de Vientos: El Salvador 1960–69* (San Salvador: CINAS, 1993), 42–47.

24. See Valle, *Siembra de Vientos*, 44–45. See also, for example, "Fidel Castro Planea Más Fusilamientos," *La Prensa Gráfica*, January 4, 1960; and "Castro Militariza al Campesino Cubano," *La Prensa Gráfica*, January 9, 1960.

25. After conducting a "survey" in Central America and the Caribbean in 1957, James A. Minotto, "a rancher and a former Mutual Security Agency chief in Portugal," warned a U.S. Senate special committee that the United States' "vital interests" in the region were "in danger of being overlooked" due to the U.S. government's "concentration on world-shaking events elsewhere." According to Minotto, although "the threat of communist subversion in those areas appear[ed]" insignificant, the rise to power of President Jacobo Árbenz in Guatemala showed "the ease with which some of these countries can be subverted to a base for mounting a Communist-led psychological offensive against the United States." Minotto called on the U.S. Senate to support the government of Carlos Castillo Armas in Guatemala, which replaced the Árbenz regime to avoid repeating "unhappy history in Guatemala from 1950 to 1954." See Ernest B. Vaccaro, "U.S. Warned to Guard Hemisphere Interests," *Washington Post*, March 26, 1957, A6.

26. Roy Rubottom, Acting Assistant Secretary of State, U.S. Department

of State, "Visit of President Lemus of El Salvador—Memo from Mr. Rubottom to Acting Assistant Secretary of State," September 24, 1958, declassified documents of the Office of Central American and Panamanian Affairs, National Archives, Washington, DC.

27. Five State Department officials, identified as Buchanan, Hall, Murphy, Olson, and Lightner, signed a "Position Paper" regarding Lemus's state visit. See U.S. Department of State, "State Visit by Salvadoran President Lemus, March 10–20, 1959, Position Paper, Communist Activities in El Salvador," 1958, declassified documents of the Office of Central American and Panamanian Affairs, National Archives, Washington, DC.

28. See "University of El Salvador Elections—the Weber Case Memorandum from C. Allan Stewart to Mr. Rubottom," and "State Visit by Salvadoran President Lemus, March 10–20 1959, Position Paper, Communist Activities in El Salvador," declassified documents of the Office of Central American and Panamanian Affairs, National Archives, Washington, DC.

29. See U.S. Department of State, "Memorandum of Conversation—Participants: Thorsten V. Kalijarvi, American Ambassador; Serafino Romualdi, Inter-American Representative of Orit; Andrew McClellan, Latin American Representative of the International Federation of Food and Drink Workers; Bruce Green, Labor Advisor USOM; William B. Sowash, Labor Reporting Officer; Subject: Various Labor Matters," State Department, March 23, 1960, declassified documents of the Office of Central American and Panamanian Affairs, National Archives, Washington, DC.

30. Lemus reportedly told Stewart and Downs that "he had been patient," tried to conduct "a democratic government" and avert repression, but "that the limits have now been reached and that the time for action had arrived." Lemus also told Stewart and Downs about the increasing "communist" influence at the university, in the trade unions, and among the press. See U.S. Department of State, "Memorandum of Conversation—Present: Lt. Col. José María Lemus, President of El Salvador; C. Allan Stewart, Director, Office of Central American and Panamanian Affairs, State Department; and Donald P. Downs, Chargé d'Affairs, U.S. Embassy in El Salvador," June 7, 1960, declassified documents of the Office of Central American and Panamanian Affairs, National Archives, Washington, DC.

31. See Almeida, *Waves of Protest*, 61.

32. Shafik Handal, a member of the PCS, became the coordinator of the Frente Unido de Acción Revolucionaria (FUAR). See Domingo Santacruz, interview by Joaquín Chávez, April 17, 2007.

33. See Manlio Argueta, interview by the author, June 22, 2012.

34. Roque Dalton claimed that state agents raped students during the raid. See Dalton, *El Salvador*, 122. Judge Alas, who personally inspected the

campus, stated that "phones, furniture, academic titles . . . blackboards, file cabinets . . . professional documents and didactic material" were destroyed during the raid. Judge Alas reported that the police and the National Guard damaged "aisles, rooms, the offices of the Rectory, classrooms, bathrooms, warehouses" as they perforated "big holes" in the walls in order to capture people who took refuge in those places. "Files, money and many other objects of the University and of employees" also disappeared during the charge. Judge Alas and the forensic experts who accompanied him showed particular indignation at the destruction of the portrait of the Salvadoran cultural icon Francisco Gavidia. See "500 Mil Cols. En Daño a La Universidad," *La Prensa Gráfica*, September 7, 1960.

35. See U.S. Department of State, "Memorandum of Conversation; Participants—H.E. President José María Lemus, Ambassador Thorsten V. Kalikarji," September 16, 1960, declassified documents of the Office of Central American and Panamanian Affairs, National Archives, Washington, DC.

36. Ibid.

37. See Almeida, *Waves of Protest*, 61.

38. See Héctor Dada, interview by the author, April 23, 2007.

39. See Binford, *El Mozote Massacre*, 38, and Valle, *Siembra de Vientos*, 119–20.

40. See Montgomery, *Revolution in El Salvador*, 52–53.

41. See Héctor Dada, interview by the author, April 23, 2007.

42. "Rompen Relaciones EEUU con Cuba," *La Prensa Gráfica*, January 4, 1961.

43. This finding supports Wickham-Crowley's depiction of Latin American universities as "political enclaves" during the 1960s. See Timothy P. Wickham-Crowley, *Guerrillas and Revolution in Latin America: A Comparative Study of Insurgents and Regimes since 1956* (Princeton, NJ: Princeton University Press, 1992), 35.

44. See Binford, *El Mozote Massacre*, 38.

45. See Michael McClintock, *The American Connection*, vol. 1: *State Terror and Popular Resistance in El Salvador* (London: Zed, 1985), 30.

46. Cited in ibid.

47. Dada considered the Directorate "the ideal Alliance for Progress regime" in that it combined an "intensely modernizing platform but before anything else, national security." Furthermore, Dada recalled that the Rivera regime, which followed the Directorate, implemented "a policy of reform of agrarian property, of defense of the interests of workers, in short, Alliance for Progress." See Héctor Dada, interview by the author, April 23, 2007. Santacruz deemed the Directorate's constitutional reform of January 1962 and Rivera's decision to tolerate the electoral participation of opposition parties

and to establish a new system of proportional representation at the National Assembly a maneuver aimed at countering the influence of the Cuban Revolution through the implementation of a limited political opening. However, Rivera closed down alternatives for the much-needed internal reforms and solely focused on the creation of the Central American Common Market, hoping that it would stimulate employment and the growth of an internal market as an alternative to the impending social crisis. See Domingo Santacruz, interview by the author, April 17, 2007.

48. Members of the Directorate were Colonel Julio Rivera; Colonel Aníbal Portillo; Major Simo; and two civilians, Dr. Antonio Rodríguez Port and Dr. José Francisco Valiente. See "Directorio Asume Poder en el País—Fue Establecida La Ley Marcial," *La Prensa Gráfica*, January 26, 1960.

49. According to Abraham Rodríguez, PDC leaders rejected the military's proposal to become the new official party because they disagreed with the practice of forming new official parties after the coups and firmly believed in the formation of "permanent opposition parties" as a precondition to democratization (Abraham Rodríguez, interview by the author, December 27, 2006). Based on the interviews she conducted with Ruben Zamora, a member of the PDC until 1980, and Hugo Carrillo, the secretary general of the PCN in the late 1980s, Montgomery offered a similar version on the formation of the PDC. See Montgomery, *Revolution in El Salvador*, 53.

50. See UPI, "500,000 Salvadorans Vote for New Congress," *Washington Post*, December 18, 1961, A12.

51. See Montgomery, *Revolution in El Salvador*, 53.

52. Ibid.

53. See Héctor Dada, interview by the author, April 23, 2007.

54. See Domingo Santacruz, interview by the author, April 17, 2007.

55. See Dalton, *El Salvador*, 137.

56. See Binford, *El Mozote Massacre*, 39.

57. Army colonel José Alberto "Chele" Medrano and U.S. Green Berets founded ORDEN in 1965 as part of the U.S.-sponsored counterinsurgency program in El Salvador. ORDEN was under the control of a state intelligence apparatus called Servicios de Seguridad (Security Services), which comprised a network of civilian informants and "the intelligence units of the National Police, National Guard, and the Immigration Service." Ibid., 45.

58. Ibid.

59. See Dalton, *El Salvador*, 137.

60. See Salvador Cayetano Carpio, "La Huelga General Obrera de Abril de 1967," in Valle, *Siembra de Vientos*, 433–34, 453–54, 457–59, and 471–82.

61. See Mélida Anaya Montes, *La Segunda Gran Batalla de ANDES* (San Salvador: Editorial Universitaria, 1972), 7–8.

62. See ibid., 40. The official press virtually silenced the numerous incidents of repression against teachers that occurred at that time.

63. See Alfredo Ramírez, "El Discurso Anticomunista de las Derechas y el Estado como Antecedente de la Guerra Civil en El Salvador (1967–1972)" (licentiate thesis, Universidad de El Salvador, Facultad de Ciencias y Humanidades, Escuela de Ciencias Sociales "Lic. Gerardo Iraheta Rosales," August 11, 2008).

64. See, for instance, "Torres ve mano roja en movimiento de ANDES," *La Prensa Gráfica*, July 17, 1971. *La Prensa Gráfica* published pictures of university students Luisa Eugenia Castillo Sol, Lil Milagro Ramírez, Salvador Orellana Montoya, Edgar Alejandro Rivas Mira, and Eduardo Sancho, identifying them as members of "El Grupo." See *La Prensa Gráfica*, July 7, 1971.

65. See Carlos López, interview by the author, April 9, 2007.

66. See "Los Seguidores de Chema Lemus," *Opinión Estudiantil*, June 1971.

67. See Montes, *La Segunda Gran Batalla de ANDES*, 87.

68. Ibid., 49.

69. Ibid., 119, 182–83.

70. Ibid., 118–19.

71. López observed, "If you wanted to keep your job you had to join the PCN, it was that simple." See Carlos López, interview by the author, April 9, 2007.

72. The sociologist Ramón Vega reproduced verbatim the testimony of David Rodríguez about the massacre at La Cayetana. At that time Rodríguez worked as a priest in Tecoluca, the parish in charge of the area where the mass killing took place. See Juan Ramón Vega, *Las Comunidades Cristianas de Base en América Central* (San Salvador: Arzobispado de San Salvador, 1987), 98–99.

73. See Facundo Guardado, interview by the author, December 6, 2006; and José Romeo Maeda, interview by the author, November 30, 2007.

74. See Gumercinda "Chinda" Zamora, interview by the author, October 10, 2008.

75. See Guadalupe Mejía, interview by the author, October 2, 2008.

76. See Hilda Mejía, interview by the author, October 10, 2008.

77. Facundo Guardado maintained that certain paramilitary commanders supported the foundation of the UTC in hamlets near Arcatao. See Facundo Guardado, interview by the author, December 6, 2006; and José "Santos" Martínez, interview by the author, December 25, 2007.

78. See Patricia Alvarenga, *Cultura y Ética de la Violencia, El Salvador, 1880–1932* (San José: Editorial Universitaria Centroamericana [EDUCA], 1996), 16.

79. See José "Santos" Martínez, interview by the author, December 25, 2007.

80. See Guadalupe Mejía, interview by the author, October 2, 2008.

81. See Facundo Guardado, interview by the author, November 12, 2007.

82. See Héctor Martínez, interview by the author, April 18, 2007.

83. See Facundo Guardado, interview by the author, November 12, 2007.

84. Ibid.

85. For a recent account of these events, see Rafael Mejívar Ochoa, *Tiempos de Locura El Salvador 1979–1981* (San Salvador: FLACSO El Salvador, 2006).

86. See Benjamin Schwarz, "Dirty Hands: The Success of U.S. Policy in El Salvador—Preventing a Guerrilla Victory—Was Based on 40,000 Political Murders," *Atlantic Monthly*, December 1998.

87. See *Diario Oficial de la República de El Salvador*, vol. 257, November 25, 1977, 2–5.

88. The UNO, LP-28, FENASTRAS, "trade unions led by the PCS" like the CUTS and CCS, and the "short-lived Partido Unionista Centrameriano" (PUCA) joined the Popular Forum. See Ochoa, *Tiempos de Locura El Salvador 1979–1981*, 30–31.

89. Ibid, 30.

90. See P.A. Aparicio, B. Barrera y Reyes, J.E. Álvarez, M.R. Revelo, and F. Delgado, "Declaración de Cuatro Obispos de la Conferencia Episcopal de El Salvador," *Estudios Centroamericanos* 359, no. 33 (September 1978): 774–75; and FECCAS-UTC, "FECCAS-UTC a los Cristianos de El Salvador y Centroamérica," September 29, 1978.

91. See O.A. Romero and A. Rivera y Damas, "La Iglesia y las Organizaciones Políticas Populares," *Estudios Centroamericanos ECA* 359, no. 33 (August 1978): 760–73.

92. Ibid.

93. Ibid., 770–71.

94. See Ester Arteaga, interview by the author, San Salvador, September 10, 2008.

95. Ibid.

96. Recently, human rights organizations in El Salvador have collected numerous testimonies of survivors of massacres perpetrated by state agents during the civil war. See, for instance, *Masacres: Trozos de la Historia Salvadoreña Contados por las Víctimas* (San Salvador: Centro para la Promoción de Derechos Humanos "Madeleine Lagadec," 2007). This book documents testimonies of survivors of the following massacres: Santa Rita, Santa Rosita,

Canoas, La Guacamaya, Rio Metayate, Palo Grande, Girones, Zacamil, San Francisco Angulo, Sisiguayo, El Calabozo, Tenango-Guadalupe, El Refugio, San Francisco Echevería, La Tigra, and Copapayo.

97. See Ron Robin, *The Cold War Enemy: Culture and Politics in the Military-Intellectual Complex* (Princeton and Oxford: Princeton University Press, 2001) 11.

98. Ibid.

99. Ibid.

100. See Elisabeth Jean Wood, *Insurgent Collective Action and Civil War in El Salvador* (Cambridge: Cambridge University Press, 2003), 234, 235.

5. Iraq, Part I *by Rick Rowley*

1. Coalition Provisional Authority, *CPA Official Documents* (Baghdad: Coalition Provisional Authority, 2010), web.archive.org/web/20100206084411/http://www.cpa-iraq.org/regulations.

2. Milan Vesely, "Who Holds Iraqi Purse Strings?" *Current Affairs,* August–September 2004, 14.

3. Marc Lacey, "Iraqi Soldiers Protest U.S. Plan to Disband Them," *New York Times,* May 26, 2003, 3.

4. "Iraqis Protest over Oil Jobs for Asians," Agence France-Presse, June 9, 2003.

5. Larry McShane, "The Latest Week in the War in Iraq, Day by Day," Associated Press, April 19, 2003.

6. "Report: U.S. Troops Fire on Iraq Crowd," United Press International, April 29, 2003.

7. Mitchell P. Prothero, "Second Day of Fighting at al-Fallujah," United Press International, April 30, 2003.

8. "Four Killed in New Clashes in Baghdad, London Warns of Lack of Security," Agence France-Presse, June 18, 2003.

9. Valentine Low, "They Were Outnumbered but Stood Their Ground, Dying Cornered by Mob; War Aftermath: How a Demonstration Against Conduct of Troops Boiled Over into Firefight That Left Six Military Policemen Dead," *Evening Standard,* June 25, 2003, 4–5.

10. Nawfal al-Obeid, "Two Dead as Riots Hit Basra for Second Day, Coalition on Alert for Islamists," Agence France-Presse, August 10, 2003.

11. Rory Mulholland, "Tensions Simmer in Baghdad After Clash Between US Troops, Shiite Protestors," Agence France-Presse, August 14, 2003.

12. "Third Iraqi City Hit by Army Veterans' Protests," Agence France-Presse, October 4, 2003.

13. Ibid.

14. Yehia Barzanji, "Gunfire Kills Two Protesters in Kirkuk; Car Bomb in Baghdad Targets U.S. Convoy," Associated Press, December 31, 2003.

15. Patrick Cockburn, *Muqtada Al-Sadr and the Battle for the Future of Iraq* (London: Simon & Schuster, 2008).

16. Naomi Klein, "Baghdad Year Zero: Pillaging Iraq in Pursuit of a Neocon Utopia," *Harper's Magazine*, September 2004.

17. Cockburn, *Muqtada Al-Sadr*, 31–32.

18. Ibid., 140.

19. "Coalition Closure of Firebrand Cleric's Iraqi Newspaper Stirs Protests," Agence France-Presse, March 28, 2004.

20. "US Tanks Deploy in Baghdad as Shiite Radicals Take to Streets," Agence France-Presse, April 3, 2004.

21. Juan Cole, "Portrait of a Rebellion," *In These Times*, May 24, 2004; and James Risen, "Account of Broad Shiite Revolt Contradicts White House Stand," *New York Times*, April 8, 2004, A1.

22. Patrick Cockburn, "Warlord: The Rise of Muqtada al-Sadr," *The Independent*, April 11, 2008.

23. Jeremy Scahill, *Blackwater: The Rise of the World's Most Powerful Mercenary Army* (New York: Nation Books, 2007), 118–24.

24. Daniel Trotta, "Clerics Warn of Mounting Anger at U.S.: Tension in Iraq: Mosque Leader Vows Holy War Unless Americans Depart," *National Post*, July 12, 2003, A10.

25. U.S. Department of Defense, "Army Maj. Gen. Swannack Jr., Live Video Tele-conference from Baghdad," news transcript, U.S. Department of Defense, November 18, 2003, www.defense.gov/transcripts/transcript .aspx?transcriptid=2959.

26. Paul L. Bremer, *My Year in Iraq: The Struggle to Build a Future of Hope* (New York: Simon & Schuster, 2006).

27. Iraq Coalition Casualty Count, icasualties.org/iraq.

28. Carol Rosenberg, "Marines Push Against Rebelling Iraqis; New Troops in Fallujah, Who Have Lost Seven in Their First 10 Days, Have Launched the 'First Significant Fight,'" *Philadelphia Inquirer*, March 28, 2004, A2.

29. Thom Shanker, "6 G.I.'s in Iraq Are Charged with Abuse Of Prisoners," *New York Times*, March 21, 2004; "UPI NewsTrack TopNews," United Press International, March 24, 2004; John Burns, "U.S. Calls for Sunni and Kurdish Rights After Turnover," *New York Times*, March 25, 2004, A1.

30. Scahill, *Blackwater*, 187–89.

31. Jeffrey Gettleman and Douglas Jehl, "Up to 12 Marines Die in Raid on Their Base as Fierce Fighting Spreads to 6 Iraqi Cities," *New York Times*, April 7, 2004, A1.

32. Pamela Constable, "U.S. and Iraqi Forces Seal Off Fallujah as Operation Looms," *Washington Post*, April 6, 2004, A12.

33. Bing West, *No True Glory: A Frontline Account of the Battle for Fallujah* (New York: Random House, 2005), 176.

34. John C. Fredriksen, *The United States Marine Corps: A Chronology, 1775 to the Present* (New York: ABC-CLIO, 2011), 338.

35. Rory McCarthy, "Uneasy Truce in the City of Ghosts," *The Guardian*, April 23, 2004.

36. Personal observation by the author, Fallujah, May 2004.

37. Fallujah residents, interview by the author, Fallujah, May 2004.

38. Robert D. Kaplan, "Five Days in Fallujah," *The Atlantic*, July/August 2004.

39. Members of the Iraqi Association of Muslim Scholars, interview by the author. In interviews, they refused to use the word "jihad" and instead favored "muqawama," meaning resistance.

40. Roel Meijer, "The Association of Muslim Scholars in Iraq," *Middle East Report*, Winter 2005.

41. John F. Burns and Christine Hauser, "Bremer Raising Pressure to End Iraqi Uprisings," *New York Times*, April 19, 2004, A1.

42. Pamela Constable, "Marines Try to Quell 'a Hotbed of Resistance,'" *Washington Post*, April 9, 2004, A1.

43. Mehdi Army fighters, imams, and leaders, including Saleh al-Obeidi, Sadrist spokesperson, interview by the author.

44. Ibid.

45. Fredriksen, *United States Marine Corps*.

46. Personal observation by the author, Fallujah, May 2004.

47. "No Longer Unknowable: Falluja's April Civilian Toll Is 600," *Iraq Body Count*, October 26, 2004, www.iraqbodycount.org/analysis/reference/press-releases/9. "Between 572 and 616 of the approximately 800 reported deaths were of civilians, with over 300 of these being women and children."

48. John Burns, "Fighting Halts Briefly in Falluja; U.S. Convoy Hit Near Baghdad," *New York Times*, April 10, 2004, A1.

49. Personal observation by the author, Fallujah, May 2004.

50. Patrick Cockburn, "Warlord: The Rise of Muqtada al-Sadr," *The Independent*, April 11, 2008, 140.

51. Rick Rowley, "The El Salvador Option," video clip, Al Jazeera English, April 30, 2009, www.youtube.com/watch?v=0dr4to5To4w&feature=bf_next&list=ELISLp_CkFOwU.

52. Michael Hirsh and John Barry, "The Salvador Option," *Newsweek*, January 8, 2005.

53. Cockburn, "Warlord," 107.

54. Coalition Provisional Authority, *CPA Official Documents*, www.iraq coalition.org/regulations.

55. Rowley, "El Salvador Option."

56. Charles Duhigg, "Sadr Army Holds Fire but Stays On at Two Holy Sites," *Los Angeles Times*, June 8, 2004, A6.

57. Precise numbers on foreign fighters and money are difficult to come by. A cache of documents seized by U.S. forces in a raid in Sinjar, however, gave a detailed picture of the traffic along at least one infiltration route. West Point's Combating Terrorism Center published the documents, which revealed a majority of fighters and money coming from Saudi Arabia. See Brian Fishman and Joseph Felter, "Combating Terrorism Center at West Point, Al-Qa'ida's Foreign Fighters in Iraq," 2007, www.ctc.usma.edu/posts/ al-qaidas-foreign-fighters-in-iraq-a-first-look-at-the-sinjar-records.

58. Rick Rowley, "The Ghost of Anbar," video clip, Al Jazeera English, September 17, 2007, www.aljazeera.com/programmes/peopleandpower/2007 /09/2008525184950170137.html; Rick Rowley, "'Re-awakening' Saddam's Tribal Strategy," video clip, Al Jazeera English, October 28, 2008, www .youtube.com/watch?v=9xgP6KvLOko.

59. Hannah Allam, "Rebel Leader Maneuvered Behind Scenes; Electrician Directed Fallujah Insurgency," *Detroit Free Press*, November 25, 2004, 3A.

60. Rowley, "'Re-awakening' Saddam's Tribal Strategy."

61. Nicholas Riccardi, "Attacks Target More Iraqi Police," *Los Angeles Times*, April 4, 2004, A11; and Sewell Chan and Scott Wilson, "Violence Leaves Iraqis in Despair; Funeral Evokes Leaders' Anxiety About Transition," *Washington Post*, May 19, 2001, A1.

62. Allam, "Rebel Leader Maneuvered Behind Scenes."

63. James Hider, "Lawless Fallujah Kills Seven Shia as 'Warning,'" *The Times* (London), June 16, 2004, 16.

64. Rick Rowley, "Beyond the Wall: Inside the Sadrist Movement," video clip, Al Jazeera English, October 25, 2008, www.aljazeera.com /programmes/peopleandpower/2008/10/2008102510584059284949.html.

65. Rick Rowley, "The Battle for Basra," video clip, Al Jazeera English, October 13, 2007, www.aljazeera.com/programmes/peopleandpower/2007 /10/2008525191459441755.html.

66. Suzanne Goldenberg and Julian Borger, "Family Says US Held Man Who Was Beheaded: CIA Links Video Execution to al-Qaida," *The Guardian*, May 14, 2004, 4.

67. "Execution of Nick Berg," video clip, Live Leak, November 1, 2006.

68. Anne Penketh, "Iraq Crisis: America's Number One Enemy Was a Killer," *The Independent*, May 12, 2004, 7.

69. Dexter Filkins, "Wanted Rebel Vows Loyalty To bin Laden," *New York Times*, October 18, 2004, A10.

70. Craig Whitlock, "Grisly Path to Power in Iraq's Insurgency; Zarqawi Emerges as Al Qaeda Rival, Ally," *Washington Post*, September 27, 2004, A1.

71. Dexter Filkins, "U.S. Plans Year-End Drive to Take Iraqi Rebel Areas," *New York Times*, September 19, 2004, A1.

72. Gheith Abdul-Ahad, "In Hideout, Foreign Arabs Share Vision of 'Martyrdom,'" *Washington Post*, November 9, 2004, A1.

73. James E. Wise and Scott Baron, *The Navy Cross: Extraordinary Heroism in Iraq, Afghanistan, and Other Conflicts* (Annapolis, MD: Naval Institute Press, 2007), 75.

74. John Patch, "Operation AL FAJR: Enduring MOUT principles make the fight for Fallujah a success," *Marine Corps Gazette*; Carl Vick, "Fighting Around Fallujah Intensifies," *Washington Post*, November 8, 2004, A1.

75. Thomas E. Ricks, *Fiasco: The American Military Adventure in Iraq, 2003–2005* (New York: Penguin, 2006).

76. Ibid., 400.

77. Mehdi Army fighters and commanders, interview by author, Baghdad, Iraq, 2008.

78. "Red Cross Estimates 800 Iraqi Civilians Killed in Fallujah," video clip, *Democracy Now!*, November 17, 2004, www.democracynow.org/2004/11/17/red_cross_estimates_800_iraqi_civilians.

79. Anthony Shadid, "Iraqi Fighters Keep Up Attacks; Sunni Cleric Says Fallujah Attracted Hundreds of Recruits," *Washington Post*, December 12, 2004, A32.

80. Alexander Cockburn, "Only One Thing Unites Iraq: Hatred of the US," *The Independent*, December 11, 2007, 30.

81. Peter Maass, "The Way of the Commandos," *New York Times Magazine*, May 1, 2005, 38.

82. Hirsh and Barry, "Salvador Option."

83. Rowley, "'Re-awakening' Saddam's Tribal Strategy."

84. Ibid.

85. Colin McMahon, "Iraq Tunes In to See Rebels Get Grilled; For Insurgents, Rough Justice on Reality TV," *Chicago Tribune*, April 17, 2005, C1.

86. Moqtada al-Sadr announced a "pact of honor" negotiated with the Association of Muslim Scholars that forbade either group from targeting Iraqis. Liz Sly, "Bombs, Attacks by Insurgents Kill 46; Spree of Violence Leaves 600 Iraqis Dead in Less Than 4 weeks," *Chicago Tribune*, May 24, 2005, C3.

87. Mehdi Army leaders, including Saleh al-Obeidi, interview by author, Najaf, Iraq, 2008.

88. "Blast Destroys Shia Shrine," *The Guardian*, February 22, 2006.

89. Ellen Knickmeyer and K.I. Ibrahim, "Bombing Shatters Mosque In Iraq; Attack on Shiite Shrine Sets Off Protests, Violence," *Washington Post*, February 23, 2006, A1.

90. Ibid.

91. "Iraqi Premier Underlines Call for Unity at News Conference on Samarra Blast," BBC Monitoring Middle East, February 24, 2006.

92. Alexandra Zavis, "Dozens of Bodies Found, Sunni Bloc Suspends Talks with Rival Parties in Wake of Shrine Attack," Associated Press, February 23, 2006.

6. Iraq, Part II *by David Enders*

1. Al Qaeda in Iraq (AQI) is an umbrella term for insurgent groups that were generally made up of Iraqis but claimed to subscribe to al Qaeda ideology and branded themselves as such. The Islamic State of Iraq (ISI) is another group that continues to operate in the country and since 2005 has often fallen under this umbrella. For many Iraqis, "Al Qaeda" became shorthand for most Sunni insurgents.

2. There is video evidence that Saddam, or someone who looked a lot like him, made the appearance described in Adhamiya that day, apparently his last public appearance before being captured by U.S. troops.

7. Afghanistan, Part I *by Jeremy Kuzmarov*

1. Quoted in Michael A. Cohen, "Tossing the Afghan COIN: The US Military's Reinvented Counterinsurgency Turns Out to Be the Same Old Brutal Game," *The Nation*, January 3, 2011, 18.

2. Robert Y. Pelton, *Licensed to Kill: Hired Guns in the War on Terror* (New York: Crown, 2006), 17–35. See also Billy Waugh with Tim Keown, *Hunting the Jackal: A Special Forces and CIA Ground Soldier's Fifty-Year Career Hunting America's Enemies* (New York: William Morrow, 2004). Military officers whom he trained were implicated in a coup against Muammar Qaddafi. In the 1990s, working in Khartoum under Cofer Black, future executive of Blackwater, Waugh was key to the arrest of the left-wing terrorist Ilich Ramírez Sánchez ("Carlos the Jackal"). Edwin Wilson was sentenced to thirty-five years in prison for illegally selling plastic explosives to Muammar Qaddafi and "false flag" recruiting, though his case was overturned by a federal court in 2003 after he proved that the CIA had requested his services.

3. On Vietnam, see Alfred W. McCoy, "Torture in the Crucible of Counterinsurgency," in *Iraq and the Lessons of Vietnam: Or, How Not to Learn from the Past*, ed. Marilyn B. Young and Lloyd C. Gardner (New York: The New Press, 2007), 241.

4. Roberto Gonzalez, Hugh Gusterson, and David Price, "War, Culture and Counterinsurgency," in Network of Concerned Anthropologists, *The Counter-Counterinsurgency Manual, or Notes on Demilitarizing American Society* (Chicago: Prickly Paradigm Press, 2008), 12; Richard Drinnon, *Facing West: On the Metaphysics of Indian-Hating and Empire-Building* (Norman: University of Oklahoma Press, 1980).

5. Virgil Ney, "Guerrilla Warfare and Modern Strategy," in *Modern Guerrilla Warfare: Fighting Communist Guerrilla Movements, 1941–1961*, ed. F.M. Osanka, introduction by Samuel Huntington (New York: The Free Press, 1962); Michael McClintock, *Instruments of Statecraft: U.S. Guerrilla Warfare, Counterinsurgency, and Counterterrorism, 1940–1990* (New York: Pantheon Books, 1992); Jonathan Schell, *The Village of Ben Suc* (New York: Harper, 1967).

6. See Malcolm Caldwell and Lek Tan, *Cambodia in the Southeast Asian War*, foreword by Noam Chomsky (New York: Monthly Review Press, 1973), x; Alfred W. McCoy, "The Secret War in Laos, 1955–1975," in *A Companion to the Vietnam War*, ed. Marilyn B. Young and Robert Buzzanco (Malden, MA: Blackwell, 2004); Marilyn B. Young, *The Vietnam Wars, 1945–1991* (New York: HarperPerennial, 1991).

7. I.F. Stone, "Anti-Guerrilla War—The Dazzling New Military Toothpaste for Social Decay," in *In a Time of Torment* (Boston: Little, Brown, 1967), 173–74.

8. See Douglas Valentine, "Provincial Reconstruction Teams and the CIA's Dirty War in Afghanistan," *Z Magazine*, February 2010, 31–35; Jane Mayer, *The Dark Side: The Inside Story of How the War on Terror Turned into a War on American Ideals* (New York: Doubleday, 2008).

9. Frank Armbruster, *A Military and Police Security Program for South Vietnam* (Hudson, NY: Hudson Institute, 1967), HI-881-RR, DOD.

10. "Phung Hoang, Monthly Report," April 29, 1971, RAFSEA, MACV, National Archives (hereafter "NA"), RG 472, CORDS, Public Safety Directorate, Field Operations, General Records, box 1; Michael T. Klare, "Operation Phoenix and the Failure of Pacification in South Vietnam," *Liberation* 17 (May 1973): 21–27; Douglas Valentine, *The Phoenix Program* (New York: Morrow, 1991); Alfred W. McCoy, *The Politics of Heroin: CIA Complicity in the Global Drug Trade*, rev. ed. (New York: Lawrence Hill, 2003).

11. "Evan Parker Jr. to Tucker Gougelmann, VCI Neutralizations," January 18, 1969, RAFSEA, HQ MACV, RG 472, NA, CORDS, Phung Hoang Division, box 1; Monthly Report, October 24, 1971, CORDS, Public Safety, box 14, folder Quality Neutralizations; Monthly Report October 24, 1971, and April 29, 1971, CORDS, Public Safety, box 13, folder Monthly Consolidated Reports; Robert Komer, "The Phung Hoang Fiasco," CORDS, Public Safety,

Phung Hoang, box 21; Iver Peterson, "Vietnam: This Phoenix Is a Bird of Death," *New York Times*, July 25, 1971, E2.

12. Frank Snepp, *Decent Interval* (Lawrence: University Press of Kansas, 2002), 31, 38; Alfred W. McCoy, *A Question of Torture: CIA Interrogation From the Cold War to the War on Terror* (New York: Metropolitan, 2006). Uncovering new evidence on this case in *Torture and Impunity: The U.S. Doctrine of Coercive Interrogation* (Madison: University of Wisconsin Press, 2012), Alfred M. McCoy reports that the Vietnamese agent survived, as the war ended before the orders to kill him were carried out. Previously he had reported that the man was actually thrown into the sea.

13. "Memo for Mr. Randolph Berkeley, Public Safety Division," November 25, 1968, RAFSEA, HQ MACV, RG, 472, NA, Public Safety Directorate, Field Operations, box 2, folder Correctional Centers; Holmes Brown and Don Luce, *Hostages of War: Saigon's Political Prisoners* (Washington, DC: Indochina Mobile Education Project, 1973), Richard A. Hunt, *Pacification: The American Struggle for Vietnam's Hearts and Minds* (Boulder, CO: Westview Press, 1995), 239.

14. See Malalai Joya with Derrick O' Keefe, *A Woman Among Warlords: The Extraordinary Story of an Afghan Who Dared to Raise Her Voice* (New York: Scribner, 2009); Tariq Ali, "Mirage of the Good War," in *The Case for Withdrawal from Afghanistan*, ed. Nick Turse (London: Verso, 2010), 51; Ahmed Rashid, *Taliban* (New Haven: Yale University Press, 2000).

15. Hannah Gurman, "Tribal Engagement and the Heavy History of Counterinsurgency Light," *Small Wars Journal*, June 6, 2010, smallwars journal.com/blog/journal/docs-temp/452-gurman.pdf; Alissa Rubin, "Afghan Tribal Rivalries Bedevil a U.S. Plan," *New York Times*, March 11, 2010; (Counter-Insurgency) Sectarian Violence RPT, 2009-10-01; "Conflict Between Tribes in Sabari," 2009-08-16, special intelligence summary, July 11, 2009, available at wikileaks.de. On economic and geostrategic interests, see Ahmed Rashid, "The New Great Game—The Battle for Central Asia's Oil," *Far Eastern Economic Review*, April 10, 1997; William Engdahl, *A Century of War: Anglo-American Oil Politics and the New World Order* (London: Pluto Press, 2004), 253–54.

16. Carlotta Gall, "NYU Report Casts Doubt on Taliban's Ties with Al Qaeda," *New York Times*, February 6, 2011; Gareth Porter, "Shattering the Myth of Taliban/Al Qaeda Ties," *Counterpunch*, February 8, 2011, www .counterpunch.org/2011/02/08/shattering-the-myth-of-taliban-al-qaeda -ties; Stanley A. McChrystal, "Commander's Initial Assessment," August 30, 2009; Noam Chomsky, in *Hegemony or Survival: America's Quest for Global Dominance* (New York: Metropolitan Books, 2003), 200, notes that the FBI merely believed the 9/11 plot came from Al Qaeda in Afghanistan, though

plotting and financing also likely traced to "Germany and the United Arab Emirates." Without court evidence, the bombing of Afghanistan was thus a war crime under international law.

17. Matthew Hoh, talk before the Tulsa Council on Foreign Relations, December 2010; "Matthew Hoh's Afghanistan: An Insider Talks," *The Nation*, January 3, 2011, 15; Anand Gopal, "Who Are the Taliban? The Afghan War Deciphered," TomDispatch.com, December 4, 2008.

18. Sonali Kolhatkar and James Ingalls, *Bleeding Afghanistan: Washington, Warlords and the Propaganda of Silence* (New York: Seven Stories Press, 2006), 65, 96; "'Killing You Is a Very Easy Thing For Us': Human Rights Abuses in Southeast Afghanistan," Human Rights Watch, July 2003.

19. Iraq Veterans Against the War and Aaron Glantz, *Winter Soldier: Iraq and Afghanistan: Eyewitness Accounts of the Occupations* (Chicago: Haymarket Books, 2008); William Yardley, "Drug Use Cited in the Killings of Three Civilians," *New York Times*, September 28, 2010, A1; Carlotta Gall, "Civilian Deaths Imperil Support for Afghan War," *New York Times*, May 6, 2007. The title of Gall's article shows the jingoistic manner in which the *Times* has covered this issue, raising concern not for the dead or commission of war crimes, but only for the impact on the efficacy of U.S. military operations and public opinion.

20. See Gareth Porter, "Kandahar Gains Came with 'Brutal' Tactics," Inter Press Service, December 21, 2010.

21. Marc Herold, "Truth as Collateral Damage: Civilian Deaths from U.S./NATO Air Strikes," *The Guardian*, October 22, 2008; "Amnesty International Lists 83 Afghan Civilians Killed in NATO Airstrike in Kunduz," Amnesty International, October 30, 2009; Tom Engelhardt, "The Wedding Crashers," TomDispatch.com, July 15, 2008.

22. Patrick Cockburn, "Who Killed 120 Civilians? The U.S. Says It's Not a Story," *Counterpunch*, May 11, 2009; Jane Mayer, "The Predator War," *New Yorker*, October 26, 2009; Fred Branfman, *Voices from the Plain of Jars* (New York: Harper, 1972). According to a recent NYU study, the drones have killed approximately 3,000 people in Pakistan, nearly one-third civilians including 176 children, with at least 1,200 injured. *Living Under Drones: Death, Injury, and Trauma to Civilians From US Drone Practices in Pakistan* (NYU and Stanford School of Law, September 2012), available at livingunderdrones.org/report.

23. In Noam Chomsky, *Hopes and Prospects* (Chicago: Haymarket Books, 2010), 240.

24. Kolhatkar and Ingalls, *Bleeding Afghanistan*, 58; Gurman, "Tribal Engagement and the Heavy History of Counterinsurgency Light"; Major Jim Gant, *One Tribe at a Time* (Los Angeles: Nine Sisters Imports Inc., 2009).

25. S. Frederick Starr, "Sovereignty and Legitimacy in Afghan Nation-Building," in *Nation-Building: Beyond Afghanistan and Iraq*, ed. Francis Fukuyama (Baltimore: John Hopkins University Press, 2006).

26. John A. Nagl, *Learning How to Eat Soup with a Knife: CIA Lessons from Malaya and Vietnam* (Chicago: University of Chicago Press, 2007), 3.

27. Martha K. Huggins, *Political Policing: The United States and Latin America* (Durham: Duke University Press, 1998); James W. Gibson, *The Perfect War: The War We Couldn't Lose and How We Did* (New York: Vintage Books, 1988), 276; Bruce Cumings, *The Korean War* (New York: Random House, 2010); Alfred W. McCoy and Nina Adams, eds., *Laos: War and Revolution* (New York: Harper & Row, 1970). Even in Malaya, thousands were herded into concentration camps and tortured by Western-trained security forces, a fact Nagl does not mention. See Mark Curtis, *Unpeople: Britain's Secret Human Rights Abuses* (London: Vintage, 2004).

28. Gabriel Kolko, *Anatomy of a War: Vietnam, the United States and the Modern Historical Experience* (New York: Pantheon, 1985); Kurt Jacobsen, *Pacification and Its Discontents* (Chicago: Prickly Paradigm Press, 2009), 48.

29. Ann Jones, "Meet the Afghan Army: Is It a Figment of Washington's Imagination?" in Turse, *Case for Withdrawal from Afghanistan*; Tim Bird and Alex Marshall, *Afghanistan: How the West Lost Its Way* (New Haven, CT: Yale University Press, 2010), 121; Yaroslav Trofimov, "U.S. Enlists Ex-Foes for Afghan Army: Soviet Era Brass Take Command Again in Alliance of Former Battlefield Rivals," *Wall Street Journal*, February 9, 2010.

30. "'Killing You Is a Very Easy Thing For Us'"; Chris Hedges, *Death of the Liberal Class* (New York: Nation Books, 2010), 50; Declan Walsh, "Afghan Civilians Accuse US-Led Soldiers of Abuse," *Boston Globe*, June 25, 2006; Antonio Giustozzi, *Koran, Kalashnikov and Laptop: The Neo-Taliban Insurgency in Afghanistan* (New York: Columbia University Press, 2009), 188; David Rohde, "The Reach of War: Kabul; Afghan Officials Deny Reports of Soldiers Beheading Criminals," *New York Times*, June 24, 2004, A11.

31. Jones, "Meet the Afghan Army."

32. Jason Motlagh, "The Afghan Army in Combat: Dazed and Confused?" *Stars and Stripes*, October 19, 2010; Brian Brady, "Drugs and Desertion: How the UK Really Rates Afghan Police," *The Independent*, March 28, 2010; Matthew Rosenberg, "Afghan Soldiers Step Up Killing of Allied Forces," *New York Times*, January 20, 2012, A1, 10.

33. Mark Hosenball, Ron Moreau and Mark Miller, "The Gang That Couldn't Shoot Straight: Six Billion Dollars Later, the Afghan National Police Can't Begin to Do Their Jobs Right—Never Mind Relieve American Forces," *Newsweek*, March 19, 2010, 29.

34. See James Glanz, "The Reach of War: U.S. Report Finds Dismal

Training of Afghan Police," *New York Times*, March 30, 2006; Ahmed Rashid, *Descent into Chaos* (New York: Viking, 2008), 204–5; Seth G. Jones, *In the Graveyard of Empires: America's War in Afghanistan* (New York: W.W. Norton, 2009), 172.

35. U.S. Army/Marine Corps, "Counterinsurgency," FM 3-24, December 2006, www.fas.org/irp/doddir/army/fm3-24.pdf; *The U.S. Army/Marine Corps Counterinsurgency Field Manual* (Chicago: University of Chicago Press, 2007), 231.

36. Huggins, *Political Policing*; and McCoy, *Policing America's Empire*.

37. American Embassy Kabul to Department of State, "Kandahar Unrest—Situation after December 1959 Riots;" Arthur Lang, End of Tour Report, February 1969 to March 1961, RG 286, NA, USAID, Operations Division, Africa and Near East, box 60, folder Afghanistan.

38. Minutes of Meeting OCB Working Group on NSC-Action 1290-d, January 18, 1955, OCB, Box 16, folder internal security; Dwight D. Eisenhower Presidential Library, White House Office, NSC Staff Papers, Operations Coordinating Board, Central File, Box 16, folder internal security; "Policy Research Study—Internal Warfare and the Security of the Underdeveloped States," Department of State, November 20, 1961, John F. Kennedy Presidential Library, Boston, MA, National Security Files, box 332. 1290-d was run by former Kansas City police chief Byron Engle, a police adviser under Douglas MacArthur in Japan, and was a precursor to USAID's Office of Public Safety (OPS), established by the Kennedy administration in 1962.

39. Albert Riedel, "Monthly Report on Civil Police Program for Afghanistan," January 29, 1958, RG 286, NA, USAID, Operations Division, Africa and Near East, box 60, folder Afghanistan.

40. Judy Dempsey, "Germany Criticized for its Training of Afghan Police," *New York Times*, October 15, 2006. On DynCorp involvement in the child-sex trade, see Robert Capps, "Outside the Law," *Salon*, June 25, 2002; Pratap Chatterjee, *Iraq Inc.: A Profitable Occupation* (New York: Seven Stories Press, 2004), 111.

41. Jones, "Meet the Afghan Army," 76; Bird and Marshall, *Afghanistan*, 123; David Bayley and Robert Perito, *The Police in War: Fighting Insurgency, Terrorism and Violent Crime* (Boulder: Lynn Riener, 2010), 21; "Training," November 3, 2006, www.wikileaks.de; "Watchdog Company Botched Afghan Police Stations," Associated Press, October 26, 2010.

42. Ken Isenberg, *Shadow Force: Private Security Contractors in Iraq* (Westport, CT: Praeger, 2009), 91–94; Renae Merle, "Coming Under Fire: DynCorp Defends Its Work in Training Foreign Police Forces,"

Washington Post, March 19, 2007, D1; Anna Mulrine, "Rogue Security Companies Threaten U.S. Gains in Afghan War," *Christian Science Monitor*, October 21, 2010; Jon Boone, "Foreign Contractors Hired Afghan Dancing Boys, WikiLeaks Cables Reveal," *The Guardian*, December 2, 2010; Chatterjee, *Iraq Inc.*

43. See D. Gareth Porter, "A Bigger Problem Than the Taliban? Afghanistan's U.S.-Backed Child Raping Police," *Counterpunch*, July 30, 2009; Nir Rosen, *Aftermath: Following the Bloodshed of America's Wars in the Muslim World* (New York: Nation Books, 2010), 465; Marc Herold, "Afghanistan: Terror U.S. Style," *Frontline*, PBS, March 11, 2009; Sayed Yaqub Ibrahimi, "Afghan Police Part of the Problem," Institute for War & Peace Reporting, June 6, 2006.

44. "Unvarnished Look at Hamstrung Fight," *New York Times*, July 25, 2010, A1.

45. Rosen, *Aftermath*, 465; Ibrahimi, "Afghan Police Part of Problem"; "Kunduz Politics of Corruption in the Baghlan Police Forces," December 5, 2005, www.wikileaks.ch/cable/12/05/2005KABUL5181.html.

46. William Fischer, "Rights: Afghan Prison Looks Like Another Guantanamo," Inter Press Service, January 15, 2008; "Pul-e-Charkhi Jail Inmates Face Awful Life," RAWA (Revolutionary Association of Women of Afghanistan) News, August 13, 2008; Deepa Babington, "Sold, Raped and Jailed: A Girl Faces Afghan Justice," Reuters, March 31, 2010; Kolhatkar and Ingalls, *Bleeding Afghanistan*, 104–5.

47. Robert Cole, *Under the Gun in Iraq: My Year Training the Iraqi Police, as Told to Jan Hogan* (Amherst, NY: Prometheus Books, 2007).

48. A classic work on Western counterinsurgency doctrine is David Galula, *Counterinsurgency Warfare: Theory and Practice* (New York: Hailer, 2005).

49. Vikash Yadav, "Animalizing Afghans: Biometrics and Biopolitics in an Occupied Zone," Association for Asian Studies Conference, Honolulu, HI, April 1, 2011; Alfred W. McCoy, "Imperial Illusions: Information Infrastructure and U.S. Global Power," in *Endless Empire: Spain's Retreat, Europe's Eclipse, America's Decline*, ed. Alfred W. McCoy, Josep M. Fradera, and Stephen Jacobson (Madison: University of Wisconsin Press, 2012).

50. Tonita Murray, "Police Building in Afghanistan: A Case Study in Civil Security Reform," *International Peacekeeping*, January 2007, 108–26.

51. Bob Woodward, "McChrystal: More Forces or Mission Failure," *Washington Post*, September 21, 2009; Rod Nordland and Sharifullah Sahak, "Afghan Government Says Prisoner Directed Attacks," *New York Times*, February 11, 2011, A6; "Break for the Hills," *The Economist*, April 28, 2011. The

prison guards may have collaborated with the Taliban prisoners and used the drug story as a ruse.

52. James Risen, "Propping Up a Drug Lord, Then Charging Him," *New York Times*, December 12, 2010, A1; Pierre-Arnaud Chouvy, *Opium: Uncovering the Politics of the Poppy* (Cambridge, MA: Harvard University Press, 2010).

53. Dexter Filkins, Mark Mazetti, and James Risen, "Brother of Afghan Leader Said to Be Paid by CIA," *New York Times*, October 27, 2009; Joya, *Woman Among Warlords*, 205; "Cables Cite Pervasive Afghan Corruption, Starting at the Top," *New York Times*, December 3, 2010, A10; Peter Dale Scott, *American War Machine: Deep Politics, the CIA Global Drug Connection, and the Road to Afghanistan* (New York: Rowman & Littlefield, 2010), 234–35.

54. Paul Fitzgerald and Elizabeth Gould, *Invisible History: Afghanistan's Untold History* (San Francisco: City Lights, 2009), 285; Pratap Chaterjee, "Paying Off the Warlords: Anatomy of a Culture of Corruption," in Turse, *Case for Withdrawal from Afghanistan*, 81–86.

55. See McCoy, *The Politics of Heroin*; and Scott, *American War Machine*.

56. Dana Lewis, "Dangerous Ride—Training Afghanistan's Police," Fox News, October 14, 2008; Carlotta Gall, "Opium Harvest at Record Level in Afghanistan," *New York Times*, September 3, 2006, A1.

57. Rensselaer W. Lee III, "Parapolitics and Afghanistan," in *Government of the Shadows: Parapolitics and Criminal Sovereignty*, ed. Eric Wilson (London: Pluto Press, 2009), 197.

58. Barnett R. Rubin, *Road to Ruin: Afghanistan's Booming Opium Industry* (Washington, DC: Center for American Progress, 2004); Patrick Cockburn, "Afghans to Obama: Get Out, Take Karzai with You," *Counterpunch*, May 6, 2009; "Wedded to the Warlords: NATO's Unholy Afghan Alliance," *Globe and Mail*, June 3, 2011.

59. "Holbrooke Calls Afghan Anti-Drug Policy Most Wasteful Ever Seen," *Progressive Review*, March 23, 2009, prorev.com/2009/03/holbrooke-calls-afghan-anti-drug-policy.html; "Farmers Attack Anti-Drug Police, Afghanistan, Four Hurt," February 2, 2007, www.wikileaks.de; James Nathan, "The Folly of Afghan Opium Eradication," *USA Today*, March 2009, 26–30; Chouvy, *Opium*, 113; Jonathan Goodhand and David Mansfield, "Drugs and (Dis)order," UK Aid, Crisis States Working Papers No. 2, November 2010, 20. For parallels with Vietnam where farmers fired back at planes sent to defoliate their fields, see Jeremy Kuzmarov, *Myth of the Addicted Army: Vietnam and the Modern War on Drugs* (Amherst: University of Massachusetts Press, 2009), 127.

60. Nir Rosen, "Something from Nothing: U.S. Strategy in Afghanistan,"

Boston Review, January–February 2010, 10; "Kunduz: New Police Chiefs Raise Hopes for Fundamental Improvements in Northeast," June 6, 2006, www.wikileaks.ch/cable/2006/06/06KABUL2862.html.

61. See, for example, "State to AID, Kunduz Authorities Turn to Militias as Security Deteriorates," October 9, 2010; "Unconventional Security Forces: What's Out There?" November 11, 2009; "Afghan Police Training: Shift to Focused District Development," November 15, 2007, www.wikileaks .ch; "Militias in Kunduz: A Tale of Two Districts," January 10, 2010, www .wikileaks.ch/cable/2010/01/10KABUL12.html; "'Just Don't Call It a Militia': Impunity, Militias, and the Afghan Local Police," Human Rights Watch, September 12, 2011. On the CIA's involvement, see Tom Engelhardt and Nick Turse, "The Shadow War: Making Sense of the New CIA Battlefield," in Turse, *Case for Withdrawal from Afghanistan,* 127–35.

62. C. Christine Fair and Peter Chalk, eds., *Fortifying Pakistan: The Role of U.S. Internal Security Assistance* (Washington, DC: United States Institute for Peace Press, 2006), 51; Jeremy Scahill, "The Secret U.S. War in Pakistan," *The Nation,* December 21/28, 2009; Elizabeth Gould and Paul Fitzgerald, *Crossing Zero: The AfPak War at the Turning Point of American Empire* (San Francisco: City Lights Books, 2011), 46.

63. Seth Jones and Christine Fair, *Counterinsurgency in Pakistan* (Santa Monica, CA: RAND Corporation, 2010), 97; "Denying the Undeniable: Enforced Disappearances in Pakistan," Amnesty International, July 2008, 9; Barbara Elias, "Pakistan: The Taliban's Godfather: Documents Detail Years of Pakistani Support for Taliban Extremists," National Security Archive, www.gwu.edu.

64. Ali, "Mirage of the Good War," 46, 53; Joya, *Woman Among Warlords,* 189.

65. Joya, *Woman Among Warlords,* 207.

8. Afghanistan, Part II *by Jean MacKenzie*

1. "Lakhdar Brahimi: Post-Taliban Mistakes in Afghanistan," Century Foundation, blip.tv/the-century-foundation/lakhdar-brahimi-post-taliban -mistakes-in-afghanistan-3558297.

2. Alex Strick van Linschoten and Felix Kuehn, "Separating the Taliban from al-Qaeda: The Core of Success in Afghanistan," Center on International Cooperation, New York University, February 2011, 4.

3. David J. Kilcullen, *Counterinsurgency* (New York: Oxford University Press, 2010), 23.

4. See Jean MacKenzie, "The Battle for Afghanistan: Helmand," New America Foundation, September 14, 2010, counterterrorism.newamerica .net/publications/policy/the_battle_for_afghanistan_helmand.

5. Joshua Partlow, "Petraeus' Comments on Coalition Attack Reportedly Offend Karzai Government," *Washington Post*, February 21, 2011.

6. Nichole Sobecki, "Afghanistan: Is Child Abuse a New Taliban Gambit?" Global Post, December 28, 2010, www.globalpost.com/dispatch/afghanistan/101227/afghanistan-war-taliban-us-medics-war-photos.

7. Jean MacKenzie, "Lost in Psy-ops," *Global Post*, February 22, 2011, www.globalpost.com/dispatches/afghanistan/lost-psy-ops.

8. U.S. Army/Marine Corps, "Counterinsurgency," FM 3-24, December 2006, www.fas.org/irp/doddir/army/fm3-24.pdf; *The U.S. Army/Marine Corps Counterinsurgency Field Manual* (Chicago: University of Chicago Press, 2007).

9. Frank Ledwidge, paper presented at forum hosted by YouGov-Cambridge, July 2011.

10. Christopher Paul, "Counterinsurgency Scorecard: Afghanistan in Early 2011 Relative to the Insurgencies of the Past 30 Years," RAND Corporation, 2011, www.rand.org/content/dam/rand/pubs/occasional_papers/2011/RAND_OP337.pdf.

11. Gareth Porter, "Ninety Percent of Petraeus's Captured 'Taliban' Were Civilians," Inter Press Service, June 12, 2011, ipsnews.net/news.asp?idnews=56038.

12. Kilcullen, *Counterinsurgency*, 20.

13. First published in "The Arab Bulletin," August 20, 1917, and available at wwi.lib.byu.edu/index.php/The_27_Articles_of_T.E._Lawrence.

14. Kilcullen, *Counterinsurgency*, 29.

15. Ibid., 30.

16. Elizabeth Rubin, "Battle Company Is Out There," *New York Times Magazine*, February 24, 2008.

17. Kilcullen, *Counterinsurgency*, 7.

18. Kate Clark, "The Takhar Attack: Targeted Killings and the Parallel Worlds of U.S. Intelligence and Afghanistan," Afghanistan Analysts Network, May 2011, aan-afghanistan.com/uploads/20110511KClark_Takhar-attack_final.pdf.

19. Kilcullen, *Counterinsurgency*, 10.

20. Eric Schmitt, "U.S. Envoy's Cables Show Worries in Afghan Plans," *New York Times*, January 25, 2010; see also "Ambassador Eikenberry's Cables on U.S. Strategy in Afghanistan," November 2009, documents.nytimes.com/eikenberry-s-memos-on-the-strategy-in-afghanistan.

21. FM 3-24, location 987.

22. See, for example, "Afghan Perceptions and Experiences of Corruption, A National Survey 2010," Integrity Watch Afghanistan, iwaweb.org/corruptionSurvey2010/Main_findings.html.

23. "Transforming Wartime Contracting; Controlling costs, reducing risks: Final Report to Congress," August 2011, Commission on Wartime Contracting, wartimecontracting.gov/docs/CWC_FinalReport-lowres.pdf.

24. Strick van Linschoten and Kuehn, 5.

25. "CIA: At Most, 50–100 Al Qaeda in Afghanistan," June 27, 2010, abcnews.go.com/blogs/politics/2010/06/cia-at-most-50100-al-qaeda-in-afghanistan.

26. Kilcullen, *Counterinsurgency*, 165.

27. Yaroslav Trofimov and Maria Abi-Habib, "Taliban Need 'Pain' to Talk, Envoy Says," *Wall Street Journal*, September 9, 2011, online.wsj.com/article/SB10001424053111904103404576558431089318822.html.

28. Jean MacKenzie, "Is Karzai Contemplating a War on NATO?" Global Post, May 31, 2011, globalpost.com/dispatch/news/regions/asia-pacific/afghanistan/110531/hamid-karzai-speech-nato.

29. Porter, "Ninety Percent of Petraeus' Captured 'Taliban' Were Civilians."

30. Stephen Grey and Dan Edge, "Kill/Capture," *Frontline*, PBS, May 10, 2011.

31. Kilcullen, *Counterinsurgency*, 9.

32. Ibid., 71.

33. Rajiv Srinavasan, "The Bus Stop," April 23, 2010, rajivsrinivasan.wordpress.com/2010/04/23/371.

34. Quoted by CBS News, "Obama, McChrystal Chat on Air Force One," October 2, 2009, cbsnews.com/2100-250_162-5357873.html.

35. Kilcullen, *Counterinsurgency*, 57.

36. Author's interview with Zaeef, Kabul, March 2009.

ABOUT THE CONTRIBUTORS

Joaquín M. Chávez is an assistant professor in the department of history at the University of Illinois at Chicago. He researches popular politics, revolution, Catholic social thought, and the Cold War in Latin America. He holds a PhD from New York University. His dissertation, *The Pedagogy of Revolution: Popular Intellectuals and the Origins of the Salvadoran Insurgency, 1960–1980*, examines the evolution of religious and political consciousness and notions of historical change among urban and peasant intellectuals in El Salvador. His recent publications include "Revolutionary Power, Divided State," in *Mapping Latin America: Space and Society, 1492–2000*, edited by Karl Offen and Jordana Dym (University of Chicago Press, 2011) and "The University for Social Change and the Legacy of Ignacio Martín Baró S.J." in *Peace Psychology: Journal of Peace Psychology* 18, no. 1 (February 2002): 68–76. Chávez has also published studies on the peace negotiations that put an end to El Salvador's Civil War and has served as an expert on peace negotiations in Nepal. He was McGill Visiting Assistant Professor in International Studies at Trinity College in Hartford, Connecticut, in 2011–12.

Born in Michigan, **David Enders** is a journalist who has been reporting from the Middle East since 2003. He won a Polk Award for his coverage of Syria for McClatchy Newspapers in 2012 and has previously written for *The Nation*, the *Virginia Quarterly Review*, the *New York Times*, and the Associated Press. He is the author of *Baghdad Bulletin: Dispatches on the American Occupation* (University of Michigan Press, 2005) and *Death of Iraq: Stories of Life Under American Occupation, 2003–2011* (with Alaa Majeed, University of Michigan Press, 2013). Enders is currently working as a producer for Al Jazeera America.

Karl Hack is the director of the Ferguson Centre for African and Asian Studies at the Open University, United Kingdom. Prior to that he was at Singapore's Nanyang Technological University, where he taught for more than a decade. He has interviewed insurgents up to and including the secretary-general of the Malayan Communist Party. Relevant publications include *Dialogues with Chin Peng: New Light on the Malayan Communist Party* (edited with C.C. Chin, National University of Singapore, 2004); *War, Memory and the Making of Modern Malaysia and Singapore* (with Kevin Blackburn, University of Hawai'i Press, 2012); and "The Malayan Emergency as Counter-insurgency Paradigm," *Journal of Strategic Studies* 32, no. 3 (June 2009). He has edited two journal special editions on insurgency: the *Journal of Southeast Asian Studies* 40, no. 3 (2009) on the origins of the Southeast Asian cold war and the *Journal of Imperial and Commonwealth History* 39, no. 4 (2011) on "Negotiating with the Enemy." He has also contributed online to RUSI website and *Small Wars Journal*.

Jeremy Kuzmarov is J.P. Walker Assistant Professor of History at the University of Tulsa in Oklahoma. He specializes in modern American history and foreign relations history and also has a background in criminological studies. He is the author of *The Myth of the Addicted Army: Vietnam and the Modern War on Drugs* (University of Massachusetts Press, 2009) and *Modernizing Repression: Police Training and Nation Building in the American Century* (University of Massachusetts Press, 2012).

Born and raised in Manila, Philippines, **Vina A. Lanzona** grew up under martial law. As a student at the Ateneo de Manila University, she was actively involved in the anti-Marcos dictatorship movement, and became part of Corazon Aquino's People Power Movement. She then pursued graduate studies in the United States, completing an MA at the New School for Social Research in New York and a PhD in Southeast Asian history at the University of Wisconsin–Madison. Her first book, *Amazons of the Huk Rebellion: Gender, Sex and Revolution in the Philippines* (University of Wisconsin Press,

2009), was inspired by her twin passions for studying revolution and the role of women in political change. She is currently an associate professor in the history department and the director of the Center for Philippine Studies at the University of Hawai'i at Manoa.

Jean MacKenzie worked in Afghanistan for nearly seven years as a journalist, consultant, and trainer. From January 2009 to July 2011 she was *GlobalPost*'s senior correspondent in Kabul; from 2004 to 2009 she headed the Institute for War & Peace Reporting in Afghanistan. Her work has taken her to the farthest corners of Afghanistan, where she has met hundreds of Afghans from all walks of life. She has created a network of Afghan reporters who gather news and information from all over the country, lending an all-important local perspective to coverage of the conflict there. MacKenzie has forged a reputation as an analyst and commentator, contributing frequently to broadcast and online projects, including National Public Radio, *PBS NewsHour*, and other major media outlets. She has recently returned from Afghanistan and lives in Cape Cod, Massachusetts, where she is working on a book about the war in Afghanistan based on her experience there.

Rick Rowley is a cofounder of Big Noise Films and has fifteen years of experience covering war and conflict. He is the director of the documentary *Dirty Wars* and has produced dozens of television documentaries from around the world for BBC's *Newsnight*, CNN International, PBS, Al Jazeera English, *Democracy Now!*, and Telesur, among others. Rowley evaded the Mexican military cordon to produce an award-winning film with the Zapatistas in 1995. He was one of the only American cameramen documenting the rebellion in Argentina in 2001 that overthrew two governments in a week. He was filming inside Jenin when Israeli tanks attacked it in 2002. He has broken many stories in his television coverage of the wars in Iraq and Afghanistan, from embedding with U.S.-funded sectarian militias to exposing the massive lawless detention system in Iraq. He is a recipient of Pulitzer, Rockefeller, Sundance, and Jerome fellowships. Links to his work can be found at www.bignoisefilms.org.

PUBLISHING IN THE PUBLIC INTEREST

Thank you for reading this book published by The New Press. The New Press is a nonprofit, public interest publisher. New Press books and authors play a crucial role in sparking conversations about the key political and social issues of our day.

We hope you enjoyed this book and that you will stay in touch with The New Press. Here are a few ways to stay up to date with our books, events, and the issues we cover:

- Sign up at www.thenewpress.com/subscribe to receive updates on New Press authors and issues and to be notified about local events
- Like us on Facebook: www.facebook.com/newpressbooks
- Follow us on Twitter: www.twitter.com/thenewpress

Please consider buying New Press books for yourself; for friends and family; or to donate to schools, libraries, community centers, prison libraries, and other organizations involved with the issues our authors write about.

The New Press is a 501(c)(3) nonprofit organization. You can also support our work with a tax-deductible gift by visiting www.thenewpress.com/donate.